An Intellectual Freedom Primer

An
Intellectual Freedom Primer

Charles H. Busha, editor

1977

Libraries Unlimited, Inc.
Littleton, Colo.

LIBRARIES UNLIMITED, INC.
P.O. Box 263
Littleton, Colorado 80160

Library of Congress Cataloging in Publication Data

Busha, Charles H
    An intellectual freedom primer.

    1. Censorship--Addresses, essays, lectures.
2. Liberty--Addresses, essays, lectures.
3. Computers--Access control--Addresses, essays,
lectures.   I. Title.
Z659.B96   323.44   77-7887
ISBN 0-87287-172-X

TABLE OF CONTENTS

This book is gratefully dedicated to

WILLIAM O. DOUGLAS

Justice of the Supreme Court of the United States,
1939-1975,

whose wisdom and courage made a lasting contribution
toward strengthening freedoms expressed in
the Bill of Rights of the Constitution of the United States.

INTRODUCTION

In its largest context, the subject of *An Intellectual Freedom Primer* is freedom of expression, a generic term which includes sub-topics such as freedom of speech, the freedom to read, freedom of the press, artistic freedom, academic freedom, the right to privacy, and other associated personal liberties. The major purpose in bringing these essays together is to provide discussions about developments in the twentieth century that have contributed to erosions of First Amendment rights—guaranteed by the Constitution of the United States. These essays should be useful to persons who wish to understand both the broader aspects of intellectual freedom and the particular sub-areas of freedom of speech, such as expression in the visual arts, performing arts, motion pictures, books and other publications, and many other media of communication and entertainment. Students of library science and educators in library schools should find this collection useful and informative. Indeed, all librarians must foster and encourage freedom of expression, as librarianship is an important link in a complex communication system which connects the past to the present.

Essays presented here include material about numerous areas of freedom of expression. In addition, contributors have offered many viable suggestions to strengthen particular freedoms. Such an inclusive approach seems especially valuable in a work which promotes intellectual freedom—a concept that is attracting more attention—because it gives the reader a broad theoretical framework with which to handle contemporary censorship problems, as well as those that will undoubtedly arise in the future. This book should demonstrate to readers that intellectual freedom is a more complex concept than the simplistic notion that it is merely the absence of censorship. Contributors make no claims of presenting unbiased views of disputes between censors and anti-censors or between the forces of intolerance and the forces of freedom. The writers who have contributed to this book are resolute in their commitment to principles of intellectual freedom and offer no apologies for their partiality.

The chief supposition underlying all essays in this work is as follows: freedom of expression is not unavoidably doomed, nor must we apathetically await the dawn of an Orwellian nightmare, provided that we remain on guard against 1) anti-democratic ideas and trends, 2) dangers of stultifying bureaucracies, 3) inhibiting restraints on personal liberties posed by collectivism, and 4) increasing threats that technology and industrialization pose to human happiness. Many of the threats to freedom discussed in this book have their origins in the complex nature of our social, political, and economic systems. For example, it is ironic that our technologically dominated age, with its emphasis on efficiency and order, has encouraged an almost imperceptible (and sometimes irrevocable) disintegration of certain freedoms in the twentieth century. Technology has advanced to the point where the use of all manner of electronic surveillance is becoming commonplace. The following ideas are also incidental products of our scientific and technological age: 1) knowledge is of little value unless it is applicable to economic gains; 2) the worth

9

of speech and literature depends upon their ability to convey practical information; and 3) knowledge is chiefly an ingredient of technical skill. Unfortunately, these all-too-prevalent ideas have contributed to an anti-intellectual climate in which a low priority is placed on the aesthetic values of knowledge and creativity. In our haste to achieve technological supremacy in the community of nations, we have placed less emphasis on the use of knowledge for the achievement of a broad, humanistic outlook of life. But if man is to view the wholeness of life, he must appreciate—at least tolerate—the creative products of human intellect: literature, art, music, dance, theater, and other contemplative endeavors. Many contemporary actions of censors and would-be censors appear to be based upon a simplistic approach to knowledge; this approach first demands to know "Of what use is it?" The struggle in the United States to overcome this narrow, utilitarian approach to scholarship or erudition—which incorporates the belief that knowledge is useful only if it can benefit social and political progress—has not been easy, nor has it been totally successful. A primary task facing all who write about the topic of individual liberties and related matters is that of defining the term *freedom*. The unabridged college edition of *The Random House Dictionary of the English Language* first indicates that freedom is "the state of being at liberty rather than in confinement or being under physical restraint." The second definition notes that freedom is "exemption from external control, interference, regulation, etc." Freedom is defined in a third statement as the "power to make one's own choices or decisions without constraints from within or without." Freedom is characterized in a fifth explanation as "civil liberty, as opposed to subjection to an arbitrary or despotic government." "Political or national independence" is included as a sixth meaning, while a seventh definition notes that freedom is "a particular privilege enjoyed." The dictionary provides nine additional definitions under the heading; moreover, a list of synonyms for freedom is also included.

Notwithstanding these dictionary definitions of freedom, B. F. Skinner has proposed in *Beyond Freedom and Dignity* a rather chilling thesis: commonly held beliefs about the nature of freedom are fictitious and misleading, and the essential element of freedom is the *avoidance of and escape from adverse conditions.* This view of freedom has been difficult for some persons to accept because it deemphasizes individual autonomy and eliminates the element of self-determination. Another disquieting opinion is expressed in Erich Fromm's classic work *Escape from Freedom*, first published in 1941. Fromm claims that man will turn to totalitarianism when he is psychologically unable to live with freedom. In 1965, Fromm pointed out in the foreword to a reprint of *Escape from Freedom* that "modern man still is anxious and tempted to surrender his freedom to dictators of all kinds, or to lose it by transforming himself into a small cog in a machine, well fed, and yet not a free man but an automaton." In *Defense of Freedom* Meyer wrote: "Freedom means freedom: not necessity, but choice; not responsibility, but the choice between accepting and rejecting duty; not virtue, but the choice between virtue and vice." In another book, *The Skinner Primer: Behind Freedom and Dignity*, Carpenter has analyzed the various concepts of freedom and has concluded: "The pragmatic 'solution' of the freedom-determinism issue holds that the problem has no unique answer, that is, it is untenable to assert that all behavior is autonomous and it is equally so to assert that all behavior is capable of complete demonstration." Thus, Carpenter tentatively concludes that some persons seem to favor the "deterministic mental set" and others are inclined toward the "freedom frame of reference." While various concepts of freedom could be placed within the determinism camp, the concept of liberty held by civil libertarians—and, incidentally, by many librarians who support intellectual freedom principles—fits squarely into Carpenter's "freedom frame of reference."

Thus, it is apparent that scholars have devoted considerable attention to the question of whether man actually has an opportunity for choice. Some scholars have argued that our lives are predetermined by an iron and unalterable sequence of cause and effect, and that our so-called "options" for choosing one way over another are illusions. However, Arthur E. Sullivan, professor of law at Harvard, stated in an Oliver Wendell Holmes Lecture at the University of North Carolina that "still we have the appearance of choice. We feel as though our wills were free; and for all practical purposes this probably is for us the same as though the choice really existed." Morton A. Kaplan of the University of Chicago wrote in *Dissent and the State in Peace and War*: "I do not believe that any society yet is a free society or that there are many autonomous human beings. But some societies contain the potentiality for future human freedom." In another discussion about freedom and the gap between natural rights and pragmatism, Henry Steele Commager wrote in *Freedom, Loyalty, Dissent*: "What are the practical consequences of a course of conduct which denies or fetters freedom? It is when we ask this question, consider its implications, and work out an answer that it becomes clear that freedom is not only a right but a necessity."

To outline what American freedoms are—or what they are not—is much easier than to attempt to define the word "freedom." Of course, freedom refers to the behavior of individuals in a group or society, and it is the domain of human behavior in which a person may act as he pleases without regard to the opinions of others. If a person actually enjoys absolute freedom, he is not restricted or punished because of his behavior by society or by its representative, the government. According to John Stuart Mill, in a truly free society, a person's freedom ends only when his actions interfere with the freedoms of others. In the complex societies produced by the modern world, no single nation permits such extensive liberties to citizens; yet, freedom to act where that action may affect others is the essence of liberty and a prerequisite for a democracy. Free societies are characterized by a decentralization of authority, so that all participants in the society have a voice in exercising control over decisions and actions. On the other hand, totalitarian societies are characterized by a concentration of power in the government and by the utilization of all sectors of the society to achieve ends determined by the government. When authority is centralized, personal freedoms are limited or non-existent; censorship is usually also practiced, so that "undesirable" materials are excluded from the channels of communication. Fortunately, citizens of the United States are able to benefit from a wide range of personal freedoms. Thus, relatively speaking, we can conclude most emphatically that Americans are much freer than the majority of the world's population.

Freedom and control are paired opposites. They form a dichotomy representing the classic conflict between permissiveness and repression—between the need in a democracy to exercise some type of restraint so that 1) social institutions can be regulated for the protection of citizens' rights and 2) individuals can exercise choice. Past and present struggles between regulators and freedom lovers have demonstrated that the United States is far from resolving this internal tension, especially in respect to freedom of speech. On the one hand, an uncomfortably large number of Americans would apparently go all out, if permitted, to limit freedoms in the name of law and order; on the other hand, some anarchists in our nation do not recognize the need for controls and would prefer to eradicate all laws, rules, and regulations. Somewhere between the extremes of overaction and inaction lies the democratic ideal—a balance between liberty and control. As world political events in recent decades have demonstrated, the criterion that distinguishes democratic from authoritarian nations is the degree of respect which the state has for the dignity and freedom of the individual citizen.

At this point, the reader has probably surmised that freedom means concrete freedoms of various kinds. Indeed, entire books have been devoted to such topics as the meanings of various concepts of freedom, the free-will *versus* determinism debate, and the characteristics and personalities of free men. Perhaps we need to recognize the relative nature of freedom, and to go on from there and attempt to define the kind of freedom with which librarians are primarily concerned.

While freedom has many meanings, and while these meanings differ considerably depending upon who is using the term, librarians have their own definition which relates to their institutions and patrons. One hears and reads a great deal about *intellectual freedom* within librarianship. In a behavioral context, the freedoms to which librarians refer are: 1) the exercise of choice without coercion in the selection and utilization of the contents of all media of human communications; 2) the citizen's ability and right to disagree and to express dissent in all communication media, as well as the library user's right of access to these recorded divergent opinions; and 3) the sense of independence and self-reliance which results from acquiring and utilizing knowledge (i.e., the informed person can select from a greater range of choices). These definitions of intellectual freedom all fall under what the First Amendment labels as "freedom of speech" and "freedom of the press"—that is, freedom of inquiry, criticism, and dissent.

Librarians use the term *intellectual freedom* as the antithesis of censorship. Operationally, the term denotes the right of persons to have access to books and information without restraint from public or private interests. Academic freedom, which protects educators from pressures in their scholarship and in their teaching, might be classed as a type of intellectual freedom under this generic usage of the term; however, intellectual freedom within the library profession is often used in reference to library users' rights to read, watch, or listen to material they want without supervision or restraint from public officials, public opinion, institutional repression, private groups, or individuals. Implicit in this concept of intellectual freedom is the conviction that freedom and ease of access to library collections are imperative if library users are to exercise their constitutional rights, particularly those expressed in the First Amendment.

The term which most appropriately serves as an antonym for intellectual freedom is *censorship*. Perhaps that word should also be defined so that readers will be clearly aware of conditions which reflect a total absence of any semblance of intellectual freedom. Most generally, censorship is regarded as the deliberate exclusion of material from the stream of communication in order to influence values, decisions, or action. Censorship has been defined by political scientist Harold D. Lasswell in the *Encyclopedia of the Social Sciences* as:

> the policy of restricting the public expression of ideas, opinions, conceptions, and impulses which have or are believed to have the capacity to undermine the governing authority or the social and moral order which that authority considers itself bound to protect.

Lasswell has also pointed out that censorship may be exercised by political or religious authorities, or even by individuals who assume a quasi-official position in respect to the enforcement of anticipated prohibitive policies. Although censorship activity has usually been associated with governmental control, Henry J. Abraham claims in the *International Encyclopedia of the Social Sciences* that censorship as an activity of private groups having both religious and secular interests is becoming more common. Insofar as libraries are concerned, the term *censorship* has been operationally defined by Robert D. Leigh in *The Public Library in the United States* as "the rejection by a library authority of a book (or other material) which the librarians, the library board, or some person (or persons) bringing pressure on them holds to be obscene, dangerously radical, subversive, or too critical of the existing mores."

At the first session of Congress under the new Constitution of the United States, a series of amendments were proposed to protect citizens from their own government. By 1791, the first ten amendments had been ratified by the states as the Bill of Rights. These amendments guarantee such basic rights as freedom of speech, freedom of religion, the right to petition the government, freedom from unreasonable search, the right to jury trial and counsel, and the right to summon witnesses. (Taken together, the freedom of speech, freedom of the press, and right of assembly are often referred to as freedom of expression.)

However, some observers have expressed doubts as to whether the Bill of Rights could be approved today were it offered as a series of constitutional amendments. Apparently, a number of citizens feel no special attachment to, or do not place a high value on, personal rights as they are spelled out in our nation's basic legal framework. Nationwide public opinion surveys have revealed that quite a number of Americans approve of the denial of basic rights to certain individuals, such as the censoring of unpopular opinions and infringements on the rights of persons accused of crime. While political and civil liberties of citizens are protected by the Bill of Rights, it is apparent that these constitutional rights are not presently revered by all Americans. For example, conservative critics of our contemporary society have complained that the courts have placed too much emphasis on constitutional rights, and that radicals, sex offenders, drug pushers, gangsters, and other persons engaged in criminal activity have benefited. These critics view the judicial emphasis on constitutional rights as a reflection of a "soft" policy toward criminal elements. According to the critics, if the government would only crack down on criminals and instigate a tougher policy, law enforcement officers would be able to effectively eradicate rising crime and juvenile delinquency. Thus, public opinion has often reflected a lack of concern on the part of some citizens for the preservation of the rights of persons to express unpopular ideas, to insure a fair and just trial for those who stand accused of criminal acts, and to preserve constitutional rights.

Nonetheless, the terms *freedom* and *equality* have become almost synonymous with the American concept of democracy. Citizens' specific rights and privileges are contained in the Constitution as amended and modified by interpretations of the judicial branch of our government. Transgressions against individual rights by the separate states are also prohibited by the First Amendment; this protection was reaffirmed in the Fourteenth Amendment. Thus, although personal rights and privileges have been clearly outlined, concepts of political freedom are sometimes difficult to implement in our everyday social and political lives. When conflicting claims about personal freedoms need to be resolved, citizens have judicial recourse for interpretations of constitutional rights. For example, numerous questions have been raised concerning the application of the Constitution to censorship cases and to questions relating to freedom of expression. Supreme Court decisions have had far-reaching implications for library services and for the development of unexpurgated collections of library materials.

In the final analysis, the essays included in this book can assist the reader to more fully understand the scope of constitutional implications for the question of freedom of expression and for problems associated with censorship. This book was conceived for the purpose of stimulating further thinking about intellectual freedom in general. Perhaps the essays which comprise *An Intellectual Freedom Primer* will also motivate the uncommitted reader to become involved in continuing efforts to lift more of the official and unofficial restrictions from our instruments of communication and expression.

Charles H. Busha

FREEDOM IN THE UNITED STATES
IN THE TWENTIETH CENTURY

Charles H. Busha

The early years of the twentieth century were greeted by an anxious and fragmented world, as governments were beset with the immediate problem of threats of open hostility. More far-reaching were the problems of applying scientific and technological advances to national aspirations and policies. Partially as a result of its physical isolation from European conflicts, then, the United States was the country where those developments were applied most advantageously and lucratively to trade and industry. Progress in creating new modes of communication led, for example, to the first scheduled radio news broadcast, made in 1920 by station KDKA (Pittsburgh) when Dr. Frank Conrad announced the victory of President Harding, and to the first public demonstration of television in Schenectady, New York, in 1928. Also, although the motion picture was invented in the nineteenth century, films were not developed as a mass medium of entertainment until the first quarter of the present century. For instance, in 1915, the most illustrious prototype of our present-day film, *Birth of a Nation*, was produced and demonstrated that the film industry had come into its own. Soon thereafter, between 1920 and 1930, most of the films produced in the world were made in the United States.

Between 1900 and 1925, unparalleled technological breakthroughs were achieved; however, social life in the United States during the first years of the century was dominated by rural customs and provincial thought. Certainly a gap existed between the level of technological and economic progress that had been achieved and the relatively unsophisticated social and cultural conditions prevalent among most citizens. During the early 1900s, then, Americans still strove to build a truly solid foundation for individual dignity, equality, and freedom.

In a political context, twentieth-century man has experienced global conflicts among nations, often in the form of intense hostility (actual or threatened) between democratic and authoritarian forces. Since 1900, individualism, tolerance, and compassion have been stringently tested by powerful and ruthless leaders, by force, and by the absence of sound judgment. Encroachments on individual liberties were made on a wide scale after the First World War by repressive governments, when totalitarianism sprang up as fascism in Italy, Spain, and Germany, and as communism in Hungary and the Soviet Union. Armed with modern techniques of communication and control, totalitarianism developed on a global scale as a creature of modern-day bureaucracies, and under the banner of absolute and intolerant ideologies, autocratic leaders were able to reduce large populations to a single malleable mass.

Despite the serious post-war economic plights of many nations during this century, however, the United States has managed to maintain a reasonable degree of stability. Now, in most phases of life, the United States and the Soviet Union have emerged as the world's dominant powers. While the political system of the

United States has been based primarily upon a democratic spirit generated by the English, French, and American Revolutions (emphasis being placed on human rights, basic freedoms, and representative government), the Soviet Union has emerged as a proponent of despotism. Thus, the rigidity and conformity demanded by the Soviet political system have been viewed by many Americans during most of the present century as the greatest challenge to democratic forms of self-government and to freedom of speech.

Intellectually, our present age has witnessed a return to reason and the enhancement of man's mind. Intellectualism has contributed to the widespread rejection of many popular, romantic myths of the nineteenth century. American thinkers were at work during the first quarter of the century forming attitudes and techniques for reforms that were often accomplished later. The status quo, including existing rigid systems of thought, was challenged as scholars explored new fields of inquiry and made increasing use of scientific methodology in their investigations. Among the leading American thinkers of the early decades of the twentieth century were William James, John Dewey, Charles Beard, Thorstein Veblen, William Z. Ripley, Richard T. Ely, Henry C. Adams, and Simon Patten. These perceptive individuals encouraged citizens to become more skeptical of static society and existing culture and to conceive of a better world.

Socially, the twentieth century could be described as a period of upward mobility for workers, the ranks of the middle class having steadily increased since 1900. Near the turn of the century, Thorstein Veblen, an economist and social scientist, published *The Theory of the Leisure Class*,[1] an attack on the predatory commercialism espoused by wealthy industrialists. Veblen and some of his contemporaries also discovered incisive intellectual implications in Darwin's theories, and thus divided thinkers into two camps, the pre- and post-Darwinians. Social theorists revealed that Herbert Spencer had used the concept of evolution to defend romantic and metaphysical ideas about life, thereby demonstrating that only nominal, superficial acceptance of new ideas had been achieved. The Spencerian metaphysical doctrine had been based upon the classical idea that man was a creature of fixed qualities—an isolated, definitive human datum. Veblen especially challenged the old theories, giving impetus to the idea of social control. He claimed that man is created by society and that no definitive, adequate method of life or absolute worthy end of action exists. Veblen also believed that the goal of production should be primarily the *use* of goods, rather than the making of profits; hence, he viewed the American business code as a barbaric tradition based upon the goal of obtaining immediate profit.[2] But not until the end of the First World War were Veblen's social and economic ideas either completely understood or realized.

Among educators, John Dewey was a strong voice in the latter years of the nineteenth century, and his ideas became even more influential in the twentieth century. Unsympathetic to authoritarianism in the classroom and to abstract learning, Dewey advocated open communication in the educational process; more exchange of ideas, suggestions, and results; and discussions about both successes and failures of previous experiences. Dewey's writings influenced the development of "progressive" education, his books *Democracy and Education*[3] and *Reconstruction in Philosophy*[4] being particularly influential in shaping American education. The educational pragmatism formulated by Dewey was labeled "instrumentalism"— an attempt to incorporate William James's individualism with Charles Pierce's social emphasis. Thus, Dewey encouraged learning by doing, looking upon the classroom as "a social clearing-house, where experience and ideas are exchanged and subjected to criticism . . . misconceptions are corrected, and new lines of thought and inquiry are set up."[5] These new educational ideas were the foundation for Dewey's dream of the creation of a popular democracy guided by intelligence.

The United States came of age in an artistic sense in 1913 with the Armory Show, an exhibition of contemporary art held in New York City. Sponsored by the Association of American Painters and Sculptors, the exhibition demonstrated that many Americans were becoming aware of a new mode of artistic sensibility. Shocked but curious citizens who attended the Armory Show viewed the abstract and vivid canvases of post-impressionist painters, whose works were freer in expression than those of beaux arts painters of the nineteenth century. Howard Mumford Jones noted that " . . . after the Armory Show, after Freud, after World War I . . . we were never again to be the nation—adolescent, picturesque, unpredictable, yearning to be loved and fearing to be outdone—that we had been between 1865 and 1915."[6]

PROGRESSIVES AND MUCKRAKERS

When President McKinley was assassinated in 1901, Theodore Roosevelt became president, and Roosevelt and the Progressive movement led the United States into the twentieth century. Indeed, the period between 1900 and the outbreak of World War I in 1914 has been labeled the "Progressive Era." However, in spite of Roosevelt's view of progressives as forward-looking conservatives, not all Roosevelt's ideas and deeds could be classified as "progressive." For example, in 1902 Roosevelt issued an extraordinary executive order which restricted the freedom of speech of federal government employees. The order, sometimes referred to as a "gag rule," had the effect of denying federal employees the right to complain about working conditions. Employees of some government agencies were not even allowed to discuss their grievances with one another. Roosevelt's gage rule forbade them

> . . . either directly or indirectly, individually or through association, to
> solicit an increase of pay or to influence or attempt to influence in
> their own interest any other legislation whatever, either before
> Congress or its Committees, or in any way save through the heads
> of the Departments in or under which they worked, on penalty of
> dismissal from the Government service.[7]

After Roosevelt's executive order was issued, Senator Robert LaFollette of Wisconsin distributed a questionnaire to federal employees in an attempt to obtain information about working conditions. Although postal employees were forbidden to respond to the survey, some workers ignored the order for silence and submitted completed questionnaires. Senator LaFollette later charged that postal inspectors had opened and read his mail to determine who had disobeyed official directives. Thus, in 1912, the repressive gag rule, in effect for ten years, was rescinded by the Lloyd-LaFollette Act.

In general, though, the Progressive Era was a period in which the quality of American life improved, and the groundwork was laid for more profound social and political reforms of subsequent decades. Among the leaders of the Progressive movement were Eugene V. Debs, Robert LaFollette, Theodore Roosevelt, Woodrow Wilson, and George W. Norris. Progressives felt that the federal government should be more than an equal match for big business; they envisaged a political system that was more democratic and responsive to citizens' needs. Herbert Croly expressed the political theory of Progressives in his work *The Promise of American Life*,[8] in which a claim was made that democracy and equality could be achieved only if the nation's economy was regulated by federal and state governments. The Progressive movement, which actually began circa 1890, was essentially an ideological and political response to an economy geared to large-scale urban and industrial centers rather than to rural areas. Progressivism was, then, a demonstration of the faith of many Americans in pure democracy and was fostered by a reaction to the adverse effects of corporate power, an increasing awareness among many citizens, and a restatement of confidence in governmental regulation of big-time business. Progressives attempted to meet new challenges by initiating basic reforms in politics, society, and the economy.

Theodore Roosevelt dubbed political journalists "muckrakers," and a muckraking movement—a corollary of Progressivism—exposed and protested the excesses of monopolies. Muckrakers supported, among other reforms, consumer protection, municipal ownership of utilities, and changes in election procedures. They attempted to rescue political and economic democracy from what they deemed to be a state of stagnation by publishing their articles in periodicals such as *McClure's*, *Collier's*, *Cosmopolitan*, and *Everybody's*. Lincoln Steffens was one notable political journalist of the Progressive Era whose articles in *McClure's Magazine* in the early 1900s, as well as his criticisms of political corruption published in books such as *The Shame of the Cities*[9] and *The Struggle for Self-Government*,[10] made him a strong voice among muckrakers. Steffens argued that if citizens wanted good government, free of political graft and corruption, they had to realize that economic and social injustices could be cured only if the people demanded reforms. In *The Shame of the Cities*, Steffens wrote:

> We are responsible, not our leaders, since we follow them. We *let* them divert our loyalty from the United States to some "party;" we *let* them boss the party and turn our municipal democracies into autocracies and our republican nation into a plutocracy. We cheat our government and we let our leaders loot it, and we let them wheedle and bribe our sovereignty from us . . . .[11]

Political liberals who led the muckraking movement examined and criticized American life between 1900 and the First World War, and Progressive causes were enhanced by that criticism. The muckrakers' ranks, comprised of journalists, novelists, sociologists, historians, and other intellectuals, included Jane Addams, Stephen Crane, Jack London, Upton Sinclair, Ida Tarbell, and William Allen White. Novelists of the naturalistic school also wrote criticisms of the harshness of American life. Frank Norris wrote *The Pit*[12] and *The Octopus*[13] —works which dealt with the struggle between farmers and the railroads—and Upton Sinclair's writings were particularly influential in obtaining certain regulations of the meat, drug, and patent medicine industries. The Hepburn Act, passed in 1906, was also a byproduct of muckraking efforts, and under its provisions, stricter government regulations on the nation's growing railroads were allowed. Too, muckrakers were primarily responsible for the establishment of the Federal Children's Bureau, an agency concerned with the protection and care of homeless and dependent children. Many of these changes, brought about by Progressives, were in reaction to political, economic, and social ills associated with industrialization, and although Progressives were committed to strengthening American democracy, they believed (unlike their forefathers) that government should regulate big business when the economic system warranted controls.

Support for the Progressives came chiefly from a growing middle class, since the political power that the individual American obtained in the first quarter of the century was achieved partially as a result of the efforts of Progressives. Political reforms endorsed by Progressives included the right to recall elected officials before the end of their terms, the establishment of the direct primary, and the right of women to vote. Progressives also worked to achieve protections for women and children who worked in industry, and by 1914, most states had passed laws establishing minimum age limits for workers. In 1912, the goals of Progressives were incorporated into President Wilson's new administration. (Wilson, a moderate Progressive, did not win a majority of the popular vote.) His program, the "New Freedom," pledged greater democracy and the expansion of economic opportunities for citizens. Hence, a number of progressive legislative acts were passed in 1913, including the Federal Reserve Act, which was designed to control the nation's banks and to prohibit unfair methods of competition in commerce. One of the most far-reaching legal changes of the Progressive Era was the so-called Income Tax Amendment, Amendment Sixteen to the Constitution of the United States. Declared effective on February 25, 1913, it contains the following provision:

> The Congress shall have power to lay and collect taxes on income, from whatever source derived, without apportionment among the several states, and without regard to any census or enumeration.

The Income Tax Amendment had an economic leveling effect in the nation for, since its passage, the opportunities for businessmen and industrialists to accumulate vast, private fortunes have been greatly decreased. Then on May 31, 1913, the Seventeenth Amendment, which provided for direct, popular election of senators, went into effect. Thus, it becomes apparent that during the Progressive Era, the American people used political means to exercise a leveling control over the nation's economy and political system and to eradicate some unfair practices.

WORLD WAR I AND PACIFISM

The First World War began in 1914 in Europe, but the United States proclaimed its neutrality at the outbreak of hostilities. Americans were at first solidly united in their determination to keep out of the European conflict, and, reflecting that attitude, President Wilson made the following comments about the war in a message to Congress on September 4, 1914: "We had no part in making it. But it is here. It affects us directly and palpably almost as if we were participating in the circumstances which gave rise to it." Non-participation in foreign alliances and in the affairs of other nations continued to be the mainstay of American foreign policy for several of the war years, even though the United States had been somehow involved in every major European conflict since the eighteenth century. The First World War was a struggle among the strong powers of the Western world for dominance in Europe, the underdeveloped areas of Africa, the Balkans, and the Pacific. Yet, despite strong isolationist and anti-war sentiments in the United States, this nation was actually very deeply involved in this power struggle in the early years of the century. Some American leaders were concerned about preserving an international situation whereby the nation would benefit from imperialism.

President Wilson was reelected in 1916, after a campaign that capitalized on the slogan "He kept us out of war." But Germany resumed unrestricted submarine warfare in 1917, and the Russian Revolution began. The spirit of isolationism in the United States soon became less intense, and President Wilson claimed: "The world must be made safe for democracy." On April 3, 1917, headlines of the *New York Times* were as follows:

PRESIDENT CALLS FOR WAR DECLARATION, STRONGER NAVY, NEW ARMY OF 500,000 MEN, FULL COOPERATION WITH GERMANY'S FOES.

American political, social, and economic ties were closer to the Allies than they were to Germany, and the German government was also generally regarded by Americans as too militaristic and authoritarian. Thus, the United States entered World War I in 1917, on the side of England and France. Congress quickly passed the Selective Service Act of 1917, invoking compulsory military service for the first time since 1863, the second year of the Civil War.

Before the nation entered the First World War, many citizens had been concerned that the United States might become involved in the conflict, and a pacifist and anti-militarist movement began in the nation in the fall of 1914. One of the first groups formed was led by Paul Kellog (editor of the social worker's magazine *Survey*), Lillian Wald (a settlement house director in New York City), and Jane Addams (founder of Hull House in Chicago). This so-called "Henry Street Group," comprised primarily of social workers, issued an anti-war declaration, which was also signed by John P. Gavit (managing editor of the New York *Evening Post*), Rabbi Stephen S. Wise (founder of the reformed Free Synagogue), and John Haynes Holmes (Unitarian minister of the Community Church in New York City). Other peace groups sprang up over the nation, and in December 1915, many of them joined ranks and formed the Anti-Preparedness Committee, later re-named the American Union Against Militarism. The ranks of proponents of anti-preparedness increased rapidly. Many pacifists, anti-militarists, and conscientious objectors organized a nationwide anti-preparedness campaign, denounced a proposed bill for national defense, and condemned the establishment of compulsory military service. Nonetheless, in 1916 the National Defense Act was passed by Congress to enlarge the regular army and to strengthen reserve forces. The Council of National Defense was also formed in 1916 to coordinate industry and other resources for national security.

After the nation entered the conflict in Europe, men who claimed exemption from military service as conscientious objectors were classified into two broad categories: those who were opposed to war on religious grounds (Quakers, Mennonites, Jehovah's Witnesses, Seventh-Day Adventists, etc.) and those whose objections were based on political, humanistic, or moral grounds (humanists, socialists, radicals, etc.).[14] In 1918, Congress also authorized the secretary of war to grant "furloughs" without pay to enlisted men who were conscientious objectors so that their services could be utilized by the Red Cross or on farms. Some conscientious objectors also served in noncombatant branches of the military services. Thus, while service was required, some freedom was allowed in the ways in which it might be rendered.

WARTIME SUPPRESSION OF FREE SPEECH

While most Americans were in favor of the nation's entry into the war by 1917, they were unsure as to the conflict's origins and objectives. The federal government became very concerned about shaping favorable public opinion, but socialists and anarchists still distributed propaganda against the war, urging young men to resist the draft. Anxious over these and other efforts to impede the war effort, Congress authorized in 1917 the creation of a Committee on Public Information to unite American public opinion behind the war. While the industrial efficiency and economic prowess of the nation were demonstrated as the United States came to grips with the emergency generated by the war in Europe, wartime agencies responsible for propaganda and the generation of public opinion were given excessive and dangerous authority over the minds of American citizens. Very shortly after war was declared, the Committee on Public Information began to manipulate communications about the war effort, as well as information about the German people, in order to persuade American leaders and citizens to accept the government's ideas, decisions, and actions concerning the war. The federal government was successful in its propaganda campaign, which stressed that involvement in the war on the part of the United States was strictly for the preservation of freedom and democracy and that Germans were perpetrating world terror because of their inherent greed and lust.

The Committee on Public Information, headed by journalist George Creel and funded generously by Congress, turned out a barrage of pro-war and anti-German propaganda, including over 100 million pamphlets. The work of the Committee was so effective that an image of the German people as "barbaric Huns" was created. To further rouse patriotic fervor, Liberty Bonds were sold at spirited rallies, and citizens who could afford, but did not purchase, bonds were often accused of giving aid to the enemy. The federal government also began to take dangerous anti-democratic steps to discourage apparent disloyalty and to stifle criticism of the nation's war efforts. The broadly constructed and notorious Espionage Act, passed in June 1917, authorized stiff penalties for dissenters. In 1918, Congress strengthened that legislation by passing sedition laws which made the old Sedition Act of 1798 look very mild indeed. The 1917 Act was strengthened by the Espionage Act of 1918, which provided for harsh punishment of persons who, during wartime,

> . . . shall willfully utter, print, write, or publish any disloyal, profane, scurrilous, or abusive language about the form of government of the United States, or the Constitution . . . or the uniform of the Army or Navy . . . .[15]

The law, aimed at persons who encouraged disloyalty to the nation or who interfered with the draft, provided for fines up to $10,000 and imprisonment for as many as 20 years. The Espionage Act's penalties were expanded in 1918 by the Sedition Act,[16] which contained provisions for punishing individuals who abused the federal government in writing. These supplementary sedition laws also allowed strict official censorship of books and newspapers, and propaganda efforts and repressive wartime laws were so effective that some books by noted German authors were permanently withdrawn from public libraries. Anything German—even German music—was suppressed.

The passage of these acts represented an all-time low in the nation's history in regard to the denial of freedom of expression. Under the Espionage Act of 1918, the government could punish criticism of its policies as though they were actual attacks on the nation itself. Anyone who dissented was likely to be labeled pro-German and a security risk to the nation.

President Wilson and other national leaders apparently did not recognize possible threats to individual liberties posed by the Espionage Act. The act became a dangerous piece of legislation used by a number of government officials to suppress or to prevent free speech—in the name of maintaining law and order. Although Attorney General Thomas W. Gregory viewed the legislation as a measure to control only the most outlandish attempts to interfere with the nation's war effort and to prevent the publication of military intelligence information, the Espionage Act became a formidable tool in the hands of persons who placed too little value on freedom of expression.

Shortly after the United States entered World War I, the mood of the nation shifted, as more and more Americans began to lend their support to the war effort. Thus, the Espionage Act was generally viewed as a logical defensive measure; little opposition was expressed by the public to the legislation. However, while the Espionage Act seemed to be reasonable in its provisions for punishment of spies and saboteurs, it was ultimately used to crush all expressions of opposition to the war. District courts tended to interpret the act broadly with ensuing violations on freedom of speech. In view of the climate of intolerance generated by the nation's official propaganda machine, and the fear of communism that gripped many Americans during the war and post-war years, the wave of repression and censorship which followed passage of the Espionage Act seems to have been inevitable. Many states also passed statutes between 1917 and 1920 that were designed to subdue opposition to war, to control sedition, to prevent criminal anarchy, and to control conspiracy. These statutes were often called "red flag laws." With the exception of William E. Borah, a highly respected and individualistic senator from Idaho, few legislators or other officials disapproved of the Espionage Act. Senator Borah was concerned about the Act's provisions for censorship of the mail, since the Post Office Department could refuse to deliver anti-war literature. Reacting to the senator's concern, administration officials pointed out that the act could not deny the right of citizens to criticize public officials, and thereby ignored Borah's true point.

During the same month in which the Espionage Act was passed, Postmaster General Albert S. Burleson requested local postal officials to forward to him any piece of mail that could harm the war effort. A flood of material was subsequently lifted from mail channels and forwarded to the postal chief. Confiscated material consisted of socialist newspapers and periodicals, including *Masses* and *American*

Socialist, conscientious objectors' leaflets, and a substantial amount of totally innocuous publications. Burleson claimed that publications containing charges that the government was involved in the war for the "wrong reasons" or for bad motives could be removed from the mails. The postmaster general had additional, rather incredible, criteria for the removal of objectionable publications from the mails:

> They can not say that this Government is the tool of Wall Street or the munitions-makers. That kind of thing makes for insubordination in the Army and Navy and breeds a spirit of disloyalty throughout the country. It is a false statement, a lie, and will not be permitted. And nothing can be said inciting people to resist the laws. There can be no campaign against conscription and the Draft Law, nothing that will interfere with enlistments or the raising of an army. There can be nothing said to hamper and obstruct the government in the prosecution of the war.[17]

Burleson was obviously reacting to socialist statements concerning war as an activity which provided increased wealth and power to members of the ruling class, but which brought suffering, death, and demoralization to workers. Risking severe public and official condemnation, American socialists at their 1917 meeting in St. Louis had denounced war as an evil "made by the classes and fought by the masses." Yet Burleson's views had the force of law behind them.

Burleson was postmaster general from 1913 until 1921. His appointment had been facilitated by his fellow Texas, "Colonel" E. M. House, Woodrow Wilson's campaign manager. An unpopular head of the U.S. Postal Service, Burleson was notorious among postal workers for his tyrannical behavior. In a history of the U.S. Postal Service, Gerald Cullinan claims that Burleson "was a coarse, vain, and excessively arrogant man, and [that] his eight years as Postmaster General are generally conceded to have been the most disastrous in the history of the postal establishment."[18]

It is apparent that the struggle to maintain basic freedom in the first quarter of the twentieth century was dealt several blows during the First World War years. Open dissent of citizens against the government's war policies in the second decade of the century was further jeopardized in 1919 by the decision of the United States Supreme Court in *Schenck v. United States*.[19] The Court unanimously upheld a lower court's conviction of the general secretary of the Socialist Party under the Espionage Act. Although Schenck, the socialist leader, was convicted for issuing pamphlets which urged draftees to oppose the Selective Service Act, there appeared to be only a slight possibility that the literature could have interfered with the draft or endangered the security of the nation. Justice Oliver Wendell Holmes argued, however, that "the most stringent protection of free speech would not protect a man in falsely shouting fire in a theater and causing panic." The Court's decision in *Schenck* established the "clear and present danger" criterion (in this case, war) as a justification for denying absolute free speech. In the Court's opinion, Justice Holmes wrote:

> When a nation is at war many things that might be said in a time of peace are such a hindrance to its efforts that their utterance will not

be endured so long as men fight and that no Court could regard
them as protected by any Constitutional right.

Justice Holmes's opinion for the Court further outlined the clear and present
danger concept as follows:

> We admit that in many places and in ordinary times the defendants,
> in saying all that was said in the circular, would have been within their
> constitutional rights. But the character of every act depends upon the
> circumstances in which it was done . . . The question in every case
> is whether the words used are used in such circumstances and are of
> such a nature that they will bring about the substantive evils that
> Congress has a right to prevent. It is a question of proximity and
> degree.

Prior to World War I, freedom of speech had been widely viewed as an absolute right—guaranteed in the First and Fourteenth Amendments and protecting expression from censorship. The concept of absolute freedom of speech was modified, however, in view of the "clear and present danger" criterion. Henry Abraham has focused attention on the Court's application of the "clear and present danger" doctrine, and he has concluded that the guideline is imperfect for restrictions on freedom of expression, but that its only alternative, legislation for or against free expression, is more incompatible with principles of democracy.[20]

The *Schenck* decision of the Supreme Court was unpopular with civil libertarians, who felt that free-speech concepts included the expression of the most hated and despicable ideas uttered, even during wartime. On the other hand, Donald Meiklejohn, author of *Freedom and the Public*, has written in reference to the *Schenck* opinion: "The urgencies of a 'hot war' situation tend to create a bias of perception to which even his admirers do not claim that Mr. Justice Holmes was entirely immune."[21]

After the *Schenck* case, another jurisdictional blow to free speech was levied in 1919 by the Court's opinion in *Abrams v. United States*.[22] The legality of the Espionage Act was again challenged in this case, which involved five Russians, including Abrams, who had been convicted for publishing leaflets that denounced capitalistic nations. The defendants had promoted the idea that capitalistic nations had interfered with the Russian Revolution of 1917. One of the leaflets that led to the conviction of the defendants was entitled "The Hypocrisy of the United States and Her Allies." It contained the following criticism of the president:

> His shameful, cowardly silence about the intervention in Russia
> reveals the hypocrisy of the plutocratic gang in Washington and
> vicinity.
> He is too much of a coward to come out openly and say: We
> capitalistic nations cannot afford to have a proletarian republic in
> Russia.[23]

Again, the Supreme Court ruled that the conviction of Abrams and his associates under the Espionage Act did not violate First Amendment guarantees for freedom of speech. However, the decision, unlike that of *Schenck*, was not unanimous.

In a dissenting opinion, Justice Holmes almost reversed his thinking in
Schenck and expressed the social utility of a wide range of opinions which serve to
counteract orthodoxy. In upholding free speech, Justices Holmes and Brandeis,
the two dissenters in *Abrams*, did not feel that the anti-capitalistic charges of the
defendants posed a threat to the government. Holmes wrote in the minority
opinion:

> In this case sentences of twenty years imprisonment have been
> imposed for the publishing of two leaflets that I believe the defendants
> have as much right to publish as the government has to publish the
> Constitution of the United States now vainly invoked by them . . .
> Every year if not every day we have to wager our salvation upon some
> prophecy based upon imperfect knowledge. While that experiment is
> part of our system, I think that we should be eternally vigilant against
> attempts to check the expression of opinions that we loathe and
> believe to be fraught with death, unless they so imminently threaten
> interference with the lawful and pressing purposes of the law that an
> immediate check is required to save the country. I wholly disagree with
> the argument of the government that the First Amendment left the
> common law as to seditious libel in force. History seems to me against
> the notion. I have conceived that the United States through many
> years had shown its repentance for the Sedition Act of 1798, by
> repaying fines that it imposed. Only the emergency that makes it
> immediately dangerous to leave the correction of evil counsel to time
> warrants making any exception to the sweeping command, "Congress
> shall make no law . . . abridging the freedom of speech."

Holmes's dissenting opinion in *Abrams* is among the notable minority opinions
of the U.S. Supreme Court that have evolved into majority opinions. In *The Supreme
Court and the Uses of History*, Charles A. Miller comments as follows about
Holmes's dissent:

> . . . whatever the cause, Holmes not only redirected his own thoughts
> but eventually that of the Court also . . . the whole range of Holmes'
> prestigious remarks on the historical background of freedom of
> expression was cited by various justices in support of their views in
> different cases.[24]

In perhaps the most famous case tried under the espionage laws, Eugene V.
Debs, founder of the Social Democratic Party in the United States and a five-time
presidential candidate between 1900 and 1920, became a symbol of uncompromising
opposition to the war and to measures designed to curb free speech. Debs was convicted under the Espionage Act because of his role as head of the socialist movement
in opposing the nation's war effort. The government claimed that Debs and the
socialists attempted to incite insubordination in the military and to obstruct recruit-
ment. Actually, Debs's chief offense was denouncement of the war. For example, at
a socialist party convention in Canton, Ohio, Debs directed the following comment to
young men: "You need to know that you are fit for something better than slavery
and cannon fodder."[25] As a result of his conviction, Debs's citizenship was revoked,

and he was sentenced to a 10-year prison term. The conviction was unanimously sustained by the nation's highest tribunal. Even though Debs was in prison in 1920, he polled 920,000 votes as the Socialist candidate for president.[26] A massive, popular campaign was conducted to obtain a presidential pardon for Debs; however, President Wilson refused to grant amnesty. In 1921, Debs's sentence was commuted on Christmas Day by President Harding, a conservative Republican, but Debs's citizenship was not restored.

The vicissitudes of Supreme Court decisions from case to case have sometimes been confusing and difficult for laymen to fathom. For example, in 1922 the Court claimed in *Prudential Insurance Co. v. Cheek* that the Constitution "imposes upon the states no obligation to confer upon those within their jurisdiction . . . the right of free speech."[27] Three years later, on the other hand, the Court's majority opinion in *Gitlow v. New York* (to be discussed in detail later in this chapter) contained the following statement:

> For present purposes we may and do assume that freedom of speech and of the press, which are protected by the First Amendment from abridgment by Congress, are among the fundamental personal rights and liberties protected by the due process clause of the Fourteenth Amendment from impairment by the States.[28]

Among domestic events during World War I, however, the Espionage Act stands as a monument to the hysteria which seized many private citizens and public officials at the outbreak of the conflict. Enacted a few months after the nation became actively involved in the conflict, the Act was the first "seditious libel" legislation passed by Congress since 1798. In his 1919 annual report, the Attorney General of the United States claimed that "the effect of the prosecutions under this Act has, no doubt, been beneficial in maintaining law and order." More than 1,500 persons were arrested during the war and post-war years for violations of espionage and sedition legislation. The harsh provisions of this legislation are among the most extreme of their kind to have been enacted in the United States; however, the constitutionality of the Espionage Act was upheld in six Supreme Court cases within a period of a year and a half after World War I.[29]

FORCES OF INTOLERANCE AND THE KU KLUX KLAN

At the turn of the century, the Ku Klux Klan, which had been quite active during the post-Civil War period, was almost inactive. In 1915, a revival of the Klan occurred, drawing inspiration from the older nineteenth century organization. While the Klan's mission after the Civil War had been to counteract attempts of carpetbaggers to establish equality for Southern blacks, the revived Klan was anti-black as well as biased against minorities such as Catholics, Jews, and foreigners. The new Klan was founded at Stone Mountain, Georgia, in October 1915. By 1929, it had gained a following throughout the South, and its membership had increased in other areas of the nation, especially in the Midwest and in the Far West. The Klan's position in the twentieth century was strengthened by an exaggerated ethnic self-consciousness among white Protestant Americans, so non-whites and non-Protestants were often victims of the Klan's bigotry. Employing tactics such as cross-burnings, floggings, and killings, Klansmen victimized persons whom they perceived as obstacles to the organization's white-supremacy campaign.

On July 4, 1923, the Knights of the Ku Klux Klan held a tri-state "Konklave" in Kokomo, Indiana. An estimated 200,000 people, including Klan members from Illinois, Indians, and Ohio, attended the meeting held in Melfalfa Park. The Klan's program consisted of a speech by the Reverend M. Kern of Covington, Indiana, who directed verbal attacks against Catholics and foreigners. A 50-piece boys' band played "America," and an address was delivered by Dr. Hiram W. Evans, the Klan's Atlanta-based national leader, who noted in his speech that major Klan activities had shifted from the South to the Midwest.[30]

The Klan capitalized on a wave of exaggerated nationalism that swept the United States after World War I. In addition, Klansmen often were looked upon as defenders of morals and virtue by persons who protested the licentiousness of the 1920s. Indeed, a new frankness was evident in the nation in literature and the theater during the post-war decade. Books, plays, and magazines that would have been totally unacceptable prior to the First World War were being enjoyed by many Americans, much to the chagrin of defenders of the Puritan ethic. Despite ardent efforts to stem the tide of sexual frankness in the arts and in literature, moralists were unable to ban such novels as *The Sun Also Rises*, *Point Counter Point*, or *An American Tragedy*. Almost all of the widely read and appreciated post-war novels were opposed by censors or would-be censors, who demanded more "wholesome" books than the novels of F. Scott Fitzgerald, Ernest Hemingway, Theodore Dreiser, Aldous Huxley, and other popular writers.[31]

Members of the Ku Klux Klan also capitalized on post-war hysteria generated by a variety of intolerant forces and used coercion, intimidation, and violence in an attempt to promote their causes. According to Francis Butler Simkins, between four and five million Americans were Klan members by 1925, and the "nationalistic, reactionary, alien-hating element in the United States during the postwar years was ripe for Ku-Klux-Klan propaganda."[32] The Klan became a political power in a number of Southern states and in Indiana and Oregon, and in 1925, robed Klansmen even marched in a parade in Washington, D.C. Arnold S. Rice, an expert on the Klan, has further described the exaggerated spirit of nationalism of the 1920s which attracted Americans to the repressive Klan:

> During the armed struggle [World War I] America mistrusted and mis-treated aliens, deprived itself of food and fuel, and poured its money into the Liberty Loan campaigns. But the war was over too quickly for the nation to spend fully its ultra-patriotic psychological feelings. In the decade following, America permitted itself to reject the League of Nations, to curtail immigration, to deport aliens wholesale, and to accept the Klan with its motto of "one hundred percent Americanism."[33]

OVERREACTIONS TO BOLSHEVISM

Both during and following World War I, Americans developed a fear of communism, a hatred of radical ideas, and a distrust of minority groups. The impact of the 1917 Bolshevik Revolution in Russia had become more apparent during the final years of the war, and many persons began to regard Marxist and Leninist principles as works of the Devil. D. W. Griffith's motion picture *Intolerance*, produced in 1916, was an apparent attempt to mirror the difficulty which men so often experience in learning to appreciate differences in other people—a warning, if not a preview, of the mood to be demonstrated in subsequent years.

After the war, a free speech issue was the constitutionality of state statutes which made it a criminal act to advocate the overthrow of the government by violent means. A former Socialist assemblyman of the New York legislature, Benjamin Gitlow, was arrested in 1919 and charged with criminal anarchy. The son of poor Russian Jewish immigrants, Gitlow had grown up in New York's lower East Side and, after the Russian Revolution of 1917, had turned from socialism to communism, and also had attempted to convert the American Socialist Party. The New York legislature had passed an anti-sedition law which made certain anti-government statements illegal. Gitlow then published an anti-capitalist manifesto that advocated the overthrow of the government, was arrested, and was convicted. Upholding the New York law, the United States Supreme Court in 1925 sustained Gitlow's sentence to hard labor for five to ten years in Sing Sing Prison. Justices Holmes and Brandeis again dissented in the case, as they had in *Abrams*; they claimed that the "clear and present danger" criterion should be applied to test the legality of Gitlow's utterances. In the opinion of the dissenting judges, Gitlow's manifesto did not represent a clear and present danger to the security of the nation.

As Bolshevism spread in Europe and military strikes occurred in Germany, Hungary, and areas along Russia's frontier, genuine concern developed in the United States over the rise of communism, and the post-war Red scare resulted in strong criticisms of persons who espoused radical ideas. The nation had hardly begun to demobilize its military activities when a new type of internal strife began with labor agitators and "Bolsheviks." Millions of Americans were fearful that an American Red revolution would break out; hence, the momentum of the labor movement and strikes by workers were viewed as dangerous signals. A Red scare gripped the nation, and extreme or unusual views about political, economic, or social changes were criticized as "un-American."

Between 1900 and 1914, more than 13 million immigrants came to the United States. Most of them were from Central, Eastern, and Southern Europe, including Poland, Russia, the Austro-Hungarian Empire, and Greece,[34] and most came in pursuit of better economic opportunities. Some of the immigrants held radical ideas that were viewed as suspect by the "native" man in the street, who in 1920 could hardly have understood very much about communism. But the winds of revolution were prevailing in Russia, and many Americans were frightened. As a result of this concern over communism, foreigners with unpopular ideas were generally held in contempt, and abridgments of the liberties of aliens were not uncommon.

Although membership in the Socialist Party, the Communist Labor Party, and the Communist Party in the United States constituted less than half of one percent of the population in 1919,[35] old prejudices and new fears, fanned by legislative investigations, were sufficient to maintain a climate in which purging seemed appropriate. During that year, Attorney General A. Mitchell Palmer began a series of operations against aliens and radicals. Unfortunately, the campaign developed into wholesale violations of some citizens' civil liberties. Worse still, Palmer's aggressive round-ups and deportations of radicals and his harassment of strikers were accomplished without official opposition, probably because President Wilson was in precarious health at that time and unable to oversee important matters of national policy. The Palmer raids have been viewed by some historians, political scientists, and other concerned citizens as one of the most scandalous episodes in American history. Although the raids did result in the arrest of a few dangerous revolutionaries, they also terrorized many innocent aliens and violated the following Fourth Amendment rights of others:

> The right of the people to be secure in their persons, houses, papers, and effects, against unreasonable searches and seizures, shall not be violated, and no warrants shall issue but upon probable cause, supported by oath or affirmation, and particularly describing the place to be searched, and the person or thing to be seized.

The raids authorized by Palmer were characterized by high-handed searches of the premises of suspects, by the seizure of personal papers and effects, and by unlawful confinement of prisoners for periods of up to five months.[36] In addition, some of the persons arrested were compelled to be witnesses against themselves. Flagrant disregard for due process of law for the accused characterized many of the activities of the raiding federal and police agents, as Attorney General Palmer and his agents—including the young J. Edgar Hoover, who later became head of the FBI— used totalitarian methods which denied individual liberties. In the face of greatly exaggerated fears of communist revolutionary movements, the federal government used police-state tactics in rounding up aliens, methods not unlike those employed in Russia, whose political system was sparking so much terror among American citizens.

Much of the national hysteria of the Red scare was generated by postal bombings in 1919 and by post-war radicalism. Attorney General Palmer claimed that 60,000 subversives were loose in the country; federal agents rounded up approximately 4,000 radicals in 33 cities on January 2, 1920.[37] Bewildered Italians, Russians, Germans, and other aliens were collected and accused of being communist agitators. Persons arrested were tried for their "crimes," but most of the aliens were actually harmless. Emma Goldman, a Russian-born anarchist leader, labor agitator, and publisher of the magazine *Mother Earth*, was among the aliens deported. She had earlier served two years in prison during World War I because of her political activism.

Although few Americans were critical of the Palmer raids, most of them gradually grew tired of the Red scare and began to pay less attention to the attorney general's overzealous activities and his unfounded charges of a grandiose plot to overthrow the government. However, super-patriots and federal agents actively pursued real and imaginary communists throughout the 1920s, and the big Red scare did not die easily. Americans ultimately came to the realization, however, that there was insufficient cause for panic. Perhaps, then, the raids conducted by Palmer represent an unfortunate adolescent deed of a growing democracy; it is hoped that our contemporary spirit of freedom will make their reenactment highly unlikely.

The Red scare subsided during the summer of 1920; however, in its wake was a tragic series of violations of citizens' rights as guaranteed in the U.S. Constitution. The intolerance of the period caused most liberal civic, social, and cultural organizations to fall under suspicion as revolutionary fronts. The Federal Council of Churches, National League of Women Voters, National Civic Federation, and National Council for the Reduction of Armaments were all labeled by one patriotic group or another as "pro-communist." In addition, books, magazines, motion pictures, and theater productions were carefully scrutinized for communist propaganda. Some schools, colleges, and universities were also accused of promoting subversive propaganda and activities. Seemingly, many Americans transferred their wartime hatred of Germans to minority groups in the nation, particularly blacks, Jews, and the foreign-born. Catholicism was also considered by some Protestants as un-American because the head of the Roman Catholic Church was a foreigner.

In New York, a joint senate and assembly committee of the state legislature was created with the power to investigate the scope, tendencies, and ramifications of "revolutionary radicalism." A four-volume report entitled *Revolutionary Radicalism; Its History, Purpose and Tactics*[38] was prepared and submitted to the New York State Senate in April 1920. The report's general introduction exemplifies the concern about anarchists in the second decade of the century, and the first two paragraphs of the massive report are reprinted here:

> In the report here presented the Committee seeks to give a clear, unbiased statement and history of the purposes and objectives, tactics and methods, of the various forces now at work in the United States, and particularly within the State of New York, which are seeking to undermine and destroy, not only the government under which we live, but also the very structure of American society; it also seeks to analyze the various constructive forces which are at work throughout the country counteracting these evil influences and to present the many industrial and social problems that these constructive forces must meet and are meeting.
>
> The Great War has shaken the foundations of European civilization. The same forces which promote civil strife in many of the countries of Europe are at work on this side of the ocean seeking to create a division in our population, stimulating class hatred and a contempt for government, which, if continued, must necessarily result in serious consequences to the peace and prosperity of this country. In doing this they are taking advantage of the real grievances and natural demands of the working classes for a larger share in the management and use of the common wealth.[39]

In fulfilling its mission, the New York Joint Legislative Committee Investigating Seditious Activities had obtained numerous warrants to search for "seditious" printed matter in such organizations as the Rand School of Social Science, the left wing of the Socialist Party, the Union of Russian Workers, and the Communist Party of America. Members of the state constabulary and the police force of New York City seized tons of supposedly "seditious" and "anarchistic" literature and arrested more than 80 persons, among them Benjamin Gitlow (previously discussed) and James L. Larkin, editors of *Revolutionary Age.* Many of the arrested persons were charged with criminal anarchy solely on the basis of written material found in their personal effects or in their offices. Some arrested aliens were deported to Russia almost immediately on the *U.S.S. Buford.*

As a result of the investigation of radicalism in New York, the legislative committee recommended the passage of a number of acts, including a law requiring public school teachers to certify that they were of good character and loyal to the state and nation; a law requiring all directors of schools, courses, and classes not under the control of the department of education to procure a license from the New York Board of Regents; and an enabling act, to allow the state commissioner of education to open more schools in factories and other non-traditional educational settings so that immigrants could be given instruction about the nation's institutions and laws and about the duties and privileges of citizens.

Because of its significance during the Red scare period, the Sacco-Vanzetti trial should also be mentioned here. The robbery and murder trial of Nicola Sacco and Bartolomeo Vanzetti, two Massachusetts Italian immigrants who were arrested and found guilty of murder, attracted considerable attention between 1920 and 1927. The conviction of Sacco and Vanzetti was vigorously protested in the nation as well as throughout the world, many critics of the trial claiming that insubstantial evidence against the two philosophical anarchists was presented in court. Other protestors claimed that the two immigrants were convicted because of prejudice against their radical views. In response to public clamor over the trial, a special commission was finally appointed by the governor of Massachusetts to investigate the case; however, the guilty verdict against Sacco and Vanzetti was sustained and they were executed. Doubts have persisted, however, to the present time about the guilt of the Italian immigrants.[40]

THE PROHIBITION ERA

Although the Anti-Saloon League had been unsuccessful in its attempt to solve what it deemed to be a "liquor problem," the federal government decided to enter into the act of curtailing the consumption of whiskey and other alcoholic beverages. Amendment XVIII to the Constitution declared Prohibition to be in force on January 23, 1919, and proscribed the manufacture, sale, or transportation of intoxicating liquors within the United States. Put into force in 1920, when Congress passed the National Prohibition Act, commonly known as the Volstead Act, Prohibition was advocated by persons who felt that the government had a moral obligation to prevent millions of their fellow citizens from drinking wine, beer, or whiskey. Prohibitionists were particularly strong in rural areas and among the ranks of religious fundamentalists. With the Volstead Act, Congress appeared to be conducting a bold experiment to determine how far legislators could go in controlling personal behavior and in restricting individual liberties. Prohibition was a sad attempt to legislate morals. Herbert Asbury, an expert on American morals, claimed that in 1920, few persons anticipated the "long train of evils" that was to be associated with Prohibition, including

> . . . the illicit breweries and distilleries, the bootleggers and speakeasies, the corruption of police and judiciary, the hijackers and their machine guns, the gang wars, the multimillionaire booze barons, the murders and assassinations, the national breakdown of morals and manners . . . [41]

During the Prohibition era, Americans could not purchase liquor except by medical prescription, nor could they give or receive a bottle of liquor. In addition, they were forbidden by law to buy or sell formulas or recipes for homemade liquors or to manufacture in their homes any intoxicant which contained more than one-half of one percent alcohol. Some libraries even entered the prohibition spirit, and in New Haven, Connecticut, and Springfield, Massachusetts, literature describing the manufacture of alcohol was withdrawn from public library shelves. However, the director of the New York Public Library, Edwin H. Anderson, did not agree with the censorship of materials about alcohol. Librarian Anderson declared: "I would no more think of forbidding readers to consult such books than I would ban books on aviation."[42] Despite the ban on alcohol, approximately 343,181 violators of the Volstead Act were arrested by federal agents during the years of Prohibition,[43] and nine million gallons of spirits, one billion gallons of malt liquor, and one billion gallons of wine, hard cider, and mash were confiscated in the decade of the 1920s.[44]

Traffic in bootlegging also lined the bank accounts of notorious criminals during Prohibition, despite the Eighteenth Amendment and the Volstead Act. The federal government spent more than $10 million dollars each Prohibition year in unsuccessful attempts to end rumrunning, but the manufacture and consumption of alcoholic beverages continued. Whether Americans drank more or fewer intoxicants during the Prohibition era has not been determined. However, many citizens refused to abide by the stringent anti-alcohol laws, and respect for law and order also declined rather dramatically during the decade. Hence, the Eighteenth Amendment should serve as a reminder that Congress can pass laws which limit citizens' social freedoms, but that such laws will not be respected when they are too restrictive or excessively oppressive.

VOTES FOR WOMEN

In 1900, only four states allowed women to vote, but by 1916 suffrage had been extended in twelve states to all citizens. Susan B. Anthony had fought vigorously for the extension of voting rights to all women and died an internationally acclaimed feminist in 1906. Her efforts were vigorously continued by other women, who became as militant in the twentieth century as Anthony had been in the nineteenth. Anna Howard Shaw, an English-born medical doctor and the first woman to be ordained in the Methodist Protestant Church, took up the cause, serving as president of the National American Suffrage Association from 1904 until 1915. Dr. Shaw's fight to obtain a constitutional guarantee of the right of women to vote was later continued by Carrie Chapman Catt.

Most suffragists were members of the National American Woman Suffrage Association; however, the more militant fighters joined the Woman's Party, which picketed the White House in 1917 and sponsored the burning of a speech by President Wilson to draw attention to its cause. But not until 1918 did President Wilson endorse the campaign to amend the Constitution so that all women could vote. One year later, the Nineteenth Amendment was ratified—72 years after the first women's rights convention in the United States was held in Seneca Falls, New York. The amendment is as follows:

The rights of citizens of the United States to vote shall not be denied or abridged by the United States or by any State on account of sex.

The Congress shall have power to appropriate legislation to
enforce the Provisions of this article.

Thus, not until the end of the second decade of the twentieth century did women in
the United States have a constitutionally guaranteed right to vote. The long labors
of the women who took part in the feminist movement were vindicated by the
attainment of that right. In 1920, Carrie Chapman Catt organized the League of
Women Voters, which has functioned to the present time as an organization for
education of all citizens to the responsibilities of voting. According to
Marjorie Fribourg, the story of the suffragists

> ... stands as a monument and as a lesson showing that peaceful methods
> of petition and assembly in the hands of dedicated citizens can bring
> about badly needed reform by the orderly processes provided for by free
> people in a free society.[45]

EVOLUTION AND ACADEMIC FREEDOM

During the 1920s, many intellectuals deplored censorship, the Puritan ethic,
and the legislation of morals (including Prohibition), and they encouraged more
sexual freedom. Too, many educated people were religious skeptics during the
period, "united in their scorn of the great bourgeois majority which they held
responsible for prohibition, censorship, Fundamentalism, and other repressions."[46]
Intellectuals were also fearful that technology's monotony and standardization
would destroy their right and ability to be themselves.

The Scopes Trial in the summer of 1925 was of significance as a modern conflict between religion and science. The languid little Tennessee town of Dayton was
the scene of the so-called "monkey trial," which attracted worldwide attention
and roused nationwide ridicule. The trial centered on the issue of whether evolutionary theory or the biblical story of creation should be taught as fact in public
schools. The roots of the Scopes Trial were in a 1925 Tennessee law which stipulated that

> it shall be unlawful for any teacher in any of the universities, normals and
> all other public schools of the State ... to teach any theory that denies
> the story of the Divine creation of man as taught in the Bible, and to
> teach that man has descended from a lower order of animals.

Shortly after Tennessee's anti-evolution law was passed, a test-case was prepared
by George Rappelyea, a Dayton mining engineer, and John Thomas Scopes, a local
high school biology teacher. The American Civil Liberties Union (discussed later in
this chapter) had previously placed an advertisement in Tennessee newspapers seeking the cooperation of a teacher who would assist in challenging the anti-evolution
law as a violation of constitutional prohibitions against the mixing of church and
state. The ACLU agreed to back Scopes in testing what was considered a repressive
law. Scopes was soon charged with a violation of the anti-evolution act, and he
became a *cause célèbre* among civil libertarians, who hoped that the case would
eventually reach the U.S. Supreme Court, where anti-evolution bills might be

declared unconstitutional. While the issue in the Scopes Trial was actually academic freedom as opposed to the rights of citizens to decide what was to be taught in public schools, in the eyes of religious fundamentalists throughout the nation, the case was a struggle between God-fearing Christians and false prophets.

William Jennings Bryan, three-time presidential candidate, former Secretary of State, and staunch critic of the evolutionary theory, volunteered to assist the prosecution. The ACLU chose Clarence Darrow, a leading defender of liberal causes, as defense attorney. After a ten-day trial, Scopes was found guilty and fined $100. In 1927, however, the verdict of the court was reversed by the Tennessee State Appellate Court on a slight technicality, and the ACLU's planned appeal to the Supreme Court was thus undercut. Although fifty years have passed since the Scopes Trial was conducted in the Bible-belt hinterlands of east Tennessee, the central issue of the trial remains alive. Civil libertarians viewed the trial as a silent victory of reason over emotionalism; however, the debate over the teaching of evolution in public schools is far from resolution and has continued in various states, including California, Michigan, Texas, and Washington.

Academic freedom is the liberty exercised by teachers and professors to pursue scholarly activities, to convey their conclusions and judgments about their findings, and to disseminate in published form the results of their research efforts and thinking. Teachers in the United States achieved widespread recognition of their right to academic freedom in the third decade of the twentieth century. This right was facilitated by the founding of such organizations as the American Federation of Teachers (1916), the American Civil Liberties Union (1920), and the American Association of University Professors (1915).[47] The American Association of University Professors (AAUP) was founded with a charter membership comprised of faculty members from 60 colleges and universities and was formed primarily as a result of concern among professors about dismissals of their colleagues.[48] Bertram Davis, a former general secretary of the AAUP, has written:

> The limits of academic freedom, or the extent to which academic freedom is tolerated, reflects, it seems to me, the limits of freedom in society itself. . . . In a society where freedom of expression is tolerated and legally protected, the professoriate will itself have a high degree of freedom.[49]

In the 1950s, academic freedom was an issue in several U.S. Supreme Court cases. In 1952, the Court upheld, in *Adler v. Board of Education*,[50] the constitutionality of New York City legislation which prohibited teachers from advocating the unlawful overthrow of the government. In a dissenting opinion, Justice William O. Douglas claimed, however, that "when suspicion fills the air and holds scholars in line for fear of their jobs, there can be no exercise of free intellect." In *Sweezy v. New Hampshire*,[51] academic freedom fared somewhat better in 1957, with the reversal of a lower court's contempt conviction of a professor who would not respond to questions relating to his involvement with "progressives." In 1958, the case *Beilan v. Board of Education of Philadelphia*[52] resulted in a decision in support of the firing of a public school teacher because the instructor would not respond to questions about alleged past communist activities. One year later, the Court ruled in *Barenblatt v. United States*[53] that suspected subversive activities in schools could be investigated by the House Committee on Un-American Activities.

WORLD WAR II AND FREEDOMS

Censorship practiced by the government during World War II was aimed primarily at preventing the dissemination of military information that might be of value to the enemy. It was voluntary, as opposed to the more inefficient and oppressive censoring measures taken during the First World War. Censorship was urged at the source of information during the 1940s, and, as a general rule, most officials of the communication media cooperated with the government. Early in the war, the War and Navy Departments began to censor all outgoing communications. Too, in 1941, Byron Price, a former executive news editor of the Associated Press, was appointed director of the Office of Censorship. The federal government had justified the Office of Censorship as an attempt to withhold some news at its source, to prevent the enemy from obtaining information, and to seek additional cooperation from the news media so that troop and vessel movements would remain secret.[54]

More than likely, censorship of an official nature will be least controversial and perhaps least opposed if exercised during periods of active hostility when citizens are united. Censorship did not become a public issue in the 1940s, as it had been in the First World War, because citizens were more united behind the nation's war efforts during World War II, while the First World War did not entirely gain the backing of the citizenry. One question that had to be answered repeatedly during that first conflict and the post-war years was: What standards are necessary to control the war effort? But a more united public opinion about the Second World War made this a less significant question in the 1940s.

The Second World War did pose another, different kind of problem in relation to personal freedoms—repressions against Japanese-Americans. Early on Sunday morning, December 7, 1941, the key U.S. Naval Base at Pearl Harbor in Hawaii was attacked by Japanese carrier-based airplanes, at the same time that Japanese envoys were negotiating in Washington, D.C., over disagreements between the United States and Japan. Most of the Pacific battle fleet of the U.S. Navy and half of the military airplanes on the island were destroyed in the attack, which took most Americans completely by surprise and which brought the nation into World War II. The Japanese military action was particularly shocking to Pacific Coast residents, who feared that the next move by the enemy might be an attack on the mainland of the United States, and that it might occur along the coast of California, Oregon, or Washington. Too, strained relationships between the United States and Japan had begun as early as 1906, when San Francisco segregated Japanese school children as a manifestation of general opposition on the Pacific Coast to Japanese immigration.

Thousands of Japanese-American citizens and Japanese aliens were concentrated in cities, towns, villages, and on farms along the West Coast, and feelings of hatred and distrust generated by Japan's attack on Pearl Harbor were transferred to these persons. Although rumors to the contrary were rampant, there was no evidence that Japanese-Americans were sympathetic or loyal to Japan. However, signs appeared in Pacific Coast store windows early in 1942 which advertised "Jap hunting licenses." Because of the shock of the attack on Pearl Harbor, and because many citizens knew little about the political goals of Japanese-American citizens, a "Yellow Peril" myth was accepted by many non-Japanese Americans, and repressions against Japanese living in the United States were initiated. A campaign for the evacuation of all Japanese from the West Coast area was initiated on January 5, 1942, in a broadcast by radio commentator John B. Hughes, a campaign also supported by newspaper editorials and by some law-enforcement officers and congressmen.[55]

On February 14, 1942, General J. L. DeWitt, commander of the Western Defense Command and Fourth Army, submitted recommendations to the Secretary of War for the evacuation and internment, under guard, of all Japanese aliens, Japanese-American citizens, and alien enemies other than Japanese from the states of Washington, Oregon, and California.[56] Five days later, on February 19, President Franklin D. Roosevelt issued an executive order which permitted the removal of persons from "national defense" areas in order to protect the nation against espionage and sabotage. The order directed

> . . . the Secretary of War, and Military Commanders . . . to prescribe military areas in such places and of such extent as he or the appropriate Military Commander may determine, from which any or all persons may be excluded, and with respect to which, the right of any person to enter, remain in, or leave shall be subject to whatever restriction the Secretary of War or the appropriate Military Commander may impose in his discretion.[57]

The president issued another executive order on March 18, 1942, which established the War Relocation Authority in the executive offices of the government,[58] and Dillon S. Myer was appointed director of the Authority. Three days later, Congress passed Public Law 503, which outlined penalties for violations of restrictions or orders with respect to persons entering, remaining in, leaving, or committing any act in "military zones." Thus, the legal framework was laid for what Edward Ennis, a member of the Justice Department, later described as "one of the most spectacular breakdowns . . . of government responsibility in our history."[59]

In the period of panic which followed the Japanese attack on Pearl Harbor, approximately 110,000 Japanese-Americans were taken from their homes on the West Coast because they were considered to be threats to national security; they were removed without hearings or trials to "relocation centers" in the interior of the nation. Properties of these citizens were seized as the Japanese were uprooted and moved to barracks, where they were placed under guard by military police. Of the persons removed, about two-thirds were American citizens; many of them had been born in the United States. After the war ended, Harold Ickes, who had been a member of President Roosevelt's administration, blamed the military for being too concerned about ungrounded fears of sabotage; he described the relocation process as follows:

> Crowded into cars like cattle, these hapless people were hurried away to hastily constructed and thoroughly inadequate concentration camps, with soldiers with nervous muskets on guard, in the great American desert. We gave the fancy name "relocation centers" to these dust bowls, but they were concentration camps, nonetheless, although not as bad as Dachau or Buchenwald.[60]

In his book about the evacuation of Japanese from the West Coast, Dillon S. Myer, who headed the removal project, discussed the episode as follows:

We all learned from first hand experience how low some of the worst of the avaricious and race-baiting segments of our population could stoop . . . We came to the realization that it is a sad fact that most people do not understand that the emotions of fear and hate are so closely associated.[61]

After the war, an editorial in the March 28, 1946, issue of the *Washington Post* pointed out that the exclusion of Japanese from the West Coast, and the detention of those persons in camps upon mere suspicion and without trial, was altogether unnecessary and was prompted by "blind racial prejudice" rather than by military considerations. In addition, the editorial quoted Supreme Court Justice Murphy's description of the act in his dissenting opinion in *Korematsu v. United States*,[62] which dealt with the constitutionality of the evacuation of civilians under the war power. Justice Murphy described the relocation process as "legalization of racism." According to the *Washington Post* editorial, "the treatment accorded this helpless minority remains a smudge upon our national honor and a threat to elementary principles of freedom."[63] Tom C. Clark, former Associate Justice of the U.S. Supreme Court, summed up the anti-Japanese movement as follows:

The truth is—as this deplorable experience proves—that constitutions and laws are not sufficient of themselves; they must be given life through implementation and strict enforcement.[64]

Audrie Girdner and Anne Loftis, authors of *The Great Betrayal*, have warned:

It has been said that any denial of the rights of a single group cheapens citizenship for all . . . the evacuation [of Japanese] cannot be relegated to a dusty corner of history. As a departure from American principles that was endorsed by the highest tribunal of the land, it will stand as an aberration and a warning.[65]

In his exhaustive study of the decision-making process surrounding the evacuation of Japanese-Americans from the Pacific Coast, Morton Grodzins has noted that " . . . the evacuation was a major event in the history of the American democracy, without precedent in the past and with disturbing implications for the future."[66]

RELIGIOUS LIBERTY

For all practical purposes, freedom of religion in the United States has been one of the most realized and solid liberties of citizens during the present century, since the government is prohibited by the First Amendment to the Constitution from establishing an official church or from interfering with citizens' religious freedoms. Religion has generally been viewed officially as a private matter in the United States, and only when religious groups have threatened to undermine laws has the government interfered with the practices of various faiths. During the twentieth century, religious liberty has also been supported by national private organizations, including the American Civil Liberties Union, the Protestants and Other Americans United for Separation of Church and State, the National Conference of Christians and Jews, the Anti-Defamation League of B'nai B'rith, and the Religious Liberty Association of America.[67] In 1936, the Religious Liberty Association of America issued a statement outlining its principles and aims, which included the following basic philosophy:

> The Association holds that the state may properly enact laws regulating the relationship of man to his fellow man, but that it has no right to pass measures which have to do with man's relationship to God or religion. The right to disbelieve may be as sacred as the right to believe. The right to dissent should be sacredly guarded.[68]

The Secretariat for Religious Liberty of the World Council of Churches, A. F. Carrillo de Albornoz, has outlined the basis of religious liberty and has listed some relevant points reached by ecumenical agreement, including: 1) freedom from legal or social coercion in religious matters, 2) freedom of religious expression and association, 3) freedom from state judgments and definitions of religious truths, and 4) freedom not to believe or not to profess any religion at all. Religious freedom has also been supported by the United Nations, Article 18 of the 1948 UN Universal Declaration of Human Rights stating:

> Everyone has the right to freedom of thought, conscience and religion; this right includes freedom to change his religion or belief, and freedom, either alone or in a community with others and in public or private, to manifest his religion or belief in teaching, practice, worship and observation.

In the United States, the policy of governmental neutrality with respect to religion has been firmly embedded in the nation's laws since Thomas Jefferson advocated "a wall of separation between church and state." Wilbur G. Katz, Professor of Law at the University of Wisconsin, has noted that religious freedom is essential in a pluralistic society because

> ... it is an integral part of religious belief. When government punishes heresy, it not only violates the freedom of the heretic but renders unfree the religious commitment of the orthodox.[69]

While the practice of exempting religious institutions from taxation is common in the United States (with roots in a European tradition originating in the fourth century), it is being attacked increasingly as an indirect subsidy to religion. Most Americans have apparently favored the principle of tax exemption for religious groups, and the U.S. Supreme Court has not yet handed down a definitive interpretation of the constitutionality of the practice under the First Amendment. Robert F. Drinan, S.J., a Catholic priest, a member of Congress, and a legal scholar, has written:

> If the trend toward the establishment of an absolute separation of church and state is to continue, it would seem logical to predict that the constitutionality of tax exemption may be challenged.[70]

However, several other issues relating to freedom of religion have been considered by the U.S. Supreme Court. In 1879, the Court, in *Reynolds v. United States*,[71] upheld the government's contention that the practice of polygamy among Mormons could not be allowed. Then in the early 1940s, a series of cases involving conflicts between religious beliefs and patriotic practices reached the court with most of the legal problems relating to religion involving practices of the Jehovah's Witnesses sect in relation to First Amendment issues. For instance, in 1936, two school children in Minersville, Pennsylvania, were informed by public school officials that they could not continue to attend classes if they refused to salute the United States flag during patriotic exercises. The children belonged to the family of Walter Gobitis, a member of the Jehovah's Witnesses sect. Gobitis objected to the flag salute required of his children, regarding the act as submission to a graven image— a performance which he and others of his religious persuasion looked upon as prohibited by biblical injunctions. The students' father filed a suit to seek relief from the financial burden of having to educate his children in another school and also to prevent the Minersville School District from requiring the flag salute.

In 1940, four years after Gobitis filed his suit, the Supreme Court ruled against him by a vote of 8 to 1. Justice Harlan F. Stone, the lone dissenter in *Minersville School District v. Gobitis*[72] maintained that the religious freedom of Jehovah's Witnesses should not be violated; however, the Court's majority opinion, written by Justice Felix Frankfurter, noted:

> The mere possession of religious convictions which contradict the
> relevant consensus of a political society does not relieve the citizen
> from the discharge of political responsibilities.

But three years after the *Gobitis* decision, a similar Jehovah's Witnesses case, *West Virginia State Board of Education v. Barnette*,[73] was considered in 1943 by the Supreme Court and resulted in a new judicial ruling quite different from the earlier decision. In West Virginia, the school flag salute ceremony was also compulsory, and a group of parents brought suit for an injunction to stop enforcement of the practice. When the case reached the Supreme Court, the earlier *Gobitis* decision was overruled by a vote of 6 to 3, and direct references were made in the *Barnette* decision as to the error of the Court's earlier opinion. The following eloquent statements were included in the *Barnette* decision:

> If there is any fixed star in our constitutional constellation, it is
> that no official, high or petty, can prescribe what shall be orthodox in
> politics, nationalism, religion, or other matters of opinion or force
> citizens to confess by work or act their faith therein. If there are any
> circumstances which permit an exception, they do not now occur to us.

In their concurring opinion, Justices Black and Douglas wrote: "Words uttered under coercion are proof of loyalty to nothing but self-interest. Love for country must spring from willing hearts and free minds."

In the three-year period between *Gobitis* and *Barnette*, some members of the Court changed their opinions. Morris L. Ernst, an expert in legal aspects of First Amendment rights, pointed out that the *Gobitis* decision was reversed because of "second thoughts among some of the justices, since seven of the nine who rendered judgment in 1940 were still on the bench in 1943."[74] Ernst went even further and declared that

> . . . a revulsion of popular feeling against the abuse heaped upon the Jehovah's Witnesses after the *Gobitis* decision had taken place among many who were inclined to respect a religious stance even if they did not agree with it.[75]

In 1940, the Supreme Court heard the case *Cantwell v. Connecticut*,[76] which was concerned with the issue of whether a Connecticut statute violated liberty and freedom of religion. State law required those persons planning to solicit money for religious purposes to secure a permit from the Secretary of the Public Welfare of Connecticut. Cantwell and other members of the Jehovah's Witnesses were arrested for solicting without the required permit when they conducted house-to-house canvasses and played a phonograph recording describing books offered for sale. The Court ruled that the statute deprived the appellants of due process of law and the right of freedom of religion.

An appeal was made in 1947 in the case *Everson v. Board of Education*[77] for the Supreme Court to determine the legality of a New Jersey statute which authorized a school board to reimburse all parents for bus transportation of students, including those enrolled in Catholic parochial schools. The New Jersey statute was challenged as a violation of the concept of separation of church and state. However, the Court ruled that while the government was prohibited from favoring religions, by the same token it could not handicap them, and public tax funds could be used to transport children to parochial as well as public schools without violating the First and Fourteenth Amendments. This decision was based upon the theory that the expenditure of tax monies for this purpose was social welfare rather than state aid to religious education. In this, as in other cases, though, critics of many court decisions relating to the church-state issue feel that the tribunal has tended to support certain laws which blur the distinction between the church and state, thus endangering a cooperative separation between government and religion.

In 1952, a controversial motion picture became the subject of a church-state issue. Although techniques for the production of motion pictures were essentially perfected in the first quarter of the twentieth century, not until the 1950s was the film legally recognized as a significant communication medium rather than pure entertainment. In 1952, the U.S. Supreme Court extended to motion pictures the same free-speech guarantees of the First and Fourteenth Amendments that had long been granted to traditional print media such as books, magazines, and newspapers. The case *Burstyn v. Wilson*[78] involved the controversial Italian film *The Miracle*, which caused so much unfavorable public reaction in New York that the license to show the motion picture was withdrawn on the grounds that it offended religious beliefs. Wilson, the New York State Commissioner of Education, had revoked the film's license. Burstyn, the film's distributor, sought redress from the courts to have the license reinstated. When the case reached the U.S. Supreme Court, justices declared in a 9-0 decision that the New York "sacreligion" statute violated the First and Fourteenth Amendments. In lifting the ban on the controversial film, the Court declared that, in respect to freedom of speech and press, the state could not prevent the expression of distasteful religious views.

In *Torcaso v. Watkins*,[79] the Supreme Court declared unconstitutional a Maryland law requiring candidates for the position of notary public to take an oath stating their belief in God. That same year, 1961, the Court considered four cases which challenged the validity of Sunday closing laws.[80] The two central issues raised in these cases were: 1) Are Sunday closing laws for businesses unconstitutional because they coincide with Christian practices? And 2) must persons who observe a day other than Sunday as a religious day of rest be exempt from the laws? The court declared that Sunday closing laws are not invalid because they do not attempt to establish Christianity as an official religion; however, the issue of forcing a Sunday closing on those persons who observe another day of rest for religious reasons was viewed as a violation of religious liberty. In one of the cases, *McGowan v. Maryland*, Justice William O. Douglas—always a champion of liberty— wrote in his dissenting opinion: "There is an 'establishment' of religion in the constitutional sense if any practice of any religious group has the sanction of law behind it."[81]

A controversial issue relating to separation of church and state was decided in 1962 in the case *Steven I. Engel et al. v. William J. Vitale, et al.*[82] The legal question considered was whether required prayers in a New York public school violated constitutional prohibitions against the establishment by the government of a religion. In New York state, the Board of Regents had recommended student recitation of the following prayer in classes each morning: "Almighty God, we acknowledge our dependence upon Thee, and we beg Thy blessings upon us, our parents, our teachers, and our country." A local school board subsequently required the utilization of the recommended prayer; however, parents of ten pupils challenged the legality of the requirement, and the U.S. Supreme Court declared by a 6-1 vote that:

> Under the First Amendment's prohibition against governmental establishment of religion . . . government in this country, be it state or federal, is without power to prescribe by law any particular form of prayer which is to be used as an official prayer in carrying on any program of governmentally-sponsored religious activity.

Thus, the Court ruled that the use of the Board of Regent's recommended prayer for New York public schools breached the constitutional demand for separation between church and state.

THE COLD WAR AND COMMUNISM

The House Committee on Un-American Activities was founded in 1938. Under the chairmanship of Congressman Martin Dies, Jr. (D-Texas), the Committee attempted to expose communist infiltration of the Congress of Industrial Organizations (CIO) and of President Franklin Roosevelt's New Deal administration. Supported by political conservatives and religious fundamentalist factions, Congressman Dies utilized the principle of guilt by association in his anti-communism campaign. After World War II, the controversial House Committee on Un-American Activities continued to pursue real or imaginary communists in labor unions, government agencies, foundations, schools, and other organizations and activities. Richard M. Nixon, then a young Republican congressman from California, was among those appointed by party leaders to the House Un-American Activities Committee, and he played a leading role in the investigation of Alger Hiss, president of the Carnegie Endowment for International Peace. Hiss was later indicted and convicted of perjury in connection with his testimony about communist activities in Washington.

Too, a national loyalty-security program for government employees was initiated by a 1947 executive order from President Harry S. Truman, which was prompted by post-World War II allegations that the government was infiltrated by communist spies. Civil libertarians criticized the government's loyalty program as a denial of a person's right to claim innocence until proven guilty, and they also objected to the singling out of government employees as potential traitors, claiming that the loyalty program was a transgression of the concept of equal justice under the law.

During the Cold War period of ideological tensions, when government officials were concerned about national security, a number of state legislatures also viewed the loyalty oath as an instrument to prevent the spread of communism. Thus, teachers in some states were required to take loyalth oaths, and even students who received federal aid in the late 1950s were required by the National Defense Education Act of 1958 to declare their loyalty to the United States government. Loyalty oaths were prerequisites for obtaining aid from the National Science Foundation as well.

Another major threat to the intellectual and civil liberties of American citizens occurred in the years immediately following World War II—a period in which deep feelings of mistrust developed between the United States and the Soviet Union. The discovery of Soviet spy rings in the nation caused some Americans to fear that communists were systematically working to gather information and to conduct espionage activities at all social and political levels, especially on the federal level. A prevailing concern came to exist among the general populace that communists were working on a large scale to undermine the American way of life. Senator Joseph McCarthy, a Republican from Wisconsin, claimed to have uncovered numerous cases of communist activity by United States citizens, including some government officials, and he helped to create and used a climate of fear of communism to charge disloyalty on the part of officials in the Department of State and the U.S. Army.

In 1950, Senator McCarthy charged in a speech delivered at Wheeling, West Virginia, that he had a list (never disclosed, however) of "card-carrying communists" who were employed by the State Department. McCarthy later made reference to the administrations of Presidents Franklin D. Roosevelt and Harry S. Truman as "20 years of treason," and the senator criticized these presidents for submitting to Russian and Red Chinese pressures. For the same reasons, he criticized General George C. Marshall, who had served in the U.S. Army as chief of staff between 1939 and 1945 and as Secretary of State between 1947 and 1949. In 1953, McCarthy expanded his charge of "softness on communism" to the Eisenhower administration.

McCarthy's accusations and emotional speeches helped to increase the public's anxiety about communism, but congressional investigations into alleged communist activities in universities, labor unions, and the motion picture industry uncovered few cases of subversive efforts by citizens. All in all, McCarthy was responsible for

157 investigations of alleged subversive activity in the nation, including an inquiry into the Voice of America and an investigation of the holdings of libraries maintained in foreign countries by the United States Information Service. It became increasingly clear in the 1950s that anti-communist charges and investigations had endangered the basic rights of many persons, and freedom of expression was dealt a heavy blow by McCarthyism, although most of the senator's charges were later found to have been largely false. A bi-partisan investigating committee, chaired by Senator Millard E. Tydings (D-Maryland), dismissed some of McCarthy's charges as "a fraud and a hoax."

However, because of McCarthy's charges, a repressive climate enveloped the nation between 1949 and 1953. McCarthyism demanded conformity as well as an uncriticial acceptance of the status quo as indiscriminate anti-communist hysteria—directed so well by Senator McCarthy—capitalized on domestic anxieties relating to a fear of communism. In equating the nation's private enterprise economic system with Americanism, followers of McCarthy also regarded any criticism of existing political, social, and economic conditions or institutions as "un-American." Persons who criticized the established order during the McCarthy era were often labeled "pinkos" or "communist sympathizers." In reference to the McCarthy-generated hysteria, Supreme Court Justice Earl Warren wrote in 1955:

> In the present struggle between our world and communism, the temptation to imitate totalitarian security methods is a subtle temptation that must be resisted day to day, for it will be with us as long as totalitarianism itself. The whole question of man's relation to his nation, his government, his fellow man is raised in acute and chronic form. Each of the 462 words of our Bill of Rights, the most precious part of our legal heritage, will be tested and retested.[83]

McCarthy's critics claimed that the senator used methods that violated democratic procedures, hampered the fight against communism, created an atmosphere of fear and suspicion among government employees, and damaged American prestige abroad. After 46 charges had been brought against the senator by his colleagues, the Senate as a body censured McCarthy by a vote of 67 to 22. Yet, although censured, McCarthy maintained the support of loyal followers over the nation. A committee called "Ten Million Americans Mobilized for Justice," headed by General George E. Stratemeyer, prepared a petition to the Senate signed by over a million citizens. Delivered in an armored car, it protested the censure of McCarthy, an indication that McCarthyism did not die easily.

The rise of McCarthy as one of the most dangerous demagogues of the twentieth century was not purely the making of the junior senator from Wisconsin; rather, it was strongly supported by a mass paranoia generated by an ignorance and fear of communism during the Cold War period. Robert Goldston concluded in his epilogue to *The American Nightmare*, a book which examined the tension and drama of the post-war anti-communist movement, that McCarthyism provided an escape valve for the anxieties of ultra-conservatism's lunatic fringe. Goldston wrote:

> McCarthyism represented, above all, a flight from reality . . . Instead of focusing public attention on the very real and deadly threats . . . it

funneled public energies into a mad-hatter's search for shadows under every bed.[84]

Civil liberties in the nation were severely challenged during the Cold War period. The rights and freedoms of some individuals were placed in jeopardy by the government in its attempt to maintain a common defense against real or imaginary, external or internal, threats to military security and the "American way of life." The ideology of communism was generally viewed as a severe challenge which might undermine the state from within, and apparently, far too few citizens and officials had mustered enough faith in the strength of democracy.

The Internal Security Act of 1950, popularly called the McCarran Act, was passed by Congress in the Cold War period in response to increasing anxieties about communism. Enacted over President Truman's veto, it required the registration of communists and communist-front organizations, denied jobs with the federal government to communists, and made deportation of aliens easier and the process of naturalization more stringent. Truman's objections to the act were based on a claim that it would allow government officials to harass citizens and inhibit the exercise of free speech. The Act certainly put freedom of association to test by its provisions. But Paul G. Kauper, an expert on constitutional law, wrote (in 1966):

> In view of the identification of the Communist Party with purposes related to forcible overthrow of government, an unlawful objective, it is appropriate to require identification of persons as Communists and disclosure of Communist activity as well as to punish under criminal legislation those in any way actively engaged in this program.[85]

In the early 1950s, Supreme Court interpretations of constitutional issues were reflections of the anti-communist temper of the times, and the Court upheld several state programs which required public employees to take loyalty oaths or to declare their backgrounds to be free of memberships in subversive organizations. In 1951, the Supreme Court upheld, in *Dennis v. United States*,[86] convictions of leaders of the American Communist Party under the Smith Act of 1940, which was the first peacetime sedition law enacted by Congress since 1798. In upholding the constitutionality of the Smith Act, the Court pushed aside Justice Oliver Wendell Holmes's "clear and present danger" criterion for determining the limits of expression.

In the *Schenck* decision of 1919, Holmes had argued that a "remote bad tendency" in a speech or pamphlet (as opposed to the aforementioned "shouting fire in a theater" analogy) was insufficient to deny free speech. According to Holmes, the free exchange of ideas was a pragmatic way to discover truth and only a "clear and present danger" could justify congressional interference with freedom of speech. The Court's abandonment in 1951 of the "clear and present danger" concept in favor of "probable danger" was viewed by dissenting Justice William O. Douglas as an abridgment of First Amendment rights. Justice Douglas expressed his ideas in a dissenting opinion in the *Dennis* case as follows:

> When ideas compete in the market for acceptance, full and free discussion exposes the false and they gain few adherents. Full and free discussion even of ideas we hate encourages the testing of our own

prejudices and preconceptions. Full and free discussion keeps a society
from becoming stagnant and unprepared for the stresses and strains that
work to tear all civilizations apart.

Full and free discussion has indeed been the first article of our faith. We
have founded our political system on it. It has been the safeguard of every
religious, political, economic, and racial group amongst us. We have
counted on it to keep us from embracing what is cheap and false; we
have trusted the common sense of our people to choose the doctrine true
to our genius and to reject the rest. This has been the only single outstanding tenet that has made our institutions the symbol of freedom
and equality.

In an area outside the strictly political, the Ford Foundation, the world's
largest endowed foundation (which administers funds on an international scale for
artistic, scientific, educational, and charitable purposes) created the Fund for the
Republic on December 9, 1952. In general, the Fund was established to explore
possibilities for liberalizing American society at the time Senator McCarthy was
hysterically goading the American public and unifying the forces of repression. In a
radio broadcast, Eric Sevareid of CBS made the following comments about the Fund
for the Republic:

A group of the most respectable and successful business and professional men in the country have banded together in a Herculean effort
to roll back the creeping tide of what is called, for want of another
word, McCarthyism.[87]

Among the Fund's areas of interest were the following: 1) restrictions and
assaults upon academic freedom, 2) due process and the equal protection of the
laws, 3) the protection of the rights of minorities, 4) censorship, boycotting and
blacklisting activities by private groups, and 5) the principles and application of
guilt by association.

Thomas C. Reeves, author of *Freedom and the Foundation*, has pointed out
that, as the tax-exempt Ford Foundation attempted to follow its own mandate,
the Fund for the Republic encountered vociferous and persistent attacks from
powerful sources, including the House Un-American Activities Committee's chairman, Francis Walter, and columnist-commentator Fulton Lewis, Jr. Professor Reeves
summarized the assumptions under which the Fund's directors operated, pointing
out that although they assumed that communism was a political conspiracy, the
directors felt that the degree of communist infiltration in the nation was actually
unknown, though exaggerated. Furthermore, Professor Reeves concluded that the
Fund's directors recognized that methods employed by anti-communist forces in
the United States during the 1950s were often deleterious to civil liberties and that
the question of communist infiltration needed to be widely discussed and studied in
order to bring about a true understanding of the so-called "internal communist
menace."[88]

Another example demonstrates that not all battles for freedom during the
Cold War period were fought in the courts. In 1955 a Charlie Chaplin film festival at
Muhlenberg College (Pennsylvania) was cancelled under pressure from the local

American Legion chapter. The American Committee for Cultural Freedom (ACCF) protested that, although it was clear that Chaplin leaned to the left politically and was anti-American, there was no reason to prevent people from enjoying his films, since they had nothing to do with communism. But Christopher Lasch has criticized the ACCF for its ambiguous defense of intellectual freedom, claiming that the Committee's objections imply

> that if Chaplin's films could be regarded as political, the ban would have been justified. The assertion that art has nothing to do with politics was the poorest possible ground on which to defend cultural freedom.[89]

In relation to Communist Party membership, the Supreme Court declared, in 1965 in *United States v. Brown*,[90] that provisions of federal law were unconstitutional which prevented persons who had been members of the Party from holding office in labor unions. In the opinion of the Court, the restrictive law was a *bill of attainder* because the person involved had never been convicted of a crime. (It should be pointed out that certain constitutional restrictions have been put on law enforcement officials to protect the general freedom of citizens. A bill of attainder is a form of legislative punishment by which a person is convicted without a court trial. But exacting punishment for crime in the United States is not the province of the legislature, and bills of attainder are prohibited by Article I, Section 9, of the U.S. Constitution. In addition, neither the states nor the federal government has the power to adopt an *ex post facto law*—i.e., to declare an act criminal and to decree *post facto* punishment for an act not criminal when committed. In other words, laws governing the conduct of citizens must be clearly outlined in advance of the undesirable or anti-social conduct; the creation of criminal laws and punishment for past actions of citizens is illegal.) Thus, the new Red scare, reminiscent of that same hysteria following World War I, seems to have only a few remnants today.

BLACKS AND CIVIL RIGHTS

At the dawn of the twentieth century, blacks in the United States had few rights, and they were subject to some of the most severe racial prejudices since the Emancipation Proclamation. Little progress was made in obtaining actual equality for black Americans during the Progressive Era; however, the early years of the century witnessed considerable activity by blacks themselves directed toward attaining their rights. The Negro Business League, founded in 1900 by Booker T. Washington of Tuskegee Institute in Alabama, encouraged black capitalism and conducted a "buy black" movement. Booker T. Washington was the primary spokesman for blacks during the early years of the century, but some blacks were disenchanted with his leadership because he accepted segregation and formulated the idea of racial conservatism. Washington's address in 1895 at the Atlanta Exposition, in which he claimed that "in all things that are purely racial we can be as separate as the five fingers, yet as the hand in all things essential to mutual progress," caused concern among blacks who felt the need for an active program to achieve civil rights.

The pattern of violence and intolerance perpetrated against blacks in America in the early part of the twentieth century has been described by John Hope Franklin in *From Slavery to Freedom*. Franklin wrote that although many blacks anticipated that the new century would usher in solutions to racial differences, "all were soon to realize that for the Negro the new century meant more violence and more bloodshed, a kind of organized brigandage of life and property."[91] At the turn of the century, most blacks in the United States lived in the South, and almost a third of the total black population was still illiterate by 1910. In addition, blacks were victims of inferior schools, unequal public transportation services, inadequate housing, and poor job opportunities.

In 1903, William E. B. Du Bois, the first black to receive a doctorate from Harvard, wrote a small volume of essays entitled *The Souls of Black Folk*,[92] in which he outlined his philosophical differences with Booker T. Washington, the Bookerites, and the so-called "Tuskegee Machine." Unhappy with existing black leadership, some young blacks also joined a group of northern Progressives in 1909—the 100th anniversary of Abraham Lincoln's birthday—and founded the National Association for the Advancement of Colored People (NAACP).[93] The NAACP was formed as a private interracial group, and, through educational programs and lobbying activities, the organization began to attack economic and social barriers against American blacks and to seek an end to racial discrimination. Under the leadership of W. E. B. Du Bois, who edited the NAACP magazine, *The Crisis*, blacks began a long struggle to obtain civil rights. Du Bois also wrote several important sociological studies about blacks, among which were *The Gift of Black Folk*[94] and *Black Reconstruction*.[95]

The Negro Medical Association was founded in 1904 by Daniel Hale Williams (who had established Provident Hospital in Chicago in 1891 as an institution for black doctors and patients who were refused jobs and services in white hospitals). Another group concerned with the expansion of civil rights to blacks, the National Urban League, was established in 1910. Placing emphasis on the improvement of the economic status of blacks, the National Urban League has been one of the most effective civil rights organizations of the twentieth century.

Just prior to the entry of the United States into the First World War, the *Defender*, a black Chicago newspaper, promoted the migration of blacks from the South to the North. Between 1910 and 1924, an estimated one million blacks moved north in search of better economic opportunities. The growth of the black population of New York's Manhattan Borough indicates the surge of black migration. In 1900, 36,246 blacks lived in Manhattan, by 1910, there were 60,534,[96] and in 1930, the black population of Manhattan had reached 224,670.[97] While many of the black migrants found a greater degree of freedom and better wages in the North, they also encountered prejudice, all forms of discrimination, and poor living conditions. As blacks gradually moved into northern urban areas occupied by whites, they were often greeted with threats and violence.

During World War I, approximately 100,000 black United States servicemen were sent to Europe,[98] but most of them were given jobs that only involved hard labor, such as unloading and transporting supplies. In that conflict, though, and despite the military's practice of open discrimination against blacks, a number of all-black units performed with distinction. Yet upon their return to the United States, black former soldiers often faced discrimination, and in some cities even violent anti-black mobs.

The Great Depression of the 1930s dampened civil rights progress, just as it slowed progress in so many other areas. Dr. Du Bois had formed a Legal Redress Committee, which in 1939 became the Legal Defense and Education Fund, but the real breaking point for blacks was World War II. During that conflict, blacks were called upon to work, fight, and die for their country, and they began to demand the rights commensurate with those responsibilities of citizenship.

The struggle for desegregation was a primary social and political issue during the 1950s since blacks began to intensify their efforts to achieve equality both during and following the Second World War. Although Congress rejected most civil-rights bills introduced during Truman's administration, the president's creation of a Committee on Civil Rights in 1946 elevated the issue of equality under the law for all citizens to the position of a national cause. Civil rights leaders took their cause to the courts in an effort to do away with the "separate but equal" doctrine that had been in effect since 1896, having been established by the Supreme Court in *Plessy v. Ferguson.*[99]

The Congress of Racial Equality (CORE) was established in 1942 by James Farmer and a group of students at the University of Chicago. Farmer was among the most active workers of the civil rights movement for more than two decades, and under his leadership, CORE began the first series of sit-in demonstrations in an attempt to desegregate public accommodations. The first sit-ins were held in Chicago in 1943; they then spread to the South as part of a move to end segregation of public transportation facilities. CORE was also responsible for the freedom rides in Alabama and Mississippi in the early 1960s, the first having been tried in 1947. After CORE's leadership passed to Floyd McKissick in 1966—and then to Roy Innis in 1968—the organization placed more emphasis on black nationalism; CORE's influence in the black civil rights movement waned in the early 1970s, and its membership declined.

The real turning point in the blacks' struggle for equality came, of course, when, in a landmark unanimous decision, the Supreme Court declared in 1954 that racial segregation in public schools violated the Constitution because it represented a denial of equal rights. In outlawing segregation, the Court handed down two decisions: *Brown v. Board of Education* (1954)[100] and *Brown v. Board of Education* (1955).[101] The first case actually condemned segregation, while the second provided guidelines for enforcing the decision in the affected states. Despite the Fourteenth Amendment, the old "separate but equal" doctrine set down by the Court in *Plessy v. Ferguson* in 1896 had allowed the separation of blacks and whites in public schools; however, little equality actually existed in at least 17 states. In the Court's opinion for *Brown* (1954), Chief Justice Warren wrote:

> We conclude that in the field of public education the doctrine of "separate but equal" has no place. Separate educational facilities are inherently unequal. Therefore, we hold that the plaintiffs and others similarly situated for whom the actions have been brought are, by reason of the segregation complained of, deprived of the equal protection of the laws guaranteed by the Fourteenth Amendment. This disposition makes unnecessary any discussion whether such segregation also violates the Due Process clause of the Fourteenth Amendment.

The *Brown* decision was met with resistance in Alabama, Georgia, Mississippi, and South Carolina; however, some progress had been made by 1960 to desegregate public schools, particularly in states bordering the old Confederacy. Although many Southerners were displeased with the Court's ruling, their resistance to desegregation gradually weakened, but in 1957, Governor Orval Faubus of Arkansas mobilized the national guard to prevent enrollment of black students in Little Rock's Central High School. President Eisenhower had been reluctant to bring direct federal force into play to desegregate public schools in compliance with the *Brown* decision; nevertheless, he challenged Faubus's action. The governor withdrew his troops, but mobs of angry whites entered the school. Eisenhower then employed federal troops to prevent violence in Little Rock, and open resistance in the South to integration gradually subsided after the Little Rock incident. By 1960, the concept of white supremacy was becoming an antiquated philosophy, but the goal of integration for blacks was far from being accomplished.

In terms of its impact on the political and social life of the nation, *Brown v. Board of Education* ranks among the most significant legal decisions of the century. With the *Brown* decision, school segregation in 17 states was eventually brought to an end, and a social and legal revolution began, since the decision precipitated laws such as the Civil Rights Act and the Voting Rights Act, as well as other social legislation.

The Civil Rights Act of 1957 established a Civil Rights Commission as a federal agency for the purpose of investigating allegations that Americans were being deprived of their rights as citizens. The Commission is solely a fact-finding agency; it has no enforcement or legal functions and serves primarily as a clearinghouse for civil rights information. The Commission later promoted the passage of both the 1965 Law Enforcement Act and the 1965 Voting Rights Act, and it has recommended stronger protections of the civil rights of gay people and of Mexican-Americans.

Discriminatory practices were widespread in the United States prior to 1964, and the Civil Rights Act passed that year represents a milestone in the political process of the nation. Blacks, Indians, Mexican-Americans, and other minorities had been discriminated against in public accommodations and housing. The Civil Rights Act was designed to eliminate discrimination in accommodations such as restaurants, motion picture theaters, hotels, parks, and other public places. To add teeth to the act, Congress permitted the U.S. Attorney General to prevent discriminatory practices in public places. The Supreme Court quickly upheld the constitutionality of the act in 1964 in *Heart of Atlanta Motel, Inc. v. United States.*[102]

Voting restrictions against racial minorities were outlawed by the Voting Rights Act of 1965, which allowed federal authorities to intervene directly to correct state or local unconstitutional procedures such as the poll tax and literacy tests. Provisions of the 1965 act were further extended by the Voting Rights Act of 1970, passed by Congress in an attempt to bring about greater participation and representation of minorities in the political process from which they had long been systematically excluded.

Another piece of legislation passed by Congress—the Civil Rights Act of 1968—included fair-housing provisions aimed at eliminating discrimination in the rental or sale of housing, other than private homes or apartments which the owner attempted to sell personally. Applicable to approximately 80 percent of all housing in 1970, these provisions help to insure open occupancy of housing.

The rights of people to assemble peaceably and to associate freely fall within the scope of the First and Fourteenth Amendments, and these liberties were put to test during the civil rights movement of the 1950s and 1960s. The Supreme Court ruled in 1958 in *NAACP v. Alabama*[103] and, in 1961, in *Louisiana ex rel. Gremillion v. National Association for the Advancement of Colored People,*[104] that the NAACP could not be compelled to disclose the names of its members. (However, it should be noted that in the case of association for the purpose of committing subversive or violent and unlawful activities, the freedom of association can be "reasonably" restrained as determined in 1928 in *Bryant v. Zimmerman*[105] and in 1959 in *Uphaus v. Wyman.*[106])

In 1967, an organization called the Brown Berets was founded to protect the rights of Mexican-Americans. Over 30 chapters and 2,000 members are claimed by the organization, which combats racial discrimination. Another civil rights movement, the American Indian Movement (AIM), was organized among the large urban concentration of Indians in Minneapolis, but AIM has sought to eliminate discriminatory practices against American Indians across the nation. Obviously the relative success of blacks has encouraged other groups deprived of their rights to seek redress for the wrongs done them.

FREEDOM OF SEXUAL EXPRESSION

The post-war decade between 1920 and 1930 experienced a moral revolution. Social attitudes of a significant number of people, especially the young, became more liberal, and the Puritan sexual ethic and Victorianism gradually lost much of their firm grip on American society, despite protests from some religious officials. In reference to those Victorian ideas that did persist during the first quarter of the century, Maurice Girodias, founder of The Olympia Press (Paris), concluded in his introduction to *The Olympia Reader* that:

> It seems hard to understand how a whole generation of men who had been through the toughest wars . . . could be reduced to the level of schoolchildren, and to be told what to read by a conglomerate of spinsters and bowler-hatted policemen.[107]

Reflecting a growing independence, American women also drastically changed their dress and appearance, and for the first time in American history, women dared to wear skirts hemmed at the knee. An unprecedented interest in sex and sexual literature also developed; newsstands were flooded with new magazines and tabloids devoted to topics such as love, the intimate lives of motion picture stars, and "true confessions."

Stimulated by the work of Europeans such as Sigmund Freud and Havelock Ellis in the early part of the century, and by changing social and moral conditions, scholars in the United States gradually approached the question of sex and began to conduct significant research about human sexuality. In 1929, two serious works dealing with the sexual behavior of average persons appeared. Based upon survey research, these works were Katherine Davis's *Factors in the Sex Life of 2,200*

Women[108] and Gilbert V. Hamilton's *Research in Marriage.*[109] These books were followed in 1932 by another study, by Robert Dickinson and Lura Beam. *A Thousand Marriages.*[110] American servicemen also returned from Europe after World War II with erotic classics and racy novels, particularly the plain green covers of the Traveler's Companion Series, published by Maurice Girodias in Paris. Ribald and erotic literature by talented writers such as Henry Miller, Lawrence Durrell, Jean Genet, Samuel Beckett, and William S. Burroughs was first published in Europe and began to find its way into the United States, where it was being increasingly read and appreciated.

Alfred Kinsey, an entomologist-turned-social-scientist, conducted sexual case studies at Bloomington, Indiana, with financial support from the Rockefeller Foundation, and his research culminated in the publication of two classic studies: *Sexual Behavior in the Human Male*,[111] in 1948, and *Sexual Behavior in the Human Female*,[112] in 1953. While the so-called "Kinsey Reports" were turgid in style and primarily of a scholarly and statistical nature, their impact on the general public was profound. The reports made Kinsey the center of a stormy controversy, and at the same time they influenced public attitudes toward sex and helped to promote sexual freedom and expression. The bicentennial issue of *Life Special Reports* (published in 1975 by Time Inc.) characterized Kinsey's Male volume as one of the "100 events that shaped America." Sociologist John S. Gagnon, who has written extensively about sexual behavior, has noted, however, that Kinsey's research "was itself an indication of changes that had already occurred in the sexual situation in the United States,"[113] and that

> if Kinsey data were correct—and the few subsequent studies tended to
> confirm many of his findings—it meant that there was a serious
> incongruity between the law and sexual conduct.[114]

Kinsey's research also paved the way for additional scientific investigations of human sexuality such as those conducted by Masters and Johnson, authors of *Human Sexual Response*[115] and *Human Sexual Inadequacy*;[116] Wainwright Churchill, author of *Homosexual Behavior among Males*;[117] and Laud Humphreys, who wrote *Out of the Closets: The Sociology of Homosexual Liberation.*[118]

Although sexually explicit materials have proliferated in recent years, participants in "clean" literature movements have demanded that materials in bookstores, libraries, motion pictures, and newspapers conform to older standards of decency. However, restrictions placed by legislators and the courts upon sexually oriented materials, especially pornography, have been relatively ineffective in controlling these materials in view of the purposes of those persons who proposed the controls. Restrictions on sexual literature have proven to be almost unenforceable and ineffectual in short-circuiting the flow of hard-core pornography, as well as in protecting the rights of citizens to read whatever they wish—including pornography if they so desire. Some pressure groups in the nation, especially the clean literature groups and societies for the suppression of vice, have sought governmental protection of society from the "dangers" of obscenity and lust. But civil libertarians feel that if such protections are to be provided, they should be the responsibility of non-government institutions, such as the family, schools, and other social groups or institutions.

Many promoters of intellectual freedom have claimed that laws designed to regulate obscene, immoral, or lascivious materials violate the First Amendment guarantees of freedom of expression and freedom of the press, this because no precise definition of the term "obscene" has been established and because anti-obscenity statutes are so vague and indefinite that they violate the principle of due process of law. Critics of anti-obscenity statutes also claim that the free press guarantee is violated unless objectionable materials can be proven to be libelous or to cause crime. Other opponents of obscenity legislation have claimed that the excuse often used by censoring agents, that their efforts are designed to protect morality, is contrary to the principles of freedom of expression.

It should be noted that all states have passed laws designed to control the publication, distribution, and sale of obscene publications. Obscene literature is also barred from the mails by federal law, and the government prohibits the importation of obscene materials into the country. In addition, the interstate transportation of obscene materials is prohibited by the federal government.

In relation to the obscenity problem, one must also be aware that court decisions in recent decades have reflected a legal trend based upon the following principles: 1) freedom of the press is not an absolute right and is subject to restraints for the protection of public or private interests, 2) states cannot impair freedom of the press because such action is contrary to the Fourteenth Amendment, and 3) laws restricting freedom of the press may be valid or invalid, depending upon the type of legal or illegal restraint imposed. Although obscenity per se has been traditionally viewed by the U.S. Supreme Court as outside protections of the Constitution, the legal problem of delineating between obscene materials and other materials which fall under constitutional safeguards has not been an easy one. Obscenity and its real or assumed effects on people have always been a thorny issue for justices of the Supreme Court. Not until 1957 did the nation's highest tribunal attempt to determine precisely whether the distribution of obscene materials was protected by the guarantees of the First Amendment.

The constitutionality of federal statutes prohibiting the distribution of obscene literature was a question in the 1957 *Roth v. United States*[119] case and in *Alberts v. California*,[120] both of which examined the legality of convictions under anti-obscenity laws. Samuel Roth, a New York businessman who sold sexually oriented publications, was convicted under federal obscenity statutes; the Supreme Court ruled that these laws did not violate provisions of the First Amendment. Guarantees of freedom of expression do not provide absolute protection for every utterance, according to the Court. On the other hand, the Court noted that all expression deemed to be of redeeming social importance is fully protected by the First Amendment, with the exclusion only of that which encroaches upon the limited area of more important interests. The Court declared, however, that obscenity does not fall within First Amendment protections for speech or press. The primary guideline established in *Roth* for determining obscenity was "whether to the average person, applying contemporary community standards, the dominant theme of the material taken as a whole appeals to prurient interest." (This guideline was used to identify what was or was not obscene from 1957 until the Court established new criteria in 1973, in *Miller v. California*,[121] which will be discussed in a later section of this chapter.)

In 1957, the Supreme Court also upheld the constitutionality of a judicial decision from a lower court in New York to enjoin an obscene book from further circulation and to order copies of the work destroyed (*Kingsley Books, Inc. v. Brown*).[122] The decision in this case and the use of obscenity guidelines set down in corollary cases show that the Court has tended to narrow its definition of obscenity so that it includes only hard-core pornography. Another obscenity case, *Kingsley International Pictures Corporation v. Regents of the State of New York*,[123] was heard by the Court in 1959. The case centered on a New York statute that allowed denial of a license for films that were obscene, indecent, immoral, inhuman, sacrilegious, or of such a nature that they could corrupt morals or incite to crime. The film *Lady Chatterley's Lover* had been denied an exhibition license by the Regents of the State of New York on the basis of the motion picture's "immoral" nature, and the decision had been sustained by the New York Court of Appeals. When the facts of the case were reviewed by the U.S. Supreme Court, the New York statute was declared to be unconstitutional because the appeals court had not upheld the legal ban on grounds of obscenity but on the premise that the film offended conventional moral standards: *Lady Chatterley's Lover* had been denied a film license because it presented adultery in a favorable light. The decision in the 1959 *Kingsley* case was not unanimous, so it demonstrates the difficulty that justices experience in arriving at definitive conclusions about censorship, as well as the Court's role in reviewing aspects of restrictive legislation on free speech.

In 1960, Justice Brennan noted in his opinion for *Ohio ex rel. Eaton v. Price*[124] that freedoms included in the Bill of Rights are recognized as fundamental under the "due process" clause of the Fourteenth Amendment, and that these freedoms enjoy the same degree of protection as they do under the Bill of Rights. (This interpretation of the Fourteenth Amendment had its roots in a 1931 case, *Near v. Minnesota*,[125] in which the Supreme Court decided that freedom of the press was so fundamental that it is subject to protection under the Fourteenth Amendment.)

Consideration was then given in 1966 in *Ginzburg v. United States*[126] to the question of whether obscenity guidelines outlined in *Roth* had been correctly applied to a case dealing with the production of allegedly obscene publications issued by Ralph Ginzburg. According to law officials, Ginzburg's publications, *Eros*, *Liaison*, and *The Housewife's Handbook on Selective Promiscuity*, violated the Comstock Act of 1873. In a 5-4 decision, the Court upheld the publisher's conviction by a lower tribunal on grounds of "pandering"—the purveying of textual or graphical matter designed to appeal to erotic interest. The Court noted in the *Ginzburg* opinion that the First Amendment does not protect materials that fall within the *Roth* definition for obscenity; the Court also noted that:

> the fact that each of these publications was created or exploited
> entirely on the basis of its appeal to prurient interests strengthens the
> conclusion that the transactions here were sale of illicit merchandise,
> not sales of constitutionally protected matter.

A former assistant district attorney of New York, Richard Kuh, pointed out in 1967, that some judges, especially justices of the U.S. Supreme Court, have been fearlessly attempting to salvage something of the anti-pornography laws but that "in the process they have burdened themselves with interminable censorship chores, have been beset with abuse for their opinions, and have ended up giving little guidance to anybody."[127] Olga and Edwin Hoyt also observed (in 1970) that

despite many conflicting judicial views, the same statutes and precedents tended
to be employed, but when judges concurred in legal decisions, it was often for very
different reasons, including diversified interpretations of existing laws.[128]

Then on June 21, 1973, the U.S. Supreme Court, both exemplifying and
adding to the confusion, issued new obscenity guidelines in *Miller v. California.*
The guidelines stipulated that *community* rather than national standards should be
used to determine whether a work is prurient, and consequently, under this
decision, the question of obscenity was left to approximately 78,200 local juries
in communities across the nation. (Prior to the *Miller* decision, the term
"community" was interpreted broadly as the nation at large.) The new obscenity
test also included the question of whether the work, taken as a whole has "serious
literary, artistic, political, or scientific value," but both of these criteria are subjective, depending upon the viewer's predispositions.

Among other people, some librarians were displeased with the *Miller* opinion
and voiced their concern in professional journals. The American Library Association filed a petition to the Court in July 1973, requesting a rehearing for the purpose
of clarification of points relating to First Amendment guarantees for free speech.
The Association of American Publishers also petitioned for an interpretation and
modification of the obscenity guidelines, claiming that the *Miller* decision "reduced
the rule of law to a matter of taste."

Dr. Paul Gebhard, Director of the Institute for Sex Research at Bloomington,
Indiana, pointed out during a 1973 interview that a "backlash effect" in public
opinion had spurred the Court to tighten controls on pornography and obscenity.
Dr. Gebhard also claimed that the producers and distributors of films, magazines,
and books containing explicit sexual materials went too far and offended the tastes
and sensibilities of some persons, producing this backlash. When questioned about
the 1973 obscenity guidelines, Dr. Gebhard claimed that the *Miller* ruling

> . . . is an infringement on individual freedom and an attempt to legislate
> taste. It is another example of the government claiming that the
> individual must be protected from himself as though he were an
> incompetent minor. This is a dangerous viewpoint since it could easily
> lead to more repressive statutes and ordinances. Our culture is still as some
> people say, erotophobic, that is afraid of sex.[129]

Writing in the *New York Law Forum*, Herbert S. Kassner, a member of the
New York law firm of Kassner & Detsky, attacked "constitutional perversions"
wrought by recent court decisions relating to obscenity. Kassner feels that the
Court's guidelines in the Miller decision for identifying obscenity are not a satisfactory solution to the problem of censorship. He concluded:

> As has often been said, the only way to insure the repeal of bad law is
> through its rigid enforcement. We now enter an era of "thought prohibi-
> tion." It will undoubtedly meet the same fate as "drink prohibition."
> How long the process will take is unpredictable. That the substantive law
> of obscenity as it exists today cannot long endure is, however,
> undeniable.[130]

Indeed, those persons who had assumed that the nation was moving toward a state of literary frankness and permissiveness in which problems of censorship appeared to be rapidly diminishing have been concerned over recent legal decisions about freedom of expression. While a temper of liberalism permeated many of the Court's decisions in the 1960s, the Court was often attacked for its liberality. Promoters of intellectual freedom felt that the liberal constitutional interpretations represented an inexorable move toward increased freedoms, but some Americans viewed these rulings as blueprints for a licentious society.

However, after the *Miller* decision was handed down in 1973, a number of organizations associated with publishing and libraries also spoke out against the new guidelines for determining what is obscene. G. Royce Smith, executive director of the American Booksellers Association (ABA) pointed out that the Association does not support any form of obscenity legislation. The ABA organized booksellers to testify before state legislatures, in the aftermath of the 1973 ruling, in cases where state lawmakers have been prompted to rewrite their obscenity laws to bring them in line with the Court's new guidelines. Kenneth McCormick, chairman of the Freedom to Read Committee of the Association of American Publishers, also urged publishers and booksellers to lobby against stricter laws on obscenity. He stated: "We're not discussing the question of obscenity and pornography only—it's a question of the freedom to read whatever you want to."[131]

Marc Jaffe, editorial director of Bantam Books, pointed out three months after the *Miller* decision was handed down that the Court's new guidelines had had little apparent impact on anti-obscenity prosecution and on editorial processes in the publishing industry. Bantam's paperback issue of *The Sex Book*, a graphically illustrated encyclopedic dictionary of sex, has encountered few censorship problems.[132] The Publisher's Ad Club also spoke out strongly against anti-obscenity legislation and indicated its intention to keep a watch over the country for attempts to tighten existing obscenity laws. Harriet F. Pilpel, a noted civil rights lawyer and a partner in the law firm of Greenbaum, Wolff, & Ernst, pointed out the difficulty of defining obscenity, and she related the *Miller* decision to "hangups" of the "upper middle-class and elderly gentlemen on the bench."[133]

The president of the American Library Trustee Association, David W. Casey, urged legislators in New York either to exempt libraries from the proposed anti-obscenity legislation or to pre-empt the local law. Addressing himself to the topic of community versus national standards, Casey stated:

> I am certain that a library board of trustees or board of education, advised by the librarians, are more qualified in the selection of books, magazines, films, etc., than a jury and prosecutor are.[134]

In March 1974, the Association of American Publishers asked the Supreme Court to adopt a "new approach" to the question of obscenity. According to the Association, "Much 'hard core' pornography continues to thrive while many works traditionally afforded First Amendment protections have fallen prey to the heavy hand of censorship."[135]

In his dissenting opinion in *Paris Adult Theater I v. Slanton, District Attorney, et al.*,[136] which was one of the four obscenity cases considered by the Court along with *Miller*, Justice William O. Douglas declared:

> What we do today is rather ominous as respects librarians. The net now designed by the Court is so finely meshed that taken literally it could result in raids on libraries. Libraries, I had always assumed, were sacrosanct, representing every part of the spectrum. If what is offensive to the most influential person or group in a community can be purged from a library, the library system would be destroyed.

Indeed, the 1973 guidelines for identifying obscenity are viewed by many practicing librarians, as well as the Office for Intellectual Freedom of the American Library Association, as among the most serious threats to intellectual freedom in the twentieth century. Promoters of intellectual freedom have claimed that the *Miller* decision paves the road for local law makers and prosecutors to function as censors, because local community standards can be used to determine whether a medium of communication is obscene. Because of the American Library Association's efforts to have the Supreme Court reconsider the *Miller* guidelines, the *New York Times* published an editorial, which is reprinted here by permission of the publisher:

Librarians Speak Up*

The American Library Association has filed a petition requesting the Supreme Court to reconsider its recent pornography rulings. The action underscores the librarians' concern over the fact that the Court's majority may have been so preoccupied with the offensiveness of pornographic motion pictures and other public exploitation of lurid sex that it paid too little attention to the potential effect of the rulings on books and libraries. Only Justice William O. Douglas, in his dissenting opinion, warned that the decision may be the signal for local vigilante raids on the nation's libraries.

Professional librarians as a group are hardly known as flaming radicals. As civil servants they find themselves in the delicate position of being the guardians of much that is necessarily controversial, while their place on the totem pole of authority gives them very little power to defend their professional opinions and their personal security. Their decision to appeal to the Supreme Court represents an expert judgment based on experience at the firing line.

What disturbs the librarians most is the fact that the rulings by Chief Justice Burger permit local standards to determine whether a work which depicts or describes sexual conduct is offensive to "the average person" in that community. The association's brief cites the observation by Justice Douglas . . .

---

* ©1973 by The New York Times Company. Reprinted from *The New York Times*, July 20, 1973, by permission.

Specifically, the petition asks the Court to review such unresolved questions as the extent to which librarians would henceforth be authorized to determine whether a book under attack had "serious" value. In more fundamental terms, the association notes that the Supreme Court has never before held that only works with serious value are protected by the First Amendment.

The librarians' concern is justified. This action by so moderate and respectable a group should give the Court an opportunity to reconsider those aspects of its pornography rulings that could encourage local vigilantism and that could diminish the First Amendment's protection of freedom by giving censors a free hand.

Prior to the 1973 ruling on obscenity, the Supreme Court had placed limitations on the government's authority to declare a medium of communication obscene. While the Court's earlier rulings had left obscene materials outside First Amendment protections, there was at least a fairly clear-cut identification procedure for such materials. Under those earlier protections, adults were allowed free choice in their selection of books, magazines, films, etc. The *Roth* decision and its guidelines were rather consistent with recommendations made later by the President's Commission on Obscenity and Pornography in 1970, which did not find evidence linking obscene materials to criminal behavior. The Commission felt that adults should be allowed to read or to view sexually oriented materials if they so desired. Regrettably, the *Report of the Commission on Obscenity and Pornography* was absolutely rejected by President Richard M. Nixon. In addition, the report, which cost the taxpaying citizens of the nation $2 million, was also rejected by the U.S. Senate by a 60-5 vote. In its 1973 decision on obscenity, the Supreme Court apparently also rejected the general recommendations of the Commission on Obscenity and Pornography.

While it is evident that there has been a proliferation of sexually oriented materials in recent years and that these works have been generally accessible in so-called "adult book stores" and from other sources, no evidence exists to establish a positive relationship between the availability of salacious materials and harm to any community or person. Unfortunately, the 1973 ruling on obscenity has opened the door for local governments to impose private morals and taste on all segments of our society. Local prosecutors can now harass distributors of certain materials to the extent that whatever is the source of objection is no longer made available. Book and magazine dealers, librarians, and film exhibitors can be prosecuted when they provide to citizens materials deemed to be offensive by local law officers. Concerned citizens and librarians are questioning whether policemen, prosecutors, and local courts can regulate the reading and viewing habits of private citizens or library users, especially since librarians have generally operated under the assumption that adults should be able to select freely their own reading materials.

In June 1974, the Supreme Court considered *Jenkins v. Georgia*,[137] the first case to be appealed and accepted for review after the *Miller* decision. Jenkins, a Georgia theater manager, was convicted by a lower court in 1971 for exhibiting the feature-length film *Carnal Knowledge*, and in an attempt to prevent further erosions of constitutional rights, the Association of American Publishers filed a brief on behalf of Jenkins, requesting the abandonment of any distinction between "hard core" and other sexual materials.[138] Attorney Louis Nizer presented arguments in the *Jenkins* case for the application of national rather than local obscenity guidelines. Nizer argued that constitutional problems should not be decided by local juries; however, the noted lawyer stated his strong belief in juries when factual matters are under consideration. Asked by Justice William H. Rehnquist to identify the difference between the tailoring of obscenity laws to the 50 states as opposed to the obscenity decisions being made in local communities, Nizer stated that it would be more natural to follow state sovereignty than to permit its fragmentation into community subdivisions.[139] After hearing the arguments, the Court declared unanimously that *Carnal Knowledge* was not hardcore pornography, and it overturned the lower court's conviction of Jenkins, the Georgia theater operator. The Court also noted that jurors may apply their own "community standards" in dealing with obscenity cases.

Other cases heard by the Supreme Court since the 1973 *Miller* decision have 1) let stand a lower court decision barring the University of Mississippi from interfering with publications of an English department magazine containing words school officials considered obscene; 2) let stand a decision declaring that a Louisiana obscenity law which barred lewd and indecent publications was unconstitutional because it was too broad and general; and 3) upheld in a 5-4 decision the federal law under which an advertisement for a commercial, illustrated version of the *Report of the Commission on Obscenity and Pornography* was barred from the mails.

The *Miller* ruling poses definite threats to individual freedoms. Local control of "obscene" materials can only lead to increasing infringements on American citizens' rights to read, see, or hear anything of interest to them without governmental interference. That the majority of Supreme Court justices believe that sexually oriented obscene materials do not fall within the scope of the free speech provisions of the First Amendment is unfortunate. Equally regrettable is the fact that the Court has determined that local standards of morality (thus local controls on morality) are necessary and proper. Consequently, the *Miller* ruling can only cause confusion and injustice as the 50 states, along with the thousands of communities therein, go about constructing their trailor-made limitations on sexual candor.

Controls on private morality, like controls on how frequently one should brush his teeth, have no place in a democratic society. When official arms of national, state, or local governments establish standards of sexual morality for all citizens, pernicious socialization results. The individual democratic spirit is crushed and forced into conformistic dogmatism.

Without a doubt, the responsibility for the latest legal debacle over the obscenity question must be placed with former President Nixon. During the 1950s and 1960s, the U.S. Supreme Court attempted to salvage something of the anti-obscenity laws and to establish more realistic guidelines at the national level for the control of offensive publications and other communication media containing sexual materials. The Court made moves to increase personal freedoms, but Mr. Nixon's conservative appointees to the high tribunal allowed the control of obscenity to be thrown back into much of the narrow, ethnocentric suppression which is frequently so characteristic of the local, grassroots level.

A regular cry from would-be censors is that increasing crime rates are the result of the availability of pornographic materials. But these cries are often from persons who fail to recognize that people predisposed to crime and other anti-social behavior are usually not interested in literary pursuits and that what people read depends heavily upon their predispositions and personal values. Would-be criminals are most likely to ferret out and read works that interest them and support their preoccupation with acts of criminality and violence. The causal relationship which censors attempt to establish between books and other media deemed harmful and grave offenses perpetrated against society simply has not been proven.

Available sexual materials are often prepared for adults who appreciate them, and, according to the First Amendment, citizens should have the right to read anything that satisfies their personal, intellectual, and emotional needs. This view was also held by Thomas Jefferson, who deplored the idea that in the United States of America the sale of a book could become a subject of criminal inquiry. Indeed, in a democratic society it is intolerable for the burden of proof to be placed on adult citizens to show why they should be able to read anything. Can we aspire to or achieve democracy if the reading of a book, whatever the subject matter may be, is illegal?

The obscenity decision in *Miller* clearly demonstrates that when the majority of the justices of the U.S. Supreme Court are devoted to defending the rights of individual citizens from gradual government encroachments, the Court will emphasize personal liberties. On the other hand, when judges are irresolute, faltering, or complacent about democracy's fundamentals, decisions about individual rights tend to be repressive. With the help of Mr. Nixon's conservative appointments to the Court, the latter condition tends to prevail presently in our nation's highest tribunal.

Public officials at the local level should keep in mind that no one has ever been forced to read or to view sexual materials. Personal choice is the determinant in this matter. Furthermore, commercial firms which sell "offensive" materials always restrict admission to their premises to adult patrons. Theaters and newspapers prominently advertise ratings given to films voluntarily by the motion picture industry, and movie attendance at X-rated films is prohibited to minors. Persons who do want access to such materials—however objectionable these may seem to others—should have that right.

EXPANDING PERSONAL FREEDOMS

Due process and assembly were at issue in 1937 in the case *De Jonge v. Oregon*,[140] when the Supreme Court decided by a 8-0 vote that De Jonge, who had been indicted for a violation of the Oregon Criminal Syndicalism Law, had been denied due process of law. De Jonge, a member of the Communist Party, had spoken at a peaceful meeting, and the state claimed that his speech violated a law restricting doctrines that advocated such actions as physical violence, crime, or sabotage. But the Court decided that the defendant was entitled to his personal right of free speech, and that he had been convicted by the lower court merely because he had taken part in a communist meeting. The Court viewed the Oregon statute as applied against De Jonge to be repugnant to fundamentals of free speech, press, and peaceful assembly.

The courts continued to cope with free speech and due process issues between the First and Second World Wars, and the general trend in Supreme Court decisions during that period was in the direction of liberalizing individual rights. Since World War II, significant legal gains have been made in bolstering the rights and personal freedoms of citizens. Then, when the ideological struggle between democracy and communism lost its momentum, restrictions on individual expression and legal convictions based on charges of espionage and subversion became less significant in the political arena.

A 1951 case involving freedom of speech, *Feiner v. New York*,[141] resulted from an arrest of a Syracuse University student, Irvin Feiner, who was convicted of creating a breach of peace by arousing restlessness among a crowd. Feiner attempted to motivate a group of spectators on the street to attend a civil rights meeting, and verbal attacks were directed against public officials and the American Legion in an inflammatory speech. Feiner claimed that his rights had been violated by police who had arrested him, but law enforcement officials stated that they were only concerned with the possibility of violence among the spectators. In a 6-3 decision, the Court ruled that the police action was not contrary to the First Amendment's provisions for free speech because Feiner's arrest was carried out to insure law and order.

While searching a Cleveland boarding house in 1957 for a bombing suspect and gambling paraphernalia, police found what they considered to be "lewd and lascivious books" belonging to Dollree Mapp. Although the police had not obtained a search warrant, they arrested Mapp, who was subsequently convicted for possession of obscene materials. When the conviction was appealed to the U.S. Supreme Court as *Mapp v. Ohio*,[142] the Court noted that evidence obtained in violation of the search and seizure provisions of the Fourth Amendment is not admissible in a state court. According to the Supreme Court's opinion in the case, the due process clause of the Fourteenth Amendment is enforceable against the states, so *Mapp v. Ohio* helped to strengthen the security of the citizen's privacy against arbitrary intrusions by the government.

During the 1960s, various sections of the McCarran Act (the Internal Security Act, discussed previously) were challenged as unconstitutional in several cases that reached the Supreme Court. In a 5-4 decision, the Court in *Communist Party v. Subversive Activities Control Board*[143] upheld the legality of registration requirements for communist-inspired or controlled groups, noting that the requirement did not violate the First Amendment. However, some provisions of the McCarran Act were later declared unconstitutional. In 1964, the denial of passports to members of the Community Party and its "fronts" was declared in *Aptheker v. Secretary of State*[144] to be a violation of the Fifth Amendment's due process clause. In 1965, registration requirements for individual Community Party members were deemed by the Supreme Court in *Albertson v. Subversive Activities Control Board*[145] to be a violation of Fifth Amendment prohibitions against self-incrimination. Also, the provisions of the McCarran Act that permitted defense facilities to refuse employment to Communist Party members were declared unconstitutional in 1967 in the case *United States v. Robel*.[146]

The rights of persons accused of crime are specified in Article 6 of the Bill of Rights; however, in the period immediately following the arrest of criminal suspects, police abuse of citizens' constitutionally guaranteed rights have not been uncommon. Legal scholar Arthur E. Sutherland pointed out that "extracting confessions in our police and prosecutorial practice has become something like a universal folk ritual." Writing on the subject of crime and confession in the *Harvard Law Review*, Sutherland also claimed:

A perfectly practical, often effective procedure, so universally followed that it continuously and monotonously appears in the law reports, is the arrest of such persons and their subjection to questioning in isolation from counsel and family or friends, with the utilization of highly developed routinized procedures, well-calculated to extract admissions of guilt from the prisoner, procedures later justified by the bland explanation that the confession was "voluntary."[147]

An example of this procedure occurred in 1940 in Florida, where police coerced a confession from a suspect who had been interrogated for six days and nights by relay terms of policemen. The Supreme Court ruled in *Chambers v. Florida*,[148] the case growing out of the incident, that confessions obtained by third-degree psychological and physical coercion are illegal.

One of the most controversial periods in the history of the U.S. Supreme Court was the 16 years in which the tribunal was headed by Chief Justice Earl Warren, a former three-term governor of California who was appointed to the Court by President Eisenhower in 1953. Under Warren's leadership, a number of landmark decisions relating to personal freedoms were handed down. In *Gideon v. Wainwright*,[149] the Court declared in 1963 that counsel must be provided for defendants in state criminal prosecutions when the accused cannot afford to retain a lawyer, and it thereby established the right of the poor to counsel. Although the defendant's right to counsel is spelled out in Article 6 of the Bill of Rights, the *Gideon* decision noted that if a defendant cannot afford the cost of employing a defense lawyer, the court must then assume the duty of appointing the accused's counsel.

More than two decades after *Chambers*, the Court further extended the rights of persons accused of crimes by ruling in *Messiah v. United States*[150] and in *Escobedo v. Illinois*[151] (both 1964) that confessions are invalid if they are obtained by police officials when counsel is not present. Confessions from defendants after indictment—or before indictment, should the defendant ask for a lawyer—are not admissible as evidence unless a defendant's lawyer was present when the confession was made. Many policemen and prosecutors were especially critical of the *Escobedo* decision, in which the Court overturned the conviction of Danny Escobedo on grounds that police had not advised him of his right to remain silent and had prevented the accused from seeing his lawyer. J. Edgar Hoover, FBI director, even blamed restrictive Supreme Court decisions for increased in acquittals and dismissals in criminal cases.

The high court's controversial decisions in favor of individual rights were not, however, limited to rights of criminals and suspects. In a case heard in 1965, a state law forbidding the dissemination of birth control information was viewed by the Court as an unconstitutional invasion of the right of privacy in *Griswold v. Connecticut*.[152]

Another "Warren Court" landmark criminal law decision was that of *Miranda v. Arizona*[153] in 1966. Despite the narrow margin of the 5-4 decision, the case helped insure a defendant's rights under police questioning and provided sweeping protections against compulsory self-incrimination. The Court declared that a suspected criminal must be informed before being questioned that: 1) he has a right to remain silent, 2) anything he says may be used against him in court, 3) he has a right to consult a lawyer and to have counsel present when he is questioned, and

4) counsel will be appointed for him if he cannot afford to employ an attorney.

Unfortunately, many Americans have been displeased with Supreme Court decisions that have resulted in safeguarding the rights of persons accused of crimes. Some law enforcement officials have been particularly critical of new regulations designed to protect defendants' rights in compliance with judicial decisions. There are strong indications that many policemen would welcome a reversal of the "Miranda rules" on interrogation in favor of a more relaxed standard, and only one justice remains on the Court who voted in favor of the *Miranda* decision— William J. Brennan, Jr.

Judge J. Edward Lumbard pointed out in *The American Bar Association Journal* in 1966 that some citizens believe that "the public interest is not receiving fair treatment and that undue emphasis has been placed on safeguarding individual rights."[154] Indeed, the "Warren Court" was so successful in curbing police abuse of power that Chief Justice Warren was the object of a nationwide campaign calling for his impeachment, the "Impeach Warren!" campaign being fueled by the John Birch Society. In response to police reactions to legal decisions of a liberal nature, William W. Turner, author of *The Police Establishment* and a former FBI agent, declared that the principal objectives of the police establishment and its lobbyist groups

> are to nullify Supreme Court decisions by legislation, legalize Big Brother devices in the interest of the "crime war," obtain more repressive laws, perpetrate the punitive theory over rehabilitation, and become a national police system.[155]

Turner also claimed that such police ambitions "are subversive to a free society" and that "in promoting a Big Blue Line as our bulwark against crime and Communism, the police lobby poses a viable threat to our democratic institutions."[156] J. Shelly Wright has pointed out also that one of the sure ways for political candidates to gain instant popularity is to "denounce crime in the streets and then accuse people in high places of being soft on criminals."[157]

DEFENDING CIVIL LIBERTIES

In 1917, the National Civil Liberties Bureau was organized as a private organization financed by private funds.[158] Originally concerned with immediate problems that grew out of the First World War (including prosecutions under the Espionage and Sedition Acts, the issue of conscientious objectors, and the question of political prisoners), the National Civil Liberties Bureau has been described as "the first organization in the history of our nation to devote itself exclusively to the defense of civil liberties, and not to the representation of a single group."[159]

In 1920, the organization was re-named the American Civil Liberties Union (ACLU). National recognition for the ACLU came in the mid-1920s, when the organization assisted defendants in the Scopes trial in Tennessee, the Sweet case in Detroit, and the Sacco-Vanzetti case in Massachusetts. Donating its services to persons involved in civil rights cases, the American Civil Liberties Union became the most active national organization concerned with safeguarding and promoting civil liberties. For more than 50 years, it has championed individual rights contained in the Declaration of Independence and the U.S. Constitution. These rights include: 1) freedom of inquiry and expression (speech, press, assembly, and religion), 2) due process of law and a fair trial for everybody, and 3) equality before the law, regardless of race, color, national origin, political opinion, or religious belief. Activities of the ACLU have included test court cases, opposition to repressive legislation, and public protests against inroads on citizens' rights. The ACLU maintains committees concerned with academic freedom, church-state relationships, communication media, due process of law, equality, free speech and association, labor and business, and privacy.

The American Civil Liberties Union has argued more cases before the U.S. Supreme Court than any other body except the federal government, and its record of legal achievements is outstanding. Several landmark cases are included in the ACLU struggle against oppression, including the flag-saluting case of the Jehovah's Witnesses and the notable freedom of expression case involving James Joyce's *Ulysses*, a novel which had been seized by the Bureau of Customs when imported into the country.[160] The ACLU has also devoted considerable attention to the efforts of blacks to exercise their full rights. Thus, in 1964, the Southern Regional Office of the ACLU was opened, and more than 160 cases have been litigated by the office since it was established.

Among the more recent activities of the ACLU is a national campaign for laws to limit government access to the intimate details of citizens' lives. An example is an advertisement which has appeared in national periodicals under the heading, "Tell us your Social Security Number and we'll tell you what your neighbors say about your sex life." The ACLU maintains that Social Security Numbers are being used as "universal identifiers," and that it is thus easy for more than 2,500 private dossier companies to obtain information about citizens' credit records, employability, and other facts and hearsay. In addition, the ACLU has fought the military practice of using secret code numbers on discharge papers as indicators of such things as alleged defective attitudes, unsanitary practices, and homosexual tendencies.

A series of guidebooks devoted to rights of various groups has also been issued by the American Civil Liberties Union, the series including books on rights of students, gay people, women, the very poor, servicemen, prisoners, teachers, and mental patients. They were written in the belief "that Americans informed of their rights will be encouraged to exercise them [and that] through this exercise, rights are given life."[161] The ACLU guide for public school students, *The Rights of Students*,[162] outlines liberties according to present laws and provides suggestions for protecting them. For example, in relation to First Amendment rights, the guidebook poses and answers such questions as:

1) Can a publication be banned because it criticizes school officials?
2) May a school ban all literature on a given subject on the grounds that the subject is too controversial and may cause disruption?
3) Can the school prevent students from inviting a speaker to their club meeting because he is too controversial?
4) Can a school prohibit students from handing out all literature, including underground newspapers, on school property?

As the guidebook for students indicates, the legal answer to all these questions is *No*. Laws pertinent to each of these issues are then carefully outlined and explained in *The Rights of Students*.

Offering services such as it does, then, the ACLU attempts to maintain freedoms for all citizens, the despised and deprived as well as the approved and affluent.

■ ■ ■

The development of freedoms in the United States during the twentieth century has been sporadic, and certainly there have been what civil libertarians would view as setbacks. The Espionage Act during the First World War, Prohibition, and the McCarthy era are proof enough that progress has not been uninterrupted. However, women attained the vote, the civil rights of racial and ethnic minorities have been assured by law, and the courts have extended to persons suspected of crimes protections of rights that were previously unrecognized. Thus, on the whole, the rights and freedoms of the individual American citizen are greater than they were at the beginning of the century.

This is not to say, however, that those freedoms, once established, are in no danger of being rescinded or eroded, and that is the focus of the remaining chapters in this *Intellectual Freedom Primer*. While a cogent discussion of automated personal data systems is included, the bulk of the chapters concentrate on freedom in various arts; but this should not be taken to mean that only in the arts should we maintain vigilance against the suppression of ideas. It should always be borne in mind that if government or private forces are allowed to control thought and expression in those activities which stimulate further thought and provide pleasure in ways both public and private, then the way has been cleared for those same forces to attempt control of even larger segments of citizens' lives, and eventually the totality of those lives.

FOOTNOTES

[1] Thorstein Veblen, *The Theory of the Leisure Class: An Economic Study in the Evolution of Institutions* (New York: The Macmillan Co., 1899), 400p.

[2] "Thorstein Veblen," in *The Oxford Companion to American History*, ed. by Thomas J. Johnson (New York: Oxford University Press, 1966), pp. 813-14.

[3] John Dewey, *Democracy and Education: An Introduction to the Philosophy of Education* (New York: The Macmillan Co., 1916), 434p.

[4] John Dewey, *Reconstruction in Philosophy* (New York: H. Holt and Co., 1920), 224p.

[5] Martin S. Dworkin, ed., *Dewey on Education: Selections with an Introduction and Notes* (New York: Teachers College, Columbia University, 1959), p. 30.

[6] Howard Mumford Jones, *The Age of Energy; Varieties of American Experience 1865-1915* (New York: Viking Press, 1970), p. 434.

[7] U.S. President. Executive Order. "Forbidding Solicitation of Increase of Pay or Attempt to Influence Legislation Except through Heads of Departments." 17 January 1902, 1p.

[8] Herbert D. Croly, *The Promise of American Life* (New York: The Macmillan Co., 1909), 468p.

[9] Lincoln Steffens, *The Shame of the Cities* (New York: McClure, 1904), 306p.

[10] Lincoln Steffens, *The Struggle for Self-Government* (New York: McClure Phillips and Co., 1906), 214p.

[11] Lincoln Steffens, *The Shame of the Cities* (New York: Hill and Wang, 1963), p. 7.

[12] Frank Norris, *The Pit: A Story of Chicago; The Epic of Wheat* (New York: Doubleday, Page & Co., 1903), 421p.

[13] Frank Norris, *The Octopus: A Story of California* (London: Grant Richards, 1901), 652p.

[14] Norman Thomas, *The Conscientious Objector in America* (New York: B. W. Huebsch, Inc., 1923), p. 97.

[15] Espionage Act. June 15, 1917, ch. 30, 40 stat. 217. *U.S. Code*, vol. 4 (1946); Sedition Act. May 16, 1918, ch. 75. stat. 533. *U.S. Code*, vol. 4 (1946).

[16] Sedition Act. May 16, 1918, ch. 75. stat. 533. *U.S. Code*, vol. 4 (1946).

[17] "Mr. Burleson to Rule the Press," *Literary Digest* 55 (October 6, 1917): 12.

[18] Gerald Cullinan, *The United States Postal Service* (New York: Praeger Publishers, 1973), p. 125.

[19] *Schenck v. United States*, 249 U.S. 47 (1919).

[20] Henry J. Abraham, *Freedom and the Court: Civil Rights and Liberties in the United States* (New York: Oxford University Press, 1967), pp. 167-71.

[21] Donald Meiklejohn, *Freedom and the Public; Public and Private Morality in America* (Syracuse: Syracuse University Press, 1965), p. 123.

[22] *Abrams v. United States*, 250 U.S. 616 (1919).

[23] *The Supreme Court Reporter* (St. Paul, Minn.: West Publishing Co., 1921), 40:18.

[24] Charles A. Miller, *The Supreme Court and the Uses of History* (Cambridge: Harvard University Press, 1969), p. 90.

[25] "Debs Arrested; Sedition Charged," *The New York Times* LXVII (July 1, 1918), p. 1.

[26] "Debs, Eugene Victor," in *The Oxford Companion to American History*, p. 235.

[27] *Prudential Insurance Co. v. Cheek*, 259 U.S. 530 (1922).

[28] *Gitlow v. New York*, 268 U.S. 652 (1925).

[29] *Schenck v. United States*, 249 U.S. 47 (1919); *Frohwerk v. United States*, 249 U.S. 204 (1919); *Debs v. United States*, 249 U.S. 211 (1919); *Abrams v. United States*, 250 U.S. 616 (1919); *Schaefer v. United States*, 251 U.S. 466 (1920); and *Pierce v. United States*, 252 U.S. 239 (1920).

[30] Robert Coughlan, "Konklave in Kokomo," in *The Aspirin Age*, ed. by Isabel Leighton (New York: Simon and Schuster, 1949), pp. 106-109.

[31] Frederick Lewis Allen, *Only Yesterday; An Informal History of the Nineteen-Twenties* (New York: Harper & Row, Publishers, 1956), pp. 113-114.

[32] Francis Butler Simkins, "Ku-Klux Klan," in *The Encyclopedia Americana* (New York: Americana Corporation, 1971), 16:550.

[33] Arnold S. Rice, *The Ku Klux Klan in American Politics* (New York: Haskell House, 1972).

[34] U.S. Department of Commerce, Bureau of the Census, *Historical Statistics of the United States, Colonial Times to 1957* (Washington: Government Printing Office, 1960), p. 56.

[35] U.S. Department of Commerce, Bureau of the Census, *Statistical Abstract of the United States* (Washington: Government Printing Office, 1974), p. 5, and U.S. Department of Commerce, Bureau of the Census, *Historical Statistics of the United States, Colonial Times to 1957*, p. 7.

[36] Robert W. Dunn, *The Palmer Raids* (New York: International Publishers, 1948), pp. 38-47.

[37] Daniel Bell, *Marxian Socialism in the United States* (Princeton, N.J.: Princeton University Press, 1967), p. 118.

[38] New York (State). Legislature. Joint Committee Investigating Seditious Activities, *Revolutionary Radicalism; Its History, Purpose and Tactics* (New York: Da Capo Press, 1971).

[39] *Ibid.*, p. 7.

[40] "Sacco-Vanzetti Case," in *The Oxford Companion to American History*, p. 700.

[41] Herbert Asbury, "The Noble Experiment of Izzie and Moe," in *The Aspirin Age: 1919-1941*, ed. by Isabel Leighton (New York: Simon and Schuster, 1949), p. 34.

[42] Ernest H. Cherrington, ed., *Standard Encyclopedia of the Alcohol Problem* (Montclair, N.J.: American Issues Publishing Co., 1928), p. 1519.

[43] John Kobler, *Ardent Spirits; The Rise and Fall of Prohibition* (New York: G. P. Putnam's Sons, 1973), p. 17.

[44] *Ibid.*, p. 283.

[45] Marjorie Fribourg, *The Bill of Rights* (New York: Avon, 1967), p. 72.

[46] Frederick Lewis Allen, *Only Yesterday; An Informal History of the Nineteen-Twenties* (New York: Harper & Row, Publishers, 1956), p. 236.

[47] William W. Brickman, "Academic Freedom," in *The Encyclopedia Americana* (New York: Americana Corporation, 1971), 1:67-68.

[48] Hans W. Baade and Robinson O. Everett, eds., *Academic Freedom; The Scholar's Place in Modern Society* (Dobbs Ferry, N.Y.: Oceana Publications, 1964), p. 8.

[49] Bertram H. Davis, "Academic Freedom, Academic Neutrality and the Social System," in *The Concept of Academic Freedom*, ed. by Edmund L. Pincoffs (Austin: University of Texas Press, 1972), p. 28.

[50] *Adler v. Board of Education of the City of New York*, 342 U.S. 485 (1952).

[51] *Sweezy v. New Hampshire*, 345 U.S. 234 (1957).

[52] *Beilan v. Board of Education of Philadelphia*, 357 U.S. 399 (1958).

[53] *Barenblatt v. United States*, 360 U.S. 109 (1959).

[54] James Russell Wiggins, *Freedom or Secrecy*, rev. ed. (New York: Oxford University Press, 1964), pp. 97-98.

[55] Dillon S. Myer, *Uprooted Americans: The Japanese Americans and the War Relocation Authority During World War II* (Tucson: University of Arizona Press, 1971), p. 16.

[56] "Evacuation of Japanese and Other Subversive Persons from the Pacific Coast," memorandum to the Secretary of War (Presidio of San Francisco, California:

Office of the Commanding General, Western Defense Command and Fourth Army, February 14, 1942).

[57] U.S. President. Executive Order No. 9066. Authorizing the Secretary of War to Prescribe Military Areas. February 19, 1942.

[58] U.S. President. Executive Order No. 9102. Authorizing the Establishment of the War Relocation Authority. March 18, 1942.

[59] U.S. Congress. House Committee of the Judiciary. *Hearings*, before Subcommittee No. 5, 83rd Congress, 2d sess. on HR 7435 (Washington, D.C.: Government Printing Office, 1954), p. 35.

[60] Harold I. Ickes, "Wartime Abuse of American Japanese Should Now Be Corrected by U.S.," column, "Man to Man," *Washington Evening Star*, September 23, 1946.

[61] Myer, p. 298.

[62] *Korematsu v. United States*, 323 U.S. 214 (1944).

[63] "Job Well Done," editorial, *The Washington Post*, March 28, 1946.

[64] Maisie Conrat and Richard Conrat, *Executive Order 9066: The Internment of 110,000 Japanese Americans* (Los Angeles: California Historical Society, 1972), pp. 110-111.

[65] Audrie Girdner and Anne Loftis, *The Great Betrayal; The Evacuation of the Japanese-Americans During World War II* (London: Macmillan, 1969), p. 482.

[66] Morton Grodzins, *Americans Betrayed; Politics and the Japanese Evacuation* (Chicago: University of Chicago Press, 1949), p. vii.

[67] Anson Phelps Stokes and Leo Pfeffer, *Church and State in the United States*, rev., one-vol. ed. (New York: Harper and Row, Publishers, 1964), p. 344.

[68] "Aims and Purposes of the Religious Liberty Association of America," issued by the Religious Liberty Association, 1936.

[69] Wilbur G. Katz, "Freedom of Worship," in *The Encyclopedia Americana* (New York: Americana Corporation, 1971), 29:539.

[70] Robert F. Drinan, *Religion, the Courts and Public Policy* (New York: McGraw-Hill, 1963), p. 10.

[71] *Reynolds v. United States*, 98 U.S. 145 (1879).

[72] *Minersville School District v. Gobitis*, 310 U.S. 586 (1940).

[73] *West Virginia State Board of Education v. Barnette*, 319 U.S. 624 (1943).

[74] Morris L. Ernst, *The Great Reversals: Tales of the Supreme Court* (New York: Weybright and Talley, 1973), p. 137.

[75] *Ibid.*, p. 141.

[76] *Cantwell v. Connecticut*, 310 U.S. 296 (1940).

[77] *Everson v. Board of Education of Ewing Twp.*, 330 U.S. 1 (1947).

[78] *Burstyn v. Wilson*, 343 U.S. 495; 72 S. Ct. 777; 96 L. Ed. 1098 (1952).

[79] *Torcaso v. Watkins*, 367 U.S. 488 (1961).

[80] *McGowan v. Maryland*, 366 U.S. 420 (1961); *Two Guys from Harrison-Allentown, Inc. v. McGinley*, 366 U.S. 582 (1961); *Braunfeld v. Brown*, U.S. 599 (1961); and *Gallager v. Crown Kosher Super Market of Massachusetts*, 366 U.S. 617 (1961).

[81] *McGowan v. Maryland*, 366 U.S. 420 (1961).

[82] *Steven I. Engel, et al. v. William J. Vitale, et al.*, 370 U.S. 421; 82 S. Ct. 1261; 8 L. Ed. 2d 601 (1962).

[83] Earl Warren, "The Law and the Future," *Fortune* 52 (November, 1955): 230.

[84] Robert Goldston, *The American Nightmare; Senator Joseph R. McCarthy and the Politics of Hate* (Indianapolis: Bobbs-Merrill, 1973), pp. 187-88.

[85] Paul G. Kauper, *Civil Liberties and the Constitution* (Ann Arbor: Ann Arbor Paperbacks, University of Michigan Press, 1966), p. 98.

[86] *Dennis v. United States*, 341 U.S. 494 (1951).

[87] Radio Reports, Inc., "Fund for the Republic: Eric Sevareid and the News at 7:30 P.M. over the CBS Radio Network," March 2, 1953, Public Documents file.

[88] Thomas C. Reeves, *Freedom and the Foundation: The Fund for the Republic in the Era of McCarthyism* (New York: Alfred A. Knopf, 1969), p. 290.

[89] Christopher Lasch, "The Cultural Cold War: A Short History of the Congress for Cultural Freedom," in *Towards a New Past: Dissenting Essays in American History* (New York: Vantage Books, 1969), p. 343.

[90] *United States v. Brown*, 381 U.S. 437 (1969).

[91] John Hope Franklin, *From Slavery to Freedom; A History of Negro Americans*, 3d ed. (New York: Vintage Books, 1967), p. 439.

[92] Du Bois, William E. B., *The Souls of Black Folk: Essay and Sketches* (Chicago: A. C. McClurg & Co., 1903), 264p.

[93] John P. Davis, ed., *The American Negro Reference Book* (Englewood Cliffs, N.J.: Prentice-Hall, 1966), p. 682.

[94] Du Bois, William E. B., *The Gift of Black Folk: The Negroes in the Making of America* (Boston: The Stratford Co., 1924), 349p.

[95] Du Bois, William E. B., *Black Reconstruction: An Essay toward a History of the Past Which Black Folk Played in the Attempt to Reconstruct Democracy in America, 1860-1880* (New York: Harcourt, Brace and Co., 1935), 746p.

[96] U.S. Department of Commerce, Bureau of the Census, *Negro Population in the United States 1900-1915* (Washington: Government Printing Office, 1918), p. 101.

[97] U.S. Department of Commerce, Bureau of the Census, *Negroes in the United States 1920-1932* (Washington: Government Printing Office, 1935), p. 62.

[98] Kelly Miller, *Kelly Miller's History of the World War for Human Rights* (New York: Negro Universities Press, 1969), p. 475.

[99] *Plessy v. Ferguson*, 163 U.S. 537 (1896).

[100] *Brown v. Board of Education of Topeka*, 347 U.S. 483; 74 S. Ct. 686; 98 L. Ed. 873 (1954).

[101] *Brown v. Board of Education of Topeka*, 349 U.S. 294; 75 S. Ct. 753; 99 L. Ed. 1083 (1955).

[102] *Heart of Atlanta Motel, Inc. v. United States*, 379 U.S. 241 (1964).

[103] *NAACP v. Alabama*, 357 U.S. 449 (1958).

[104] *Louisiana ex rel. Gremillion v. National Association for the Advancement of Colored People*, 366 U.S. 293 (1961).

[105] *Bryant v. Zimmerman*, 278 U.S. 63 (1928).

[106] *Uphaus v. Wyman*, 360 U.S. 72 (1959).

[107] Maurice Girodias, ed., *The Olympia Reader* (New York: Grove Press, 1965), p. 13.

[108] Katherine Davis, *Factors in the Sex Life of 2,200 Women* (New York, Harper, 1929), 430p.

[109] Gilbert V. Hamilton, *Research in Marriage* (New York: Alfred and Charles Boni, Inc., 1929), 570p.

[110] Robert L. Dickinson and Lura Beam, *A Thousand Marriages: A Medical Study of Sex Adjustment* (London: Williams, 1932), 482p.

[111] Alfred C. Kinsey, W. B. Pomeroy, and C. Martin, *Sexual Behavior in the Human Male* (Philadelphia: Saunders, 1948), 804p.

[112] Alfred C. Kinsey, W. Pomeroy, C. Martin, and P. Gebhard, *Sexual Behavior in the Human Female* (Philadelphia: Saunders, 1953), 842p.

[113] John S. Gagnon, "Sex Research and Social Change," *Archives of Sexual Behavior* 4 (1975):111-41.

[114] *Ibid.*

[115] William H. Masters and Virginia E. Johnson, *Human Sexual Response* (Boston: Little, Brown, 1966), 366p.

[116] William H. Masters and Virginia E. Johnson, *Human Sexual Inadequacy* (Boston: Little, Brown, 1970), 467p.

[117] Wainwright Churchill, *Homosexual Behavior Among Males: A Cross Cultural and Cross Species Investigation* (Englewood Cliffs, N.J.: Prentice-Hall, 1971), 347p.

[118] Laud Humphreys, *Out of the Closets: The Sociology of Homosexual Liberation* (Englewood Cliffs, N.J.: Prentice-Hall, 1972), 176p.

[119] *Roth v. United States*, 354 U.S. 476 (1957).

[120] *Alberts v. California*, 354 U.S. 476 (1957).

[121] *Miller v. California*, 413 U.S. 15 (1973).

[122] *Kingsley Books, Inc. v. Brown*, 354 U.S. 436 (1957).

[123] *Kingsley International Pictures Corporation v. Regents of the State of New York*, 360 U.S. 684 (1959).

[124] *Ohio ex rel. Eaton v. Price*, 364 U.S. 263 (1960).

[125] *Near v. Minnesota*, 283 U.S. 697 (1931).

[126] *Ginzburg v. United States*, 383 U.S. 463 (1966).

[127] Richard H. Kuh, *Foolish Figleaves? Pornography in and out of Court* (New York: The Macmillan Co., 1967), p. 323.

[128] Olga C. and Edwin P. Hoyt, *Censorship in America* (New York: Seabury Press, 1970), pp. 51-55.

[129] *Daily Herald-Telephone*, Bloomington, Indiana (August 4, 1973):4.

[130] Herbert S. Kassner, "Obscenity Leads to Perversion," *New York Law Forum* No. 3 (Winter 1975).

[131] "Obscenity Ruling Strongly Opposed at Ad Club Lunch," *Publishers Weekly* 204 (October 29, 1973):22-23.

[132] *Ibid.*

[133] *Ibid.*

[134] "Trustee Tells State: Exempt Librarians from Obscenity Laws," *Wilson Library Bulletin* 48 (December 1973):294.

[135] "AAP Asks Supreme Court for 'New Approach' to Porno," *Library Journal* 99 (March 15, 1974):722.

[136] *Paris Adult Theater I v. Slanton, District Attorney et al.*, 413 U.S. 92 (1974).

[137] *Jenkins v. Georgia*, 94 S. Ct. 2750 (1974).

[138] "AAP Asks Supreme Court for 'New Approach' to Porno," *Library Journal*, p. 722.

[139] *New York Times* (June 25, 1974), 18:3.

[140] *De Jonge v. Oregon*, 299 U.S. 353 (1937).

[141] *Feiner v. New York*, 340 U.S. 315; 71 S. Ct. 303; 95 L. Ed. 295 (1951).

[142] *Mapp v. Ohio*, 367 U.S. 643 (1961).

[143] *Communist Party v. Subversive Activities Control Board*, 367 U.S. 1 (1961).

[144] *Aptheker v. Secretary of State*, 378 U.S. 500 (1964).

[145] *Albertson v. Subversive Activities Control Board*, 382 U.S. 70 (1965).

[146] *United States v. Robel*, 19 L Ed. 2d 508 (1967).

[147] Arthur E. Sutherland, "Crime and Confession," *Harvard Law Review* 79 (1965):39.

[148] *Chambers v. Florida*, 309 U.S. 227 (1940).

[149] *Gideon v. Wainwright*, 372 U.S. 335 (1963).

[150] *Messiah v. United States*, 377 U.S. 201 (1964).

[151] *Escobedo v. Illinois*, 378 U.S. 478 (1964).

[152] *Griswold v. Connecticut*, 381 U.S. 479 (1965).

[153] *Miranda v. Arizona*, 384 U.S. 436 (1966).

[154] J. Edward Lumbard, "New Standards for Criminal Justice," *American Bar Association Journal* 52 (May 1966):431.

[155] William W. Turner, *The Police Establishment* (New York: Tower Publications, 1968), p. 248.

[156] *Ibid.*, pp. 248-49.

[157] J. Skelly Wright, "Crime in the Streets and the New McCarthyism," *New Republic* 153 (October 9, 1965):10.

[158] Donald Johnson, *The Challenge to American Freedoms; World War I and the Rise of the American Civil Liberties Union* (Lexington: University of Kentucky Press for the Mississippi Valley Historical Association, 1963), p. 96.

[159] *Ibid.*, p. 194.

[160] *United States v. One Book Entitled Ulysses*, 72 F.2d 705 (2d Cir 1934).

[161] Alan Levine and others, *The Rights of Students: The Basic ACLU Guide to a Student's Rights* (New York: Avon Books, 1973), p. vii.

[162] *Ibid.*

PRIVACY AND SECURITY IN AUTOMATED PERSONAL DATA SYSTEMS

Stephen P. Harter

The Freedom of Information Act, signed into law by President Lyndon Johnson in 1966 and amended in November 1974, is based on the principle of the people's right to know—the right to be informed of government's past, present, and intended activities.[1] The Watergate affair and cover-up, as well as the recently reported illegal activities of the CIA, have excited citizens' interest in the activities of their government and their protests against governmental secrecy in the conduct of these affairs. However, the central concern of the present chapter is not with freedom of information but with a principle that is to a certain degree in conflict with the principle of freedom of information—the issue of the preservation of the privacy and sanctity of the individual citizen, of his physical person, his thoughts, actions, personal businesses and pleasures. Indeed, while "freedom of information" implies a public right to examine government files openly, this right of access is not absolute. Provisions of the Freedom of Information Act and its amendments include certain exemptions—in particular, a provision which prohibits access to files which could not be disclosed without a "clearly unwarranted invasion of personal privacy."[2] This chapter examines the concept of personal privacy, especially as it relates to the use of the electronic computer and supportive information technologies to store, transmit, and communicate personal data records.

Today, rational decision making and policy formation seem to demand ever-increasing quantities of accurate, pertinent, and current information. Government at all levels requires an extraordinary amount of personal data on which to base new legislation, to evaluate the status and effect of programs and institutions, and to plan in a comprehensive and rational way for such pressing social needs as adequate energy resources, balanced ecological and economic systems, crime control, highway construction and maintenance, water regulation, education, taxation, and national defense. In addition, the twentieth century has witnessed the proliferation of new services to citizens such as Social Security, Medicare, unemployment compensation, and other programs of social welfare by government at all levels, but particularly by the federal government. The provision of these services requires a considerable bureaucracy and an enormous volume of governmental record-keeping.

Moreover, the private sector also possesses a seemingly insatiable appetite for data concerning individuals. The banking, credit, and insurance industries collect quantities of data about our financial dealings; detailed pecuniary histories on each of us are maintained. Doctors and hospitals keep complete records of our medical histories, wherever we may seek their services. Commercial airlines, motels, and hotels maintain files on our physical comings and goings, while the telephone company records the numbers of those to whom we teletransport our voices. Thus, our society is, quite literally, an information-based society. As we have noted, much of the information collected represents personal, private data concerning individual citizens. Because of this fact, the term "dossier society" is a particularly appropriate description of what we have become.[3]

To place our discussion of Man as a keeper of records into historical perspective, it should perhaps be observed that record-keeping is anything but a new phenomenon. Homo sapiens has been collecting, recording, analyzing, and preserving data since the time he first learned to represent ideas symbolically. The earliest examples of writing, from the civilizations of Egypt, Sumer, and Babylonia, are mostly business, legal, and religious records. Recorded on rolls of papyrus and clay tablets and preserved in the first libraries, many of these records have survived to the present day, telling us much about commercial, religious, and political life in the earliest civilizations.[4] Indeed, it is probable that the growing need of ancient societies to collect, record, and maintain data files may in significant measure have been responsible for the invention of writing. Clearly, the distinction between ancient societies and our own in the matter of record-keeping is only a matter of degree. Even so, three disturbing trends can be identified as particularly characteristic of today's dossier society.

First, the nature of the data being collected is widely diverse. Much of this information is increasingly personal and confidential in nature, leading a growing number of private citizens, congressional committees, and groups in the private sector to be vitally concerned about possible violations of personal privacy. The nature of and the necessity for many instances of data gathering have been questioned, both in the public and private sectors. The accuracy of personal data and the possible harm to individuals resulting from inaccurate data are also sources of concern.

Second, our data and information processing technologies have radically changed in the past few decades. The use of the electronic computer and direct access storage devices have made possible the accurate and efficient maintenance of enormous libraries or data banks of information, and the possibility of retrieving, inspecting, modifying, creating, or deleting particular data records or fields, all virtually instantaneously. In addition, the communications technologies permit the transmission of data records over thousands of miles, theoretically allowing users of a computerized data library to examine the contents of the library or to otherwise interact with it from anywhere on the globe, regardless of the library's physical location. Unfortunately, these capabilities imply unique disadvantages as well as advantages, especially with reference to the problem of guaranteeing the security of confidential and private information.

Employment statistics and projections released by the Department of Labor clearly demonstrate the growing impact of the computer in our society.[5] In the decade since 1960, the number of persons employed in computer-related occupations quadrupled to 765,000 in 1970, and this number was projected to swell to one million by 1980. However, this expected growth rate of 30 percent over the decade of the 1970s is considerably reduced from the growth characterizing the previous decade, at least in part because by 1970, the "untapped new customer base" had already been greatly reduced. For this reason, little or no overall growth was projected in computer-related employment in transportation, communications, electric, gas, sanitary services, and government, while the largest existing market was predicted to lie in the services, such as hospitals, educational institutions, and libraries. The Department of Labor projects that the greatest future growth in computer-related occupations will occur in service industries. Estimates have been made that the gross cost of goods and services related to the computer totaled more than 20 billion dollars in 1972,[6] and that by 1975, approximately three percent of the work force in the United States would be working directly with computers.[7] The pervasiveness of the computer in our society has implications for the education of our youth as well. Mumford and Sackman, in their summary of the proceedings of a 1974 international conference on "Human Choice and Computers," observed that "computer literacy will be essential for informed human choice in the future," and they recommended that all children over the age of ten be instructed as to the use and potential of the computer.[8]

A final characteristic of the dossier society which distinguishes it from earlier civilizations is that the volume of data collected, recorded, and analyzed is growing exponentially, is *exploding*, in both the private and public sectors. In the state of California alone, 1973 estimates of the number of existing data bases have ranged between 8,000 and 10,000, 45 percent of which contained some personal data.[9] Data almost appears to feed upon itself, creating a need for more data, and causing an ever-increasing flood of information.

In part, the information explosion is a reflection of the increasing complexity of our society. It is also probably closely related to technological improvements in computer speed, efficiency, and storage capacity, as well as exponential decreases in per-unit computing costs. The net result of all of these developments has been a considerable reduction in the expense associated with large-scale record keeping. Thus, a third explanation for the information explosion was suggested by Arthur Miller, in his careful study *The Assault on Privacy*. Professor Miller describes our affliction by a new social virus—"data-mania." Given birth by the information technologies, data-mania was characterized by Miller as an obsession with data:

> Its symptoms are shortness of breath and heart palpitations when con-
> templating a new computer application, a feeling of possessiveness about
> information and a deep resentment toward those who won't yield it, a
> delusion that all information handlers can walk on water, and a highly
> advanced case of astigmatism. . . .[10]

There is perhaps more truth in Miller's description of this malady than many members of the information professions would care to admit; however, the purpose of this essay is not to explore further the social and psychological factors under-lying the creation and the perpetuation of the dossier society. Whatever its origin, one cannot deny that the dossier society exists, and that it poses an increasing threat to personal privacy. Growing public realization of this threat was reflected in the Congress, which, since 1966, has conducted numerous hearings and investigations of the problem. These concerns culminated in the "Privacy Act of 1974," signed into law by President Ford on December 31, 1974.[11]

In the remainder of this chapter, the motivation underlying the provisions of the Privacy Act of 1974 will be explored in some detail, and the most significant events leading to its passage will be outlined. The chapter will conclude with an examination of the act itself, and with a brief speculation concerning possible future legislation.

THE CONCEPT OF PRIVACY

Privacy can be viewed from a number of perspectives, virtually ensuring that a precise definition of the concept acceptable to every reader would be difficult to formulate. Nevertheless, several characteristic elements of privacy can readily be identified. Alan Westin, in his seminal work *Privacy and Freedom*, emphasized the necessity of an individual's removing himself from society in his exercise of personal privacy, and said further that the act should be effected of his own free will: " . . . privacy is the voluntary and temporary withdrawal of a person from the general society through physical or psychological means. . . ."[12] The concept of "person" can be expanded from the purely physical to encompass psychological, emotional, and spiritual attributes—"attitudes, beliefs, behavior, and opinions."[13] The idea that privacy is intimately related to several basic relations which may exist between two human beings is brought out by Charles Fried in a valuable essay on the nature of privacy: "[Privacy is] . . . necessarily related to ends and relations of the most fundamental sort: respect, love, friendship, and trust."[14] With respect to personal data, Fried defined privacy as " . . . the *control* we have over information about ourselves."[15] But probably the most well-known definition of privacy was provided by Supreme Court Justice Louis Brandeis in 1928: " . . . the right to be let alone—the most comprehensive of rights and the right most valued by civilized men."[16]

Perhaps the concept of privacy can be most clearly illustrated by contrasting it to another, equal human need—the need to communicate, share, and participate in a larger society.[17] The health and vitality of individuals require that a balance be struck between these competing needs, and we are constantly made aware of this conflict between privacy and participation in the conduct of our everyday lives. To varying degrees, every human being has a need to communicate with others of his species—to give up part of himself by sharing some of his personal ideas, thoughts and actions, by being near others, in both a physical and a psychological sense. Each of us has a need to feel part of a social unit larger than ourselves, physically, intellectually, and emotionally. At the same time, we are aware of a need to hold something of ourselves back, to hoard certain attitudes, thoughts, and emotions, and to keep particular facts about ourselves private. At times we feel the need to be alone in a physical sense as well.

As Charles Fried convincingly argued, the most fundamental relations between humans—respect, love, friendship, and trust—can exist only if the *possibility* of privacy exists.[18] The giving implicit in the intimate relations of love and friendship requires the voluntary relinquishment of a certain amount of privacy to the beloved; privacy is thus a necessary condition for these relations to exist. Without the possibility of privacy, participation loses meaning and significance, and intimate relations are impossible. According to Fried,

> . . . intimacy is the sharing of information about one's actions, beliefs, or emotions which one does not share with all, and which one has the right not to share with anyone. By conferring this right, privacy creates the moral capital which we spend in friendship and love.[19]

On the other hand, if participation with other human beings is impossible, such as in the case of total isolation, it is impossible to conceive of the existence of privacy.

It is the *possibility* of privacy which permits the existence of true intimacy, and conversely.

In *Privacy and Freedom*, Alan Westin carefully and thoroughly explores the dual needs for privacy and participation of members of primitive as well as modern societies, and of animals as well as men. Westin's study strongly suggests that these needs are not unique to modern man, nor even to the species, but are in some sense characteristic of animal life in general:

> ... the animal's struggle to achieve a balance between privacy and participation provides one of the basic processes of animal life. In this sense, the quest for privacy is not restricted to man alone, but arises in the biological and social processes of all life.[20]

But it is not only on the individual level that a tension or balance exists between privacy and participation. Society has a need to preserve and enforce its social norms and paradigms in order to perpetuate itself. This need inevitably entails a degree of psychological and physical surveillance over its citizens, and a consequent loss of personal privacy. The conflict thus defined between the common good and the sanctity of the individual member of society is probably as old as societies themselves. Indeed, the way in which a society resolves this conflict, that is, the relative balance maintained between these needs within the society, defines an important difference between a liberal democratic society and a totalitarian society. In a multitude of forms, "Big Brother" watches over the citizens of totalitarian societies, monitoring, recording, and evaluating their most private words and deeds. Thus the regime is forced to oppose the concept of privacy as contrary to the best interests of the state:

> The modern totalitarian state relies, in varying degrees, on secrecy for the regime and full surveillance for all other groups. Both fascist and communist literature are replete with attacks on the idea of privacy as "immoral," "antisocial," and part of "the cult of individualism."[21]

Clearly, if Charles Fried's analysis is correct, totalitarian societies in their most extreme forms preclude the possibility of the existence of love, friendship, trust, and respect. The most familiar explication of this thesis is perhaps George Orwell's *1984*.[22] Modern democratic societies, on the other hand, are biased in favor of the individual. For example, a fundamental tenet of the Western democratic system of jurisprudence is that an accused person is presumed innocent until proven guilty. Thus, our society prefers to allow possible law breakers to go free than to wrongly imprison a man.

The conflict between the good of the state and the sanctity of the individual can also be characterized as a conflict between individual privacy and the famous American virtue of *efficiency*.[23] According to this view, the state gives up a measure of efficiency so that the individual might enjoy personal liberty. Thus, in societies in which efficiency is valued too highly, personal privacy inevitably suffers, and the quest for efficiency may well represent the single greatest source of danger to the loss of personal privacy in the modern world. This danger is in fact exacerbated by the nature of modern data processing technologies, a claim which will be explored in some detail in another section of the chapter.

PRIVACY AND THE LAW

The concept of privacy has been the central subject of analysis from a legal point of view in several excellent publications.[24] For comprehensive discussions of the privacy issue in the law, the reader is referred to these studies.

The modern legal attitude toward the subject of privacy probably had its origins[25] in an article published in the *Harvard Law Review* in 1890 by Samuel D. Warren and Louis D. Brandeis.[26] In their seminal article, Warren and Brandeis traced the development of the concept of privacy in common law. From the legal concept of protecting an individual's land and physical possessions arose the concept of intangible property belonging to the realm of the mind, such as works of literature and art. With this interpretation of privacy, the legal concept of protection of personal privacy may be said to constitute an extension of the concept of protection of personal property. However, Warren and Brandeis considered this view to be somewhat strained, and suggested an important alternate hypothesis: that the principle underlying the right of an individual to protect his private writings and other productions—his right "to be let alone"—is a quite different principle, the right of an individual to protect his inviolate personality. Thus Warren and Brandeis proposed a *new* legal principle, that of the citizen's right to privacy.

The concept of privacy is implicit in the Bill of Rights and in the Fourteenth Amendment, though never referred to by name.[27] The First Amendment affirms the individual citizen's right to freedom of religion, freedom of speech, freedom of the press, and the right to assemble peaceably, thus protecting citizens' private thoughts and actions. The Third and Fourth Amendments protect a person from the unlawful occupation of his home, and search and seizure of his personal papers and effects; thus, the privacy of the individual's living space and personal property is legally recognized. The Fifth and Fourteenth Amendments to the Constitution declare that a citizen may not be deprived of "life, liberty, or property, without due process of law," thus protecting the individual from unwarranted governmental intrusion on his person or private property. The Fifth Amendment also stipulates that an individual cannot be compelled to testify against himself—to reveal private information which might incriminate him. Finally, the Ninth Amendment is a catch-all, stipulating to the people that if any of their personal rights have been omitted from the Constitution, that these rights shall not be considered to have been denied or disparaged. The Ninth Amendment implies the possibility of the existence of a body of fundamental, inalienable rights—such as, perhaps, privacy—not explicitly enumerated in the Constitution.

Thus, if a unifying concept in the Bill of Rights and the Fourteenth Amendment exists, it might be argued that it is precisely the recognition of the sanctity of the thoughts, actions, personal property, and homes of individual citizens—the assertion that citizens enjoy the fundamental right to privacy in these areas. Since the protection of privacy is implicit in several constitutional goals, it has been argued that privacy should be a newly declared constitutional right, cutting across other constitutional rights. This argument is detailed in what has become the Supreme Court's "primary analytical model of privacy,"[28] the plurality opinion of Justice William Douglas in *Griswold v. Connecticut*, in 1965.[29] The 7-2 *Griswold* ruling invalidated a Connecticut statute which prevented the dissemination of birth control information, on the grounds that the law invaded marital privacy. Justice Douglas's argument in its essence contended that since privacy is incident to several constitutional goals, it should be declared a goal in itself. As William Coyle has observed, the *Griswold* decision is an excellent example of the Supreme Court's responsiveness to current community mores.[30] In our highly technological society, protection of privacy has become a source of increasing concern to citizens, and the interpretation of the Constitution provided in *Griswold v. Connecticut* reflects these community concerns.

Since the early part of the twentieth century, court decisions in the United States have established a common law pattern which tends to support the extension of the right of individuals to personal privacy,[31] as outlined in the Warren and Brandeis paper and in *Griswold*. Such cases include the unauthorized use of a person's name or photograph for personal advantage, the wiretapping and bugging of private conversations, the intrusion into a delivery room by a non-physician, and the extensive surveillance in various forms maintained by General Motors over the personal life of Ralph Nader. Then in 1973, in *Roe v. Wade*,[32] the concept of privacy was recognized by the Supreme Court to include the right of an individual to decide on an abortion, thus voiding a Texas law that prohibited abortions except in the case of medical advice for the purpose of saving the mother's life.

Even though a number of court decisions have supported the legal concept of privacy, the lack of an operational, unambiguous definition of privacy has caused the courts to be relatively cautious to apply the concept.[33] Arthur Miller has enumerated other weaknesses of the common law approach to privacy.[34] First, because of the paucity of relevant decisions, the common law approach is relatively insensitive to the varied ways in which privacy may be violated, in the sense that at present only a few "pigeon holes" exist into which violations can be classified. Second, the necessity for the injured party to go to court to seek redress for a violation, in addition to being costly and emotionally upsetting, may in many cases, because of the ensuing publicity, aggravate the injury. This is particularly true in the privacy context. A final weakness of the common law approach is especially apparent when applied to violations resulting from the misuse of the new methods of information handling—particularly the electronic computer and the communications technologies. Under the existing structure, a citizen may never learn that his privacy has been violated; there is no provision in common law to assure the *participation* of the citizen in decisions relating to the dissemination and accuracy of data pertaining to his own life.

The unobtrusive danger of privacy violation that results from the unauthorized distribution of personal information, whether accurate or inaccurate, obviously is present in manual as well as automated personal data systems; however, the danger is greatly increased by the use of modern data processing technologies. This claim will be documented in a later section of the chapter. The deficiencies of the common law approach have led a number of observers to suggest that common law is insufficient to protect personal privacy and that protective legislation should be enacted for this purpose. Present and contemplated federal and state legislation, of which the Privacy Act of 1974 is the most conspicuous example, reflects these concerns. We turn now to an examination of the several issues motivating the passage of this act.

THE ISSUES

The Watergate and related affairs had a significant role to play in focusing full public awareness on flagrant governmental violations of individual privacy. More than a decade prior to Watergate, however, concerned citizens increasingly began to worry about the privacy problem, concern being stimulated by the development of new and powerful privacy-invading technologies. Of these technologies, the ones most familiar to the general public are the capability of transmitting audio signals by bugging, the recording of conversations by means of directional microphones, and telephone tapping. In addition to new methods of audio snooping, the development in the photographic technologies of miniaturization, and the use of infra-red film and the telephoto lens made it possible to record our actions as well as our words. The specter of an Orwellian society began to concern an increasing number of citizens, and their concern was reflected in the Congress, which began to conduct hearings and studies on the subject of privacy invasion.

Two of the earliest sets of hearings were conducted in 1965 and in the years following, by Senate and House subcommittees chaired by Edward Long of Missouri and by Cornelius Gallagher of New Jersey, respectively.[35] Originally concerned with the general subject of the invasion of personal privacy by government in all of its many manifestations, the two subcommittees reacted vigorously to a proposal that the Bureau of Budget establish a centralized National Data Service Center. Congressman Gallagher summarized the concerns of his subcommittee in his opening remarks to his colleagues:

> What we are looking for is a sense of balance. We do not want to deprive ourselves of the rewards of science; we simply want to make sure that human dignity and civil liberties remain intact. We would like to know just what information would be stored in a national data center; who would have access to it; who would control the computers; and, most importantly, how confidentiality and individual privacy would be protected. Thought should be given to these questions now, before we awaken some morning in the future and find that the dossier bank is an established fact, and that liberty as we knew it vanished overnight.[36]

The primary purpose of the proposed Data Center was to facilitate the coordination and use of statistical data by social scientists and other researchers and users in the areas of poverty, health, economics, urban renewal, education, voting habits, and other topics about which data were gathered by the Census Bureau, the Internal Revenue Service, and other government agencies. In a report submitted as justification for the proposed Center, Bureau of Budget consultant Edgar S. Dunn, Jr. identified the greatest deficiency of the existing federal statistical system as "its failure to provide access to data in a way that permits the association of the elements of data sets in order to identify and measure the interrelationship among interdependent or related observations."[37] Dunn's report proposed the use of general purpose statistical records to solve the incompatibility of records problems, and to permit the association of records and data elements maintained by several agencies for a variety of purposes. In essence, Dunn's complaint centered on the failure of the existing federal data system to permit the *linking* of data records on a single individual from a variety of agencies. The proposed system would remedy this deficiency, essentially by standardizing the format in which data would be recorded.

The overall reaction of members of the Senate and House subcommittees to the Bureau of Budget proposal was quite negative. Persistent questioning of government and other witnesses clearly established that little thought had been given by systems planners and government administrators to the potential problems posed by the issues of data confidentiality and violations of personal privacy. Recently enacted, as well as proposed, privacy legislation owes a considerable debt to the Gallagher and Long hearings, which brought most of the issues and problems with which we are concerned to the public attention for the first time. The proposal for a National Data Center served as a catalyst; it set into motion a decade of continuous debate and study concerning the effect on personal privacy of automated personal data systems, these studies being conducted by the Congress, by national foundations, by state and local governments, by private industry, and by individual citizens. A number of issues have been defined as characterizing the problem.

First, a major fear of observers has been that computers would be used by government to pull together data on individuals from dozens of now separate files, creating a central dossier on each citizen. Such a dossier might contain comments made by our elementary teachers on our intellectual, psychological, and social development, our complete credit history, a list of all the courses we took in college and the books we checked out of the library there, our military service record, our complete employment history, our financial status over the years, our medical history since birth, and a detailed record of any brushes we may have had with the law over the years. Of course, most of these files, and many others, exist today, albeit in separate and individual locations and maintained by different agencies. It is the centralization of these files into a single dossier data bank which has caused consternation among many observers. Representative Frank Horton, a member of the Gallagher Committee, has described his fears as follows:

> . . . one of the most practical of our present safeguards of privacy is the fragmented nature of present information. It is scattered in little bits and pieces across the geography and years of our life. Retrieval is impractical and often impossible. A central data bank removes completely this safeguard.[38]

Most of the present data maintained in record form about individuals were gathered by an agency *for a specific purpose*. Thus, while it may be entirely correct and necessary for a hospital to have access to a patient's medical record, in general, it is clearly not appropriate for one's employer, banker, teacher, or president to have access to that record. Moreover, data subjects are seldom notified that their file, maintained by agency A, for a specific purpose, is being sent to agencies X, Y, or Z, usually for an altogether different purpose. The issue is primarily one of data confidentiality, having to do with whether or not the data subject has knowledge of and has given consent to the agency's intention to share personal data with other agencies. Disclosure of a person's file to other agencies without his knowledge and consent has been said to constitute a violation of a "moral contract" between agency and individual.[39] In response to President Nixon's executive order which permitted inspection of more than three million farmers' tax returns for statistical purposes (the first time in our history an entire class of citizens was singled out for such disclosure[40]), Arkansas Representative Bill Alexander commented,

> ... informed consent ... is the difference between a democratic form of government and a totalitarian one. It is the difference between servants and masters. And, this is something they have apparently forgotten downtown. The people are the masters and the Government is their servant—not the other way around.[41]

The danger of confidential personal data being obtained by unauthorized persons is obviously greatly increased in a centralized dossier file, unless specific security precautions are taken. The issue of data confidentiality also arises in the increasing use of the communications and computer technologies in the creation and maintenance of personal data systems. The problem of guaranteeing data security in computer systems, as well as the issue of centralized data banks, will be discussed in somewhat more detail later in the chapter.

A related issue arises from the increasing use by agencies and institutions of the Social Security Number (SSN) as a universal personal identifier. Though not specifically prohibited by law, the SSN was never intended by the Congress to be used in this way. In fact, the concept of a universal personal identifier for every citizen (a national Birth Certificate Number) was formally proposed in 1948 by the National Office of Vital Statistics, but because of strong public opposition to the idea, was eventually dropped.[42] Thus, the growing use, both in the private and public sectors, of the SSN as a universal personal identifier is a de facto version of an earlier plan overwhelmingly rejected by the people.

From an administrative viewpoint, there are a number of advantages of the use of a common numbering system. The efficient linking of records from various agencies and institutions is obviously made possible, especially when the records are in machine-readable form and the linking can be accomplished rapidly by computer. In addition, file merging and updating is facilitated, and the incidence of file error is probably reduced. The concept of a universal personal identifier is, however, abhorrent to many Americans, who deplore what they view as the dehumanizing implications of its use and fear the threat posed to personal privacy. Another aspect of the universal personal identifier lies in its permanence—by definition, it follows each of us from birth to death. This is clearly contrary to a rich American tradition permitting and even encouraging citizens to make new lives for themselves. Vance Packard comments:

> America's frontiers were largely settled by people seeking to make a fresh start. They were often seeking to get away from something unpleasant in their past, either painful episodes, misdemeanors, poverty, or oppression. Today with episodes of our past increasingly being recorded in central files and computers the possibility of the fresh start is becoming increasingly difficult. The Christian notion of the possibility of redemption is incomprehensible to the computer.[43]

In addition to the increased utilization of the Social Security Number as a universal personal identifier, other aspects of modern personal data record systems also appear to the general public as dehumanizing, especially practices suggested by or arising from the use of modern computer and communications technologies for the maintenance of such systems. Each of us is all too familiar with information practices which seemingly arise more from considerations of cost/benefit ratios, efficiency, expediency, or convenience than from human considerations. Practices which strike many individuals as depersonalizing include the computerization of billing procedures, the production and sale of mailing lists, and the reduction of one's identity to a number or a series of holes in a cardboard card. Human considerations today seem to be increasingly overruled in favor of the concept of utility. It is perhaps precisely because of this fact that many citizens fear and mistrust the computer as the ultimate symbol of efficiency in our civilization.

Another significant concern arises from a tendency of agencies to gather more, and seemingly increasingly irrelevant, yet personal, data on individuals. A few examples of this practice in federal personal data banks will perhaps serve to illustrate this point.

Item. Air traffic controllers employed by the Federal Aviation Agency have been required to complete psychological tests composed of questions such as the following:

- I think the spread of birth control is essential to solving the world's economic and peace problems. (a) yes, (b) uncertain, (c) no.

- I would like to see a move toward (a) eating more vegetable foods to avoid killing so many animals, (b) uncertain, (c) getting better poisons to kill the animals which ruin farmer's crops (such as squirrels, rabbits, and some kinds of birds).

- I admire the beauty of a fairy tale more than that of a well-made gun (a) yes, (b) uncertain, (c) no.[44]

Item. In a form distributed by the Census Bureau for the Department of Health, Education and Welfare, some elderly, disabled, and retired people "were pressured" to answer a 15-page form which included in part the following questions:

- Do you have any artificial dentures?

- What is the total number of gifts that you give to individuals per year?

- What were you doing most of last week?[45]

Item. Applicants for positions in several federal agencies have been required to complete psychological tests containing such intensely personal questions as:

- My sex life is satisfactory.

- I have no difficulty in starting or holding my bowel movements.

- I like poetry.

- I loved my Mother.

- I am considered a liberal "dreamer" of new ways rather than a practical follower of well-tried ways. (a) true, (b) uncertain, (c) false.[46]

A final crucial issue concerns the relative *powerlessness* of citizens with regard to their own dossiers. Even though obsolete data, exaggeration, irrelevancies, and outright errors may exist in personal files, very frequently data subjects are not even notified that a file about them is being maintained, and if notified, are not permitted to review their file or to make corrections in it. This powerlessness is magnified in automated systems. For example, many readers have probably experienced the frustration of attempting to correct a billing error in an accounting system maintained by computer. Even in 1971, a survey conducted by *Time* magazine and the American Federation of Information Procession Societies revealed that 34 percent of the persons interviewed had experienced a problem "because of a computer."[47] A significant study conducted for the Department of Health, Education and Welfare summarized the issue as follows:

> . . . the net effect of computerization is that it is becoming much easier for record-keeping systems to affect people than for people to affect record-keeping systems.[48]

In a massive study of personal data banks maintained by the federal government, conducted over a four-year period and released late in 1974, Senator Sam Ervin's Subcommittee on Constitutional Rights found that in more than 42 percent of the government data banks which were reported by the agencies as maintaining such files, subjects of dossiers were not notified that information concerning them was being gathered and filed, and approximately one-third of data bank subjects are not permitted to examine their dossiers. The confidentiality of data files was also found to be a serious problem by the Ervin subcommittee, with more than 60 percent of the data bases analyzed being accessible, to a greater or lesser extent, to other agencies. More than 25 percent of the reporting agencies with data bases provide direct access to such information, either by routine distribution or by communication link with a computer. Singled out as particularly troublesome cases in this respect were the Internal Revenue Service and the Selective Service System. Despite the fact that both agencies issue a pledge of confidentiality to data subjects, who incidentally are required by law to provide personal data, established procedures permit the dissemination of this information to other agencies.[49]

Before we proceed to discuss the concept of data security in somewhat more detail, a final mention should be made of the role of the computer in respect to violations to personal privacy. There has been a pronounced tendency for some commentators to identify the computer as the principal villain in the piece, as the *cause* of information practices which represent invasions of privacy, such as the gathering of more personal data, the sharing of confidential data, etc. Aside from the obvious observation that computers do precisely what they are programmed to do by man, this conjecture has not received total support from factual evidence. In particular, the results of a careful study, directed by Alan Westin and supported by the National Academy of Sciences,[50] tended to allay to some extent fears of what actually was and was not occurring in operational computerized personal data systems. Investigators conducted on-site visits to 55 private and governmental organizations which utilized sophisticated computer/communications systems, spending in most cases one to three full days at each site. In addition, more than 1,500 questionnaires, distributed to and returned by managers of agencies in a number of different fields, both public and private, were analyzed. Published in 1972, the final report contains profiles of 14 advanced systems and reaches a few somewhat unexpected conclusions.

First, centralized computer systems, such as that proposed for the National Data Center in the mid-1960s and widely assumed by various writers to have proliferated since that time, were found to be essentially nonexistent, principally because the organizations that planned such systems tended to grossly underestimate the problems and costs involved in creating them. And, contrary to much speculation (for example, by Westin himself[51]), computerization was found not to have increased the content of personal data collection and recording, although this on-site impression was to some extent contradicted by the survey results.[52] No evidence was found of alterations in pre-computer practices with respect to the sharing of confidential data with other organizations; to the contrary, "customary practices have been reproduced with almost mirrorlike fidelity."[53] The overall findings of the study group demonstrated that computerization tended to reproduce both the practices and policies of pre-computer systems.

Generally speaking, then, the broad issues with which we are concerned characterize all personal data systems, manual as well as automated. On the other hand, there is no question that the problem of data security posed by the use of the computer and communications technologies is a difficult one, and that, theoretically at least, the centralization of personal data records implies a very real threat to privacy. Thus, the electronic computer should be considered as a device which intensifies various aspects of the problem but which cannot in any sense properly be held responsible for them.

DATA SECURITY IN PERSONAL INFORMATION SYSTEMS

> The latest and potentially the greatest threat to privacy is the recording, storing, and dissemination of personal information by computers.
>
> The International Commission of Jurists[54]

This introduction to the difficult and complex problem of providing data security in personal information systems will begin by making a distinction between the concepts of privacy, confidentiality, and security, as these terms are used in the literature and in the present chapter. In the earlier treatment of the topic in this essay, the concept of privacy was viewed as a philosophical, social, and legal concept referring to individual persons. Privacy essentially refers to the desirable or actual degree of interaction between a person and the larger society of which he is a part. With respect to private and personal information, privacy is germane to an individual's willingness to share data concerning himself with others. Confidentiality and security, on the other hand, are administrative and technical concepts which apply to data and data systems. Confidentiality refers to the extent to which particular data are or should be made accessible to others, while security has reference to those specific technical means by which the desired degree of confidentiality is to be ensured. These means may involve physical devices such as locks and guards, intellectual devices built into computer software and intended to frustrate unauthorized access, and other devices.

Developments during the past two decades in the computer and communications technologies have radically improved the speed by which information can be retrieved and the ease with which networks of data banks and users can be established and maintained. The development of computer networks is encouraged primarily by two innovations, the concept of *time-sharing* and the possibility of interacting with the computer in an "on-line" mode. A user is on-line in a computer system if he is communicating with the computer by means of a terminal, connected to the central computer through a direct communications hook-up, that is, by means of satellite, cable, microwave, or even ordinary telephone lines. Users interact with the computer by entering instructions on a typewriter-like keyboard and receiving responses printed on paper or on a cathode ray tube screen. In this way, users may obtain and process data virtually instantaneously on terminals located in their homes or offices, perhaps thousands of miles from the physical location of the computer and data bank. And because portable terminals are now commonplace, it is not even necessary for the user and his terminal to occupy a fixed physical location. The concept of time-sharing refers to the simultaneous use of a central computer by many users. In an on-line, time-shared network comprised of a central computer, one or more data banks, dozens or even hundreds of terminals and users, the rapid speed of the computer can provide each user with the illusion that he alone is in contact with the machine.

The operation of an on-line, time-shared information network poses special problems in data security which are not present in manual systems or even in dedicated batch-processing computer systems. The use of communications terminals means that a potential penetrator need not be physically present at the data bank to obtain confidential information, and therefore that each terminal in the system must be provided with security protection devices. Indeed, if access is normally gained by dialing a telephone number, a terminal from outside the system could be used to gain entry to the system. Moreover, if communication takes place over ordinary telephone lines, those lines can be tapped. Penetration of an on-line, time-shared data system has been characterized as an act which involves relatively little physical risk, small probability of detection, anonymity, and, if the penetration has been successful, little evidence that the act has even taken place.[55]

Space does not permit more than a very brief reference to some types of data security devices. For detailed treatment of aspects of the topic, the reader is referred to works listed in two comprehensive bibliographies on the subject prepared by the Rand Corporation.[56] The first and most obvious type of protective device is physical in nature, that is, locks, doors, shields on communications cables, and security guards. Physical devices protect the hardware itself from intrusion; they are effective mainly against unauthorized persons who might attempt to obtain access to computer systems or data files. However, according to a National Bureau of Standards report,[57] these "intruders" present the *least* threat to the compromise of confidential data. The NBS report described three classes of persons who possess authorization to access the system under certain specified circumstances, but for whom access to particular data or programs is not authorized. Systems must obviously be secured against access by these classes of persons as well as by intruders. The classes identified in the report include: "consumers"—the users of the system, "producers"—the analysts and programmers who design and implement specific subsystems, and "servicers"—the systems programmers, computer operators, and data entry personnel who maintain these systems. According to the report, these classes of individuals present the greatest threats to data confidentiality, in the order in which they are listed above. In particular, the report states that those who service the system constitute the maximum threat, enjoying generally unrestricted access to any program or data in the system.

To offer a degree of protection against improper use of data by the consumers, producers, and servicers of a personal data system, various protective devices other than physical are available, such as special identification systems, the use of passwords, encryption (scrambling or coding) of data, and administrative controls placed over the use of the system. The design of adequate computer security systems has become a major topic of research in computer science, and the magnitude of the problem was very clearly brought out by a report that IBM recently committed 40 million dollars to a five-year major research effort related to data security.[58]

To point out in a dramatic way the inadequacies of present data security systems, perhaps we should briefly discuss the somewhat peripheral area of computerized crime. In a practical sense, the state-of-the-art of present computer security systems can be measured by its success in thwarting computer criminals. According to this yardstick, much needs to be done; "compucrime" is on the increase, and, like rape, the number of reported cases is believed to constitute only a small fraction of the actual number of violations.[59] The Stanford Research Institute has published a revealing report, entitled *Computer Abuse*,[60] which summarizes the results of a careful study of the misuse of the computer as a consequence of malicious intent. The appendix to the report contains 148 case summaries, including instances of embezzlement, fraud, sabotage, and theft of programs and data. Some of the most successful and bizarre of these include the cases of a chief accountant who embezzled $1,000,000 from his company, a data center employee who embezzled $2,750,000 from the Youth Corps, the three night-shift computer operators who stole three million customer addresses, and an alleged two billion (sic) dollar fraud perpetrated by an insurance company. In their summary of findings, the study team commented that most known cases of computer abuse were discovered accidentally, and hypothesized that computer abuse can in future years be expected to increase rapidly to significant proportions. As to the source of computer abuse, the report singles out computer professionals as the major threat. Authors of the report make the following comments with respect to security protection devices:

> Technological methods to control computer abuse are necessary but not sufficient. Legal and social remedies must also be considered.[61]

As these comments suggest, even the most perfectly designed security system will be to some extent vulnerable to its designers. Safeguards beyond technological improvements in security design are clearly required. These are basically of two types. First, legal sanctions are needed, to specify unfair and illegal information practices, to specify procedures by which victims of such practices may bring suit to recover damages, and to define acts punishable by criminal penalties. In this way, a set of psychological deterrents to the misuse of personal data can be established.

Several provisions of the Privacy Act of 1974, to be discussed in detail in the next section of the chapter, make explicit such a set of definitions. The second way in which the threat to personal privacy offered by systems programmers and others in the computer-related professions can be reduced originates from the improvement of ethics, standards, and attitudes within the members of these professions themselves. Commenting with respect to this situation, one observer stated in 1972:

> [There is] growing dissatisfaction with the failure of the computer world to keep its own house in order. There has been virtually no exemplary pursuit of excellence, neither in professional standards nor in services for computer users.[62]

At least two study groups have recommended that data-processing personnel need to develop standards of professional conduct and ethical behavior.[63] In all fairness, it should be observed that the computer professions are relatively very young. Programming is more of an art than a science, and most programmers learn their craft by informal rather than formal means. A set of meaningful professional ethics cannot be expected to be developed and adhered to overnight. Even so, some computer-related professional organizations, somewhat belatedly and probably to a considerable extent in reaction to growing public dissatisfaction, have either adopted or considered the adoption of a code of ethics governing behavior or a bill of rights regarding the proper use of personal data. Obviously a considerable gap exists between the formal adoption of such a code by a professional group and the inculcation of its principles into the consciences of its members. Nevertheless, all efforts in this direction should be applauded as being positive approaches, if not total solutions, to the problem of protecting data confidentiality.

THE PRIVACY ACT OF 1974

Many of the specific provisions of the Privacy Act of 1974 can be traced to a study conducted by former Health, Education and Welfare Secretary Elliot Richardson's "Secretary's Advisory Committee on Automated Personal Data Systems." The committee was established in reaction to the growing public concern regarding the infringement of personal rights and liberties—in particular, the right to privacy—resulting from the use and misuse of automated personal data systems. The membership of the committee was broadly based, composed of 27 representatives from state and federal governments, private industry, the legal profession, organized labor, the university and research communities, and three private citizens. Beginning their work in 1972, the Secretary's Advisory Committee reviewed written materials and heard testimony from more than 100 witnesses who represented some 50 organizations. The work of the committee is noteworthy because of the strong influence of its report on later federal legislation.

A major recommendation of the study, entitled "Records, Computers, and the Rights of Citizens,"[64] is the enactment of a federal "Code of Fair Information Practice" for all automated personal data systems. According to the report, the five basic principles on which such a code should rest are:

- there must be no personal data record-keeping systems whose very existence is secret

- there must be a way for an individual to find out what information about him is in a record and how it is used

- there must be a way for an individual to prevent information about him that was obtained for one purpose from being used or made available for other purposes without his consent

- there must be a way for an individual to correct or amend a record of identifiable information about him

- any organization creating, maintaining, using, or disseminating records of identifiable personal data must assure the reliability of the data for their intended use and must take precautions to prevent misuse of the data.[65]

Based on these principles, the report specified a set of minimum standards that defined fair information practice, both with respect to personal data systems and with respect to statistical data systems. Violations of any of these proposed "safeguard requirements" would be prohibited by law, and subject to both civil and criminal penalties.

The proposed safeguard requirements are essentially rather specific elaborations of the five principles enumerated above. For example, the fourth principle states that a data subject must have the capability of correcting or amending data records which concern him. The safeguard requirements which reflect this principle specify that:

> any organization maintaining an administrative automated personal data system shall maintain procedures that (i) allow an individual who is the subject of data in the system to contest their accuracy, completeness, pertinence, and the necessity for retaining them; (ii) permit data to be corrected or amended when the individual to whom they pertain so requests; and (iii) assure, when there is disagreement with the individual about whether a correction or amendment should be made, that the individual's claim is noted and included in any subsequent disclosure or dissemination of the disputed data.

In addition, such organizations should give public notice of

> the procedures whereby an individual can (i) be informed if he is the subject of data in the system; (ii) gain access to such data; and (iii) contest their accuracy, completeness, pertinence, and the necessity for retaining them.[66]

The committee also took a strong position against the increasing use of the Social Security Number as a universal personal identifier, and recommended that the utilization of these numbers by agencies be limited to those "sparing" uses specifically provided by congressional legislative mandate. Moreover, the committee recommended that persons should not be coerced into providing their Social Security Numbers for any other than such uses. Finally, the committee recommended that violations of safeguard requirements be subject to criminal as well as civil penalties; that provision be made for injunctions to prevent violations; and that individuals be given the right to bring suit to recover damages and costs of litigation for unfair information practices.

Public Law 93-579, known as the "Privacy Act of 1974," is the most conspicuous result of a decade of national debate on privacy and automated data systems. Signed into law by President Ford on December 31, 1974, the act formalizes many of the proposals outlined in *Records, Computers, and the Rights of Citizens* and earlier studies. The passage of the Privacy Act of 1974 demonstrated a remarkable degree of bipartisanship among members of the Congress. Considered as a whole, the sponsors of the act represented a wide range of political ideologies; a House version of the bill was cosponsored by Representatives Goldwater and Koch, while the original Senate version was authored by Senators Ervin, Percy, Muskie, Ribicoff, Jackson, Goldwater, and Baker. The bill was passed in both houses of Congress by overwhelming majorities, and it became law 270 days after the date of its passage, or roughly at the end of September 1975.

Senator Ervin, speaking for the Committee on Government Operations, eloquently stated the purpose of the Senate version of the bill:

> [Its purpose is to] promote government respect for the privacy of citizens by requiring all departments and agencies of the executive branch and their employees to observe certain constitutional rules in the computerizing, collection, management, use and disclosure of personal information about individuals.

> It is to promote accountability, responsibility, legislative oversight, and open government with respect to the use of computer technology in the personal information systems and data banks of the Federal government and with respect to all of its other manual or mechanized files.

> It is designed to prevent the kind of illegal, unwise, overbroad, investigation and record surveillance or (sic) law-abiding citizens which has resulted in recent years from actions of some over-zealous investigators, from the curiosity of some government administrators, and from the wrongful disclosure and use of personal files held by Federal agencies.

> It is to prevent the secret gathering of information or the creation of secret information systems or data banks on Americans by employees of the departments and agencies of the Executive branch.

> It is designed to set in motion a long-overdue evaluation of the needs of the Federal government to acquire and retain personal information on Americans, by requiring stricter review within agencies on criteria for collection and retention of such information.

It is also to promote observance of valued principles of fairness and individual privacy by those who develop, operate, and administer other major institutional and organizational data banks of government and society.[67]

Some of the major provisions of the Privacy Act of 1974 will be discussed here. First, the act specifies that any individual on whom a personal data record is maintained by a federal agency must promptly be permitted by that agency to review his record and to correct or amend inaccurate, irrelevant, obsolete, or incomplete data. In addition, each agency is required to maintain in its records only data relevant to purposes mandated by legislative statute or by presidential order. In consequence, if a citizen wishes to inspect the record maintained on him in, say, the Internal Revenue Service's Master File, the White House Talent Bank, the Selective Service System's Registrant Information Bank, or one of the 57 personal data banks maintained by the Veterans Administration, he now possesses the legal right to do so. Furthermore, if he believes certain data to be incorrect, obsolete, or not relevant to the agency's purpose, he may request that his record be amended. The agency must then amend the record, as requested, or state its reasons for the refusal.

The Privacy Act of 1974 further requires that federal agencies announce publicly in the *Federal Register*, at least annually, a complete description of personal data bank systems they maintain, including the categories of individuals on whom records are kept, the uses to which the records are put, and policies and procedures by which persons can gain access to their personal records and challenge their contents. The Office of the Federal Register has compiled a set of extracts from all agency descriptions of personal record systems published in the *Federal Register* prior to October 10, 1975, including descriptions of agency rules for processing requests for information.[69] Another useful publication for citizens interested in exercising their right to examine and challenge agency records is a brochure describing these rights in easy-to-read language, published by the American Civil Liberties Union.[70]

In another section of the Privacy Act of 1974, federal agencies are required to establish appropriate security measures to protect the confidentiality of personal data records. The act also explicitly states that identifiable personal data shall not be used for a purpose other than that for which the data were collected, or disclosed to other agencies, without written consent of the data subject. The force of this section is somewhat blunted by the fact that it admits no fewer than eleven exemptions. Even so, the spirit of the provision rightly appears to regard the use of personal data for purposes other than that for which they were gathered as an *unusual* circumstance, and one which must be justified, in writing, by the agency requesting such use.

Thus, all five of the principles outlined in *Records, Computers, and the Rights of Citizens* are represented in the Privacy Act of 1974. In addition, the act was given teeth by the Congress, which specified civil remedies by means of which the subject of an unfair information practice as a result of intentional or willful agency action may bring suit to recover damages. Moreover, such violations of the act by agency employees were made punishable by criminal penalties.

Federal agencies exempted by the Privacy Act of 1974 include the CIA, the Secret Service, and all agencies whose primary function is with law enforcement.

Other exemptions are for purely statistical systems, whose purpose is to determine suitability of persons for federal employment or promotion, and for National Archives historical records. In a strong reaction to the prevalent practice of law enforcement agencies gathering data on individuals merely because they are exercising their First Amendment right to freedom of expression, as seen in recent years with many Viet Nam War protesters, the Privacy Act of 1974 prohibits this practice ". . . unless expressly authorized by statute or by the individual about whom the record is maintained. . . . " The language of this provision unfortunately also contains what may become a popular loophole: ". . . or unless pertinent to and within the scope of an authorized law enforcement activity."[71]

The invasion of privacy resulting from having one's name and address sold or rented was also addressed by the Act, which prohibited this practice by federal agencies. Also prohibited was the denial by any federal, state, or local agency to any person of any rights or privileges due to him by law as a result of his refusal to disclose his Social Security Number. Thus, citizens can no longer be required to provide their SSN merely because it makes a convenient identifier. However, this section of the law applies only to the establishment of *new* information collection systems; agencies maintaining a system prior to January 1, 1975, are exempted if disclosure of the SSN for purposes of identification was required by specific statute or regulation. Unfortunately, these restrictions on the use of the SSN as a personal identifier were in part nullified by an amendment to the Tax Reform Act of 1976, signed into law by President Ford in October 1976. This amendment expands the use of the SSN by state and local governments for several specific purposes.

A final provision of the Privacy Act of 1974 established a Privacy Protection Study Commission. Its purpose is to study automated personal data systems maintained by agencies (in both the private and public sectors), and to formulate recommendations to the President and to the Congress with respect to the application of the principles and procedures of the Privacy Act of 1974 to these organizations, either by administrative action, federal legislation, or voluntary adoption. Specifically cited as desirable areas for study were interstate transfer of information, the use of Social Security Numbers and other universal identifiers in personal data banks, and the misuse of statistical information systems. A total of $1,500,000 was appropriated by the Congress to carry out the work of the Commission for fiscal year 1975, 1976, and 1977. Since its formation, the Privacy Protection Study Commission has held a series of public hearings, each on a particular kind of record-keeping system, including educational records, employment and personnel records, credit records, insurance records, and medical records. The Commission will produce its final report on June 10, 1977, after which date it will cease to exist. Two other federal agencies investigating public policy on privacy-related concerns are the Commission on Federal Paperwork and the Office of Telecommunications Policy.

A SPECULATIVE LOOK AT
FUTURE PRIVACY LEGISLATION

A clue as to what might be expected in future privacy legislation can be inferred from an examination of the compromises made between the Senate and the House resulting in the Privacy Act of 1974. The original version of Senate Bill 3418[72] called for the establishment of a Federal Privacy Board, the purpose of which was to see that the various other provisions of the bill were carried out. Taking a more conservative approach, at President Ford's insistence,[73] and also on the recommendation of the Domestic Council Committee on the Right to Privacy,[74] the House objected to the introduction of yet another layer of federal bureaucracy, and preferred the establishment of a privacy study commission. As part of the compromise between House and Senate, provisions for such a commission eventually became part of the Privacy Act of 1974. It should be observed, however, that the study commission will enjoy a life of only two years, and that there was and remains considerable sentiment for an independent privacy board. If federal agencies appear to be unable to enforce and implement the privacy safeguards enumerated in the Privacy Act of 1974, we may surely look for the establishment of an independent enforcement board to ensure that the provisions of the act are being carried out effectively.

Another Senate measure dropped from the final bill would have broadened the bill's provision concerning the denial of service to an individual because he refused to disclose his Social Security Number, this by applying the provision to the private sector as well as to federal, state, and local government. Much undoubtedly depends on the recommendations contained in the final report of the Privacy Protection Study Commission; however, it appears that privacy legislation of 1976 and the future will almost certainly address itself to personal data systems maintained by the private sector, not only in regard to the Social Security Number, but also with respect to many of the other provisions of the Privacy Act of 1974. Indeed, Representatives Goldwater and Koch introduced such a bill on January 23, 1975, rather appropriately numbered H.R. 1984. Space does not permit an examination of the numerous provisions of this proposed legislation, but in general, its effect is to extend the Privacy Act of 1974 to state and local governments and to the private sector. In addition, the bill calls for the establishment of a Federal Privacy Board, having the following functions: 1) to publish an annual Data Base Directory containing the names and characteristics of all personal data systems; 2) to make rules for the purpose of ensuring compliance with the law; 3) to conduct, or cause to be conducted, any research as may be necessary to ensure implementation of the Act; and 4) to assist organizations in complying with the various provisions of the Act. To ensure compliance with the law, the Board would moreover have the power to: 5) examine information systems and records pertaining to personal data systems; 6) order organizations violating provisions of the Act to halt violations, enforceable in civil action; 7) delegate its authority to the states, if satisfied that such delegation would provide adequate enforcement; and 8) conduct open hearings on petitions for exemptions from the provisions of the Act. In addition, the Board would be required to issue an annual report of its activities to the Congress and the President. A final provision of H.R. 1984 would grant data subjects the right to examine the *source* of personal information in the system.

Congressman Koch explains the motives for this provision as, "An individual should have the right . . . to know who his or her accuser is."[75]

Action on privacy legislation can certainly be expected at the state level as well as the national level in the near future. The swelling of public feeling on the issue is well illustrated by a two-day conference (held in Philadelphia on September 5, 1974) of the governors of the thirteen original states. One of the four resolutions considered by the governors called for the passage of a constitutional amendment "to include proper restraints on all public and private information-gathering agencies and on the dissemination of criminal justice information in order to further protect the individual citizen's privacy." After much heated debate, a diluted version of the resolution was adopted.[76] In another state action, California voters amended their constitution in November 1972 to include privacy as an inalienable right of all people,[77] and in December 1974, California Assembly Bill No. 150 was referred to the Committee on Judiciary. A.B. 150 contains a number of provisions based on the Code of Fair Information Practice and provides civil remedies and criminal penalties for the failure of organizations, in both the public and private sectors, to comply with these provisions. Sponsors hoped for Governor Brown's support, but he vetoed both A.B. 150 and a second bill. While the private sector in California does not support privacy legislation, the bill's sponsors are working closely with representatives of banking, credit, insurance, and other industries, and most active opposition is reported to have been eliminated.[78] California legislators undoubtedly learned a valuable lesson from the Ohio experience with privacy legislation. On January 3, 1974, Ohio State Senator Aronoff introduced an Ohio "Code of Fair Information Practices," modeled on the recommendations outlined in *Records, Computers and the Rights of Citizens*, and very similar to the Privacy Act of 1974.[79] Its provisions applied, however, to the private sector as well as to government data banks. The Ohio experience with privacy legislation demonstrates very clearly the extent to which the private sector opposes such legislation as well as the power that sector can wield. In the five open hearings held following the introduction of Senator Aronoff's bill, not a single witness spoke against it. In the floor debate itself, even though only one Ohio senator spoke in opposition to the bill, and only one senator asked a question, the bill was defeated, 21-10, on June 5, 1974.[80] The explanation was a "feverishly" determined lobbying effort led by the Ohio Council of Retail Merchants and the Ohio Manufacturers Association. Senator Aronoff outlined what he took as constituting the main fears of the private sector which were responsible for the defeat of his bill: the fear of "new, expensive, and untested procedures . . . of hurting credit operations . . . of limiting the use of the Social Security Number . . . of limiting 'in-house' access . . . of law enforcement officials . . . of hasty action . . . of new bureaucratic regulation." The crux of the objections probably center on the *cost* of implementing privacy legislation. This fear received some support in a recently published computer simulation study of the probable cost of privacy, in which five typical personal data systems were examined. The study concluded that the cost of privacy will amount to more than 10 percent of annual operating costs in law enforcement, personnel, and insurance systems, a jolting 45 percent in medical record systems, and a whopping 146 percent in credit systems. The differences for the five systems reflect the number and size of data records, the mode of access desired, the number of potential users of the data system, and the number of expected transactions.[81]

As a result of the intense lobbying effort mounted by business and industry, the new Ohio privacy legislation sponsored by Senator Aronoff and others,[82] introduced in February 1975, deals only with personal information systems maintained by the state and local government and excludes similar systems maintained by the private sector. The new version of the bill succeeded in passing the Ohio legislature. Though thwarted by lobbyists for the time being, government leaders in Ohio and elsewhere who are interested in applying the principles of the Privacy Act of 1974 to the private sector can be expected to renew their efforts in the future.

At least six states have passed versions of the Privacy Act of 1974, applying to state and local government, and legislation has been introduced in several other states. In all, there are more than 200 state statutes relating to some aspect of the confidentiality of various types of record-keeping systems.[83]

The problem of preserving privacy in personal data systems is not, of course, limited to the United States. For example, in an international conference on "Human Choice and Computers" held in 1974 and sponsored by the International Federation of Information Processing Societies, representatives of 35 information processing groups from around the world proposed the development of an international computer Bill of Rights. Such a code, law, or agreement would enumerate principles of fair information practice, and the rights of individual citizens with regard to computers, stressing, but not limited to, the use of the computer in maintaining personal data systems.[84] Legislation is being considered or has actually been enacted by the governments of several Western nations other than the United States. By the end of 1973, West Germany, Sweden, France, Great Britain, and Canada had either enacted privacy legislation or were actively studying the question.[85] We are very likely to witness increased international efforts, both by government and by the private sector, to deal with the privacy issue in the future.

CENTRALIZED NATIONAL DATA CENTERS: QUIS CUSTODIET IPSOS CUSTODES?

Public outcry which followed publicity concerning the proposed National Data Center effectively squelched government plans for such a center, at least for a time. But because of the increased efficiency of centralized systems, the plan periodically resurfaces. In a paper released as part of the Rand paper series,[86] the issue of centralization versus decentralization was given careful examination from a theoretical point of view. The authors argued that a properly designed centralized system would offer superior privacy protection because of its relatively high public visibility and the resulting high degree of public scrutiny directed toward it. This was to happen because individuals will be more likely to examine and challenge a single data record as opposed to a multitude of records, as under the Privacy Act of 1974; because in the event of a "sudden, unconstitutional change of government as a result of a *coup d'état* or the occupation of the country by a foreign power,"[87] the physical destruction of personal records would be facilitated in a centralized system; and finally, because data security measures can be implemented more efficiently and economically in a centralized system.

Despite the plausible ring of the authors' argument, a nagging doubt remains. Knowledge is power, and the potential power to be gained by access to full and complete personal dossiers belonging to any particular set of citizens staggers the imagination. The chronicle of Richard Nixon's fall from power, as well as that of some of his cronies, demonstrated quite clearly that many of the most highly placed public officials in the land—ironically, most of them lawyers—were not in the least reluctant to suspend their moral, ethical, and legal obligations to the citizens of this nation and to themselves. In some cases, this suspension was perhaps believed to be for the good of national security; in others, it was for the more mundane purpose of "screwing our enemies." Awe and possibly fear of power, especially fear of the power of the presidency, almost certainly was an important factor. It would be difficult in the extreme to protect vulnerable personal data against access by a highly placed data bank official asked to bend the rules for national security in the name of the president. If the Watergate affair can be used as a yardstick, such an official would be very likely to comply with unethical or even illegal requests.

In this regard, it has been noted that the weak link in any security system designed for the protection of personal privacy is the management of the system.[88] One can only speculate about what Mitchell, Haldeman, Dean, or Nixon would have attempted to do had a centralized data file of personal dossiers existed and been available in 1973, or how the managers of such a system would have reacted in the event of an illegal request. On the other hand, our knowledge of what was actually attempted and accomplished in the Watergate and related affairs is enough to give us considerable pause.

In his testimony at joint hearings before two Senate subcommittees, Alan Westin speculated about what might have happened if Watergate had taken place in 1980 or 1984, when many more government files had been automated, and when the spread in the use of the Social Security Number as a universal personal identifier would have made linkage of all of these files as well as many other files in the private sector—health, education, credit, banking, insurance, etc.—an elementary feat. By this time, the White House would have been fully staffed with computer systems experts and information specialists. Replacing the basement room of tape records might be a network of terminals linked to a computer in Camp David, providing data files on "enemies," "possible leakers," "disloyal radicals," "biased pressmen," and presumably many others.

> In such a Watergate 1984 setting, the plumbers of 1972 would have become the filers of 1984 and the dossiers on the Ellsbergs, Schorrs, Eagletons, O'Briens, Muskies, and Fondas would have been produced far more effectively than by such crude measures as wiretaps, breakins, and double agents. And where there were obstacles to be overcome, the Chairman of the Federal Privacy Board would be a latter-day Charles Colson ready to leak his grandmother's file to help reelect the President, and he would have unlocked the doors.[89]

If nothing else, Watergate's lesson for us is that illegal or unethical requests placed by men occupying the highest seats of power are not often refused, and that far less than a *coup d'état* or occupation by a foreign power is required for such a breakdown to occur. Indeed, the possibility of access by *anyone* to comprehensive personal data files is a chilling thought. As Congressman Gallagher stated, "We cannot be certain that such dossiers would always be used by benevolent people for benevolent purposes."[90] Moreover, it is not necessary to ascribe evil motives to system managers or politicians to question seriously the wisdom of establishing centralized personal data systems. As Justice Louis Brandeis observed in his famous dissenting opinion in *Olmstead v. U.S.* against the conduct of unauthorized wire tapping by government agencies, personal liberties are more threatened by ignorance than by evil intentions:

> Experience should teach us to be most on our guard to protect liberty
> when the government's purposes are beneficent. Men born to freedom
> are naturally alert to repel invasions of their liberty by evil-minded rulers.
> The greatest dangers to liberty lurk in insidious encroachment by men of
> zeal, well-meaning but without understanding.[91]

Certainly from a purely economic point of view, centralization and inter-connection of computer systems is a desirable course of action, and hence is a predictable occurrence unless other, disruptive forces are brought to bear. In this respect, a strong analogy can be established between the concept of an information utility and the established communication and transportation utilities of the telephone, telegraph, and railroad. For economic reasons, communications and transportation services historically tend to integrate into larger systems and networks. It is simply cheaper and more efficient for independent systems to share facilities and data, when this is appropriate, than it is to maintain independence. Thus, as with the older utilities, interconnection and centralization represent the way of the future. Commenting in 1965 with respect to the proposed National Data Center, Paul Baran warned of the inevitable evolution of such a system:

> Today we are building the bits and pieces of separate automated infor-
> mation systems in both the private and government sectors that so
> closely follow the pattern to the present integrated communications
> structure that a de facto version of the system you are now pondering is
> already into the construction phase. It is in many ways more dangerous
> than the single data bank now being considered. There is no culprit. No
> one set out to build our system. It's like little Topsy in Uncle Tom's
> Cabin who said, "Never was born. I 'spect I grow'd."[92]

Baran's observations are even more appropriate today than they were a decade ago. Giant information systems and networks have indeed evolved, and continue to proliferate and swell. In the federal government alone, the report of Senator Ervin's Subcommittee on Constitutional Rights documents the existence of 858 government data banks, containing an estimated one and one-quarter billion records on individuals. In his introduction to the Subcommittee's Report, Senator Ervin complained at length concerning the general attitude of Executive Branch agencies toward the release of information regarding data banks under their control. Because the senator's comments are highly significant, they are reprinted here at length:

> Some reports are evasive and misleading. Some agencies are high-minded
> and take the attitude that the information belongs to them and that the
> last person who should see it is the individual whom it is about . . . Find-
> ing out about these systems has been a difficult, time-consuming, and
> frustrating experience. The inherent aversion of the Executive Branch to

informing Congress and the people about what they are doing is not restricted to matters of high-policy, national security, or foreign policy. An attitude approaching disdain infects even requests for basic non-sensitive data such as this survey sought. The subcommittee met evasion, delay, inadequate and cavalier responses, and all too often a laziness born of a resentment that anyone should be inquiring about their activities. Some agencies displayed their arrogance by not replying at all. With others, extracting information was like pulling teeth.[93]

Evidently a gentleman even in the most adverse of circumstances, Senator Ervin concluded, "These remarks should not detract from our appreciation for the fine cooperation the subcommittee received from a great many agencies." Because of the attitude his subcommittee encountered, Senator Ervin added that perhaps the most important effect the survey may have is to bring a realization of the absolute necessity of replacing the *voluntary* approach necessarily followed by the subcommittee with a *statutory* requirement that all federal agencies maintaining data banks fully and accurately report on their contents.[94]

According to the Ervin subcommittee,[95] one of the most troubling aspects of their survey was the extent to which it revealed a lack of Congressional authorization for an astounding proportion of data banks. No fewer than 84 percent of the data banks analyzed failed to cite express statutory authority for their existence—that is, no specific congressional mandate for the establishment and maintenance of the data bank was provided. Though derivative or implied authority—authority deriving from or implied by programs which themselves derived from express statutory mandate—was cited by most data banks, fully 18 percent of reporting agencies cited no statutory authority whatever. The White House, for example, tersely commented that the question regarding statutory authority was "not applicable" to three of its files.

For a number of reasons, the 858 data banks summarized in the six-volume, several-thousand-page final report of the Ervin subcommittee cannot be regarded as more than a sample of data banks maintained by federal agencies.[96] For one thing, the Departments of Commerce, Defense, and Justice, as well as the Office of Management and Budget, curiously stated that such data as an individual's Social Security Number, salary, race, sex, history of drug addiction, and other similar data were not, in their view, "personal" information, and data bases containing this information were not reported. A number of relatively sensitive "intelligence" systems, as well as other more routine files, known by other means to the committee, were not reported. The State Department reported only two personal data banks that came within the scope of the survey. Some agencies simply refused to supply any information at all. In this regard, the Department of the Interior was identified by the report as being a particularly bad example; not a single personal data base was reported to exist in the Department. Even more disturbing to the subcommittee was the response of the General Services Administration, which made *no mention* of their developing plans for a vast new telecommunications network of data banks, called FEDNET.

Requests for bids for FEDNET were issued in February 1974 for up to nine data centers, several thousand remote terminals, and a GSA-funded telecommunications network.[97] In addition, the FEDNET system was to have the capability of indefinite expansion by the addition of other agencies to the system. Shockingly, the GSA did not intend to have FEDNET be subject to congressional authorization or review, and hence it would, as originally conceived, be closed to public scrutiny. Concern over FEDNET was publicly expressed by several senators and representatives. In addition, President Ford, as Vice President, stated before a national computer conference:

> I am concerned that Federal protection of individual privacy is not yet developed to the degree necessary to prevent FEDNET from being used to probe into the lives of individuals. Before building a nuclear reactor, we design the safeguards for its use. We also require environmental impact statements specifying the anticipated effect of the reactor's operation on the environment. Prior to approving a vast computer network affecting personal lives, we need a comparable privacy impact statement. We must also consider the fallout hazards of FEDNET to traditional freedoms.[98]

In reaction to these concerns by government leaders, plans for FEDNET have now been dropped, ostensibly. However, a new plan for linking computers and data banks belonging to federal agencies has been proposed by the General Services Administration. Called AIDS—Automated Integrated Digital Services—the new system would link such agencies as the Veterans Administration, the Internal Revenue Service, the Department of Agriculture, and many others. Because it regards AIDS as an "enhancement" of the existing system rather than a "new" system, the GSA has not seen fit to consult the Congress on these plans.[99] The name may have changed, but planning by the GSA on a FEDNET-like system continues.

CONCLUDING REMARKS

Privacy is clearly an idea whose time has come. Though not mentioned by name in the Constitution, we have seen that the concept of privacy is implicit in many of its amendments, and that it has become increasingly important in the common law. We have the mentality of the Nixon administration to thank for the overwhelming congressional support for the Privacy Act of 1974 and for the privacy legislation certain to come in the future, although similar legislation would probably have passed eventually without the revelations of the Nixon years. Several years prior to Watergate, thoughtful observers were aware of the losses of personal privacy posed by automated personal data systems, and the Congress has been moving toward privacy legislation in this area for more than a decade. Even so, one cannot help but suspect that perhaps the major motivating force today behind privacy legislation is a reaction to the Watergate mentality and to the events of Watergate. If true, this fact may have an unfortunate effect, should the Nixon years one day begin to dim and lose significance in the public eye. There is an obvious danger of losing interest in privacy as an issue if it is tied too closely with a series of events such as Watergate. On the other hand, Watergate provides a real-world example of the kinds of excesses that can result if the government gives too little consideration to the preservation of personal privacy. We should not, and cannot, forget Watergate as a symbol of these excesses.

From the earliest years of the computer to the present time, the general public has played an essentially passive role in the conception and design of computerized personal data systems. But the computer and communications technologies are tools of man, and in the final analysis should have a significant positive effect on the overall quality of life to justify their use. While the overwhelming beneficial effects of the computer are obvious in some of its applications, such as in the conduct of scientific research, they are not so clear in the case of its unrestricted use in the maintenance of automated personal data systems. The general public has had virtually no effect on the development of these systems. In consequence, mass information utilities have been designed, to a considerable extent, in the private sector by men guided by the profit motive and in the public sector by men motivated by their quest for the famous American ideal of efficiency. And, " . . . almost nowhere in sight is deliberate social planning of individual services for maximum benefits to every citizen over the long run."[100] Although the passage of the Privacy Act of 1974 represents a giant step forward, deliberate social planning is still desperately needed. For example, the vital question of whether the advantages of a centralized system such as FEDNET outweigh the possible detrimental consequences is moot, but it is a question which the people and the Congress must ultimately bring themselves to face in open debate and national soul-searching. If we do not, citizens are likely to have FEDNET or its equivalent presented one day as a *fait accompli*. It is the American people who are ultimately responsible for what a free and democratic government does in their name. As Harold Sackman has observed,

> When you peer into the face of the computer, do not be surprised to discover the reflection of yourself.[101]

FOOTNOTES

[1] An excellent source book on the legislative history of the Freedom of Information Act and its amendments is: U.S., Congress, House, Committee on Government Operations, and Senate, Committee on the Judiciary, *Freedom of Information Act and Amendments of 1974 (P.L. 93-502)*, Source Book: Legislative History, Texts, and Other Documents, 94th Cong., 1st sess., Joint Committee Print (Washington, D.C.: Government Printing Office, 1975).

[2] *Ibid.*, p. 10.

[3] Arthur R. Miller, *The Assault on Privacy: Computers, Data Banks, and Dossiers* (Ann Arbor: University of Michigan Press, 1971), p. 20.

[4] Elmer D. Johnson, *Communication: An Introduction to the History of Writing, Printing, Books and Libraries*, 4th ed. (Metuchen, N.J.: Scarecrow Press, 1973).

[5] U.S., Department of Labor, Bureau of Labor Statistics, *Computer Manpower Outlook*, Bulletin 1826 (Washington, D.C.: Government Printing Office, 1974).

[6] Harold Sackman, *Computers and Social Choice*, P-4915 (Santa Monica, Calif.: Rand Corporation, 1972), p. 2.

[7] Donn B. Parker, Susan Nycum, and S. Stephen Oüra, *Computer Abuse*, Microfiche no. PB-231 320 (Springfield, Va.: National Technical Information Service, 1973), p. 79.

[8] Enid Mumford and Harold Sackman, *International Human Choice and Computers: Conference Retrospect and Prospect*, P-5258 (Santa Monica, Calif.: Rand Corporation, 1974), p. 18.

[9] U.S., Department of Commerce, National Bureau of Standards, *Privacy and Security in Computer Systems: A Summary of a Conference Held at the National Bureau of Standards, Gaithersburg, Maryland, November 19-20, 1973*, NBS Technical Note 809 (Washington, D.C.: Government Printing Office, 1974), p. 10.

[10] Miller, *The Assault on Privacy*, pp. 22-23.

[11] P.L. 93-575, "The Privacy Act of 1974."

[12] Alan R. Westin, *Privacy and Freedom* (New York: Atheneum, 1967), p. 7.

[13] Oscar M. Ruebhausen and Orville G. Brim, Jr., "Privacy and Behavioral Research." In: U.S., Congress, Senate, Committee on the Judiciary, *Computer Privacy, Hearings*, before the Subcommittee on Administrative Practice and Procedure, on S. Res. 25, 90th Cong., 1st sess., March 14-15, 1967, p. 208.

[14] Charles Fried, "Privacy," *The Yale Law Journal* 77 (1968): 477.

[15] *Ibid.*, p. 482.

[16] The quotation is found in: Vern Countryman, "The Diminishing Right of Privacy: The Personal Dossier and the Computer," *Texas Law Review* 49 (1971): 868.

[17] Westin, *Privacy and Freedom*, pp. 8-63.

[18] Fried, "Privacy," pp. 475-93.

[19] *Ibid.*, p. 484.

[20] Westin, *Privacy and Freedom*, pp. 10-11.

[21] Arthur J. Sills, "Information Systems: The Privacy Issue." In: *Conference on Information Systems Coordination, Washington, D.C., June 1968, Proceedings* (Chicago: Council on State Governments, Committee on Information Systems, 1968), p. 58.

[22] George Orwell, *1984* (New York: Harcourt, Brace & World, 1949).

[23] J. J. Hellman, *Privacy and Information Systems: An Argument and an Implementation*, P-4298 (Santa Monica, Calif.: Rand Corporation, 1970), pp. 24-25.

[24] "Privacy in the First Amendment," *Yale Law Journal* 82 (1973): 1462-80; Sam J. Evin, Jr., "Privacy and Government Investigations," *University of Illinois Law Forum* 1971 (1971): 137-53; Samuel D. Warren and Louis D. Brandeis, "The Right to Privacy," *Harvard Law Review* 4 (1890): 193-200; Miller, *The Assault on Privacy*; Westin, *Privacy and Freedom*; and William E. Coyle, "The Ninth Amendment and the Right of Privacy: The Griswold Case" (unpublished Ph.D. dissertation, Florida State University, 1966).

[25] Miller, *The Assault on Privacy*, p. 70.

[26] Warren and Brandeis, "The Right to Privacy."

[27] "Privacy in the First Amendment."

[28] *Ibid.*, p. 1475.

[29] *Griswold v. Connecticut*, 381 U.S. 479 (1965).

[30] Coyle, "The Ninth Amendment."

[31] Miller, *The Assault on Privacy*, pp. 171-76.

[32] *Roe v. Wade*, 410 U.S. 113 (1973).

[33] "Privacy in the First Amendment," p. 1476.

[34] Miller, *The Assault on Privacy*, pp. 187-89.

[35] Senator Long was the chairman of the Subcommittee on Administrative Practices and Procedures of the Senate Committee on the Judiciary. Representative Gallagher chaired the Special Subcommittee on Invasion of Privacy of the House Committee on Government Operations.

[36] U.S., Congress, House, Committee on Government Operations, *The Computer and Invasion of Privacy, Hearings*, before a subcommittee of the Committee on Government Operations, 89th Cong., 2d sess., July 26-28, 1966, p. 3.

[37] *Ibid.*, p. 255.

[38] *Ibid.*, p. 6.

[39] *Ibid.*, "Statement of Charles A. Reich, Professor, Yale Law School," pp. 22-33.

[40] U.S., Congress, House, Committee on Government Operations, *Information from Farmers' Income Tax Returns and Invasion of Privacy*, H. Rept. 93-598, 93d Cong., 1st sess. (Washington, D.C.: Government Printing Office, 1973), p. 1.

[41] *Ibid.*, p. 24.

[42] Westin, *Privacy and Freedom*, p. 304.

[43] House Committee on Government Operations, *The Computer and Invasion of Privacy*, p. 12.

[44] U.S., Congress, House Committee on Government Operations, *Special Inquiry on Invasion of Privacy, Pt. 2, Hearing*, before a subcommittee of the Committee on Government Operations, 89th Cong., 2d sess., May 24, 1966, p. 16.

[45] U.S., Congress, Senate, *Protecting Individual Privacy in Federal Gathering, Use and Disclosure of Information*, S. Rept. 1183 to accompany S. 3418, 93d Cong., 2d sess. (Washington, D.C.: Government Printing Office, 1974), p. 12.

[46] *Ibid.*, p. 13.

[47] Parker, Nycum, and Oüra, *Computer Abuse*, p. 44.

[48] U.S., Department of Health, Education and Welfare, *Records, Computers, and the Rights of Citizens*, Report of the Secretary's Advisory Committee on Automated Personal Data Systems (Washington, D.C.: Government Printing Office, 1973), p. xx.

[49] U.S., Congress, Senate, Committee on the Judiciary, *Federal Data Banks and Constitutional Rights: A Study of Data Systems on Individuals Maintained by Agencies of the United States Government*, prepared by the Staff of the Subcommittee on Constitutional Rights, as Part III of the Subcommittee's Study of Federal Data Banks, Computers, and the Bill of Rights, Vol. 1 (Washington, D.C.: Government Printing Office, 1974), pp. xlii-xliv.

[50] Alan F. Westin and Michael A. Baker, *Databanks in a Free Society: Computers, Record-Keeping and Privacy*, Report of the Project on Computer Databanks of the Computer Science and Engineering Board, National Academy of Sciences (New York: Quadrangle/The New York Times Book Co., 1972).

[51] Westin, *Privacy and Freedom*, p. 161.

[52] Westin and Baker, *Databanks*, pp. 420-24.

[53] *Ibid.*, p. 253.

[54] U.S., Congress, Senate, Committee on Government Operations and the Committee on the Judiciary, *Privacy: The Collection, Use and Computerization of Personal Data, Joint Hearings*, before the Ad Hoc Subcommittee on Privacy and Information Systems of the Committee on Government Operations and the Subcommittee on Constitutional Rights of the Committee on the Judiciary, on S. 3418, S. 3633, S. 3116, S. 2810, S. 2542, 93d Cong., 2d sess., June 18-20, 1974, p. 117.

[55] Rein Turn and H. E. Petersen, *Security of Computerized Information Systems*, P-4405 (Santa Monica, Calif.: Rand Corporation, 1970), p. 2.

[56] M. Kathleen Hunt and Rein Turn, *Privacy and Security in Databank Systems: An Annotated Bibliography, 1970-1973*, R-1361-NSF (Santa Monica, Calif.: Rand Corporation, 1974); and Annette Harrison, *The Problem of Privacy in the Computer Age: An Annotated Bibliography* (Santa Monica, Calif.: Rand Corporation, 1967).

[57] U.S., Department of Commerce, *Privacy and Security in Computer Systems*, pp. 8-10.

[58] A. G. W. Biddle, "A Call for Non-Proprietary Security Systems." In: U.S., Department of Commerce, National Bureau of Standards, Approaches to *Privacy and Security in Computer Systems*, NBS Special Publication 404 (Washington, D.C.: Government Printing Office, 1974), p. 19.

[59] Alan M. Adelson, "Embezzlement by Computer," *Security World* (1968): 26-27, 40.

[60] Parker, Nycum, and Oüra, *Computer Abuse*.

[61] *Ibid.*, p. 6.

[62] Sackman, *Computers and Social Choice*, p. 19.

[63] Republican Task Force on Privacy, quoted in: U.S., Congress, House, 93d Cong., 2d sess., Nov. 21, 1974, *Congressional Record*, 230, p. 10970; and Department of Health, Education and Welfare, *Records, Computers, and the Rights of Citizens*, p. 141.

[64] *Ibid.*

[65] *Ibid.*, pp. xx-xxi.

[66] *Ibid.*, pp. 59-64.

[67] U.S., Congress, Senate, 93d Cong., 2d sess., Dec. 17, 1974, *Congressional Record*, 120, p. 21819.

[68] Senate Committee on the Judiciary, *Federal Data Banks and Constitutional Rights*, Vol. 6, pp. 3429-98.

[69] *Protecting Your Right to Privacy—Digest of Systems of Records, Agency Rules and Research Aids* (Washington, D.C.: Office of the Federal Register, 1975).

[70] American Civil Liberties Union, *The Privacy Act: How It Affects You; How to Use It* (1975), 24p.

[71] P.L. 93-573, "Privacy Act of 1974," sec. 3, e-7.

[72] S. Res. 3418, 93d Cong., 2d sess. (1974).

[73] "Privacy: Bill Limits Federal Government," *Congressional Quarterly* (January 11, 1975): 100.

[74] Douglas W. Metz, "The Domestic Council Committee on the Right of Privacy," *Bulletin of the American Society for Information Science* 1 (1974): 18.
Established by President Nixon in February 1974, Committee members include the Vice President, the Attorney General, the Secretaries of the Treasury, Defense, Commerce, Labor, and Health, Education and Welfare, the Chairman of the Civil Service Commission and the Directors of the Office of Management and Budget, the Office of Consumer Affairs and the Office of Telecommunications Policy.

[75] Unpublished statement by Representative Edward I. Roch, enclosed with letter dated May 15, 1975. (Mimeographed.)

[76] Al Robbins, "Computers and the Bill of Rights," *The Nation* 219 (1974): 260-61.

[77] Mike Cullen, "Remarks by Assemblyman Mike Cullen, California State Legislature to the Data Processing Management Association," Sacramento, California, May 21, 1975, p. 1. (Mimeographed.)

[78] Letter from Charles A. Mobley, Senior Consultant to Assemblyman Mike Cullen, to the author, October 8, 1975.

[79] Ohio Senate Bill 418, "Code of Fair Information Practices," 1974.

[80] Senate Committee on Government Operations and the Committee on the Judiciary, *Privacy*, "Statement of Hon. Stanley Aronoff, State Senator from Ohio, on Behalf of the National Legislative Conference," pp. 212-38.

[81] Robert C. Goldstein and Richard L. Nolan, "Personal Privacy Versus the Corporate Computer," *Harvard Business Review* 53 (1975): 62-70.

[82] Ohio Senate Bill 99, 1975.

[83] *A Compilation of State and Federal Privacy Laws* has been published by the editors of *Privacy Journal*. More than two hundred statutes are included in the compilation.

[84] Mumford and Sackman, *International Human Choice and Computers*, pp. 27-28.

[85] Willis H. Ware, *Computers, Personal Privacy and Human Choice*, P-5149 (Santa Monica, Calif.: Rand Corporation, 1973), p. 15.

[86] Rein Turn, Norman Z. Shapiro, and Mario L. Juncosa, *Privacy and Security in Centralized vs. Decentralized Databank Systems*, P-5346 (Santa Monica, Calif.: Rand Corporation, 1975).

[87] *Ibid.*, p. 18.

[88] Hellman, *Privacy and Information Systems*, p. 55.

[89] Senate Committee on Government Operations and the Committee on the Judiciary, *Privacy*, p. 68.

[90] House Committee on Government Operations, *The Computer and Invasion of Privacy*, p. 3.

[91] *Olmstead v. U.S.*, 277 U.S. 438 (1928).

[92] House Committee on Government Operations, *The Computer and Invasion of Privacy*, p. 122.

[93] Senate Committee on the Judiciary, *Federal Data Banks and Constitutional Rights*, Vol. 1, p. iv.

[94] *Ibid.*

[95] Facts contained in this and the following paragraph were derived from: Senate Committee on the Judiciary, *Federal Data Banks and Constitutional Rights*, Vol. 1, "Summary of Findings," pp. xxxvii-lix.

[96] See *Federal Personal Data Systems Subject to the Privacy Act of 1974; The First Annual Report of the President for Calendar Year 1975*. Two volumes. (Washington, D.C.: Government Printing Office, 1976), and *Protecting Your Right to Privacy—Digest of Systems of Records; Agency Rules; Research Aids* (Washington, D.C.: Office of the Federal Register, 1976).

[97] Senate Committee on Government Operations and the Committee on the Judiciary, *Privacy*, pp. 2253-54.

[98] U.S. Senate, *Protecting Individual Privacy*, p. 11.

[99] "Son of FEDNET," *Privacy Journal* 2 (No. 9) (July 1976): 1.

[100] Sackman, *Computers and Social Choice*, p. 14.

[101] *Ibid.*, p. 19.

FREEDOM OF THE VISUAL ARTS:
The Role of Governments

Yvonne Linsert Morse

The repression of the visual arts is an ancient practice, having originated apparently with attempts to maintain religious icons and symbols that were believed to possess magical powers. Primitive cultures often felt that natural stones were the dwelling place of spirits or gods, so rocks were used as tombstones, boundary stones, or objects of religious veneration. By carving or otherwise modifying stones into more recognizable forms, ancient people attempted to express the souls or spirits of rocks. Both the abstract faces of the menhirs and the more realistic forms of the hermae of ancient Greece developed out of boundary stones.[1]

Ancient works of art were used to convey ideas through stylized, abstract, or realistic representations of human and animal forms. An example of the artisans' use of symbolic forms in an early civilization is the Aztec rain-god Tlaloc, whose statue is given shape by use of the forms of sacred rattlesnakes that were believed to embody the power of lightning. The serpent in Aztec art thus became a portrayal of a rattlesnake, a sign for lightning, and by extension, a being through whose power thunderstorms could be celebrated or even induced. Art historian E. H. Gombrich has pointed out that, "If we try to enter into the mentality which created these uncanny idols we may begin to understand how image-making in these early civilizations was not only connected with magic and religion, but was also the first form of writing."[2]

Early works of art, therefore, were not created merely for enjoyment or decoration; their purpose was more often of a practical nature. The magical power of visual representation could keep early man alive both in this world and in the unknown; sacred objects could "break the drought, end famine, stay a pestilence, or turn the tide of battle."[3] Examples may be seen in the scenes of everyday life which decorate the tombs of Egypt's kings and queens. The style of these numerous portrayals was considered to be successful in maintaining eternal life; thus, they seldom varied through hundreds of years. Individual creativity in design was not the primary responsibility of ancient artists, as artistic efforts were more commonly used to stimulate the favor of the gods and to create harmony between man and a mysterious, often hazardous world.

Plato considered the visual arts to be the most potentially dangerous of man's creative efforts because of their power to convey ideas. Therefore, he felt that all artistic production should be subjected to rigid censorship of both form and content. This concept is presently accepted by some persons—and especially by totalitarian governments.

Censorship of the visual arts has included repressions based on economic, social, political, moral, or esthetic grounds by government and religious officials, as well as by groups of citizens, individuals, or society in general. This chapter examines the regulatory roles of governments on artistic expression during the twentieth century, which has witnessed the rise and fall of regulatory bodies ranging from the artist's censorship of his own work, through local institutions and governments, to the censorial pressures of national governments. In the succeeding sections of this chapter, examples of various types of repression will be discussed in an effort to provide a general overview of censorship of the visual arts. Local and national governmental repressions will be treated in greater detail. Developments in Soviet Russia, Nazi Germany, and the United States have been chosen for close examination because they reflect the widest ranges of political thought and action— far left to far right. In addition, these countries are examples of both closed and open societies. Although Soviet Russia and Nazi Germany developed in the twentieth century as closed societies with opposite ideologies, it is interesting to note their similar viewpoints concerning censorship of the visual arts. By presenting the similarities and differences among the three societies in respect to censorship of the visual arts, it is hoped that the reader will better understand the many social forces that affect visual creativity. The United States was chosen as an example of an open society which has been able to adapt to changes in morality in a constantly changing society. The acceptance of the modern world as presented in works of art further increases and deepens understanding of today's society. For instance, the revival of past traditions such as quiltmaking and stitchery, and the interest in "naturalness" in food and other facets of everyday living have been reflected in an increasing awareness and appreciation of more representational works of art.

Although this chapter is devoted mainly to the relationship between Western art and governments, mention must also be made of the status of artistic expression in Eastern countries, particularly in China. Conditions affecting artistic freedom in China have been quite similar to those in the West: religion and art were allied, and tradition dictated acceptable styles and patterns. When China became a communist state, the fate of the nation's artists was not unlike that of their Russian counterparts. Restrictions were imposed in China so that the Communist Party line would be followed, and economic ruin befell any artists who ignored prescribed limits. A recent episode relating to Chinese art will illustrate how artistic expression remains subservient to the whims of politics in some countries. In December 1974, an exhibit of Chinese jade was put on display at the National Gallery of Art in Washington, D.C. Many of the exhibited pieces of jade were ancient, having been discovered only recently during archeological excavations in China. At a preview showing of the jade, reporters, newsmen, and foreign diplomats accompanied Mrs. Betty Ford and other distinguished guests on a tour of the display. However, news representatives from several countries with whom China has political disagreements, including South Korea, Taiwan, South Africa, and Israel, were not permitted to view the exhibit, this at the request of the Chinese delegation. Ordinarily, this restriction would not have been readily accepted because of the possibility of adverse publicity. In the interests of world peace and political harmony, however, the politically motivated demands of the Chinese were honored. Nevertheless, it does appear strange that a foreign government could influence American officials to impose restrictions on freedom of the press. This episode illustrates the power of a closed over an open society; it also serves as a reminder that vigilance is necessary if a democratic society is to remain free and open.

MORALITY AND THE ARTS

Governmental control of the visual arts has usually been accompanied by religious repression. That combined control has taken two forms: 1) tacit official approval of censorship by religious groups, such as the destruction in sixteenth century England of religious art, encouraged by Thomas Cranmer under Henry VIII; and 2) unified repressions by both government and religious bodies. Although this chapter does not contain a discussion of the traditional alliance of religion and art, the effect of religion on both the production and destruction of art cannot be overlooked or underestimated. In many instances, factions within some religious groups have argued violently to preserve their own symbolic representations. For example, the struggle within the Catholic Church between the Iconoclasts (the image destroyers) and the Iconodules (the image worshippers)—both of the late Ancient and Early Byzantine periods—persisted for more than 100 years. Large numbers of sacred images depicted in mosaics, paintings, and carvings were destroyed.[4] Iconoclasts were especially active 800 years later, during the Protestant Reformation of the sixteenth century, when Calvinists, Huguenots, Puritans, and Lutherans destroyed sculptures, stained glass, tapestries, wood carvings, metalwork, and illuminations. Protestants tended to disregard the higher pleasures of art as they associated the fine arts with the old church and the establishment.[5]

Portrayal of human nudity and sexual activity in the visual arts has often resulted in official harassment, also. Citizens who feel moral indignation and righteousness have always been eager to judge what their fellow citizens should see or hear. Works by Renaissance genius Michelangelo have even been censored. The colossal nude figures of "The Last Judgment" fresco in the Sistine Chapel shocked Michelangelo's contemporaries when the work was completed in 1541, and Pope Paul IV eventually issued instructions for draperies to be painted over especially provoking parts of nude figures in the work. Throughout the succeeding years, other popes commissioned artists to add even more veils, draperies, skirts, and clouds to obscure areas of the fresco that were deemed to be distasteful to sensitive eyes. Pope Clement VIII even entertained the idea of destroying the entire painting because of the "obscenity" of the nudes.[6] Reproductions of the frescoes have been banned in various parts of the world during the past 400 years. In addition, reproductions of Michelangelo's statue "David" have also persistently provoked censors, and as recently as 1969, a bookstore in Sydney, Australia, faced obscenity charges because a poster of the statue was displayed. One year later, four men were arrested in the same city for selling obscene publications, including a photograph of "David."[7] In many communities, including Florence, Italy, where the statue was created, small reproductions of the famous biblical figure may be purchased with or without a figleaf.

At times, artists have exercised a certain amount of self-censorship. Potentially offensive works have not always been allowed adequate exposure, and consequently, some artists have not benefited from certain of their own works either professionally or financially. For example, Diego Rivera, the well-known Mexican artist, declined to show three photographs of his mural "Portrait of America" at an exhibit in Mexico City. As a result of quarrels with Communist Party leaders, Rivera had been expelled from the Party, and since he wanted to be reinstated, he chose not to show the three photographs because he felt that Party authorities might be offended by his generally sympathetic portrayal of the United States.[8]

Public institutions, including libraries, have also banned or restricted access to pictorial matter that could be considered obscene and potentially damaging to young people. During the 1960s, Gertrude Gscheidle, director of the Chicago Public Library, was responsible for two such repressive incidents. The first occurred when Ms. Gscheidle directed the removal of eight works of art by George C. Kokines from a library exhibit. Although the banning of Kokines's paintings was opposed by several concerned citizens and by two members of the library's board, Ms. Gscheidle defended her action with a claim that the art works were suggestive, and that her action was not censorship but a "question of taste."[9] The second incident at the Chicago Public Library, in the spring of 1967, was provoked by a print entitled "Ozymandias," which depicted a nude man and woman and was included in a print exhibit of the works of Letterio Calapai. Ms. Gscheidle felt that the objectionable print was not in keeping with the purposes of the library's Art Department and that children were apt to be adversely affected. The librarian's demand that the print be removed led to protests by the artist and cancellation of the entire exhibit in the library. Calapai commented that "to remove one print from a carefully planned exhibition of a body of my works is like tearing the page from a serious book."[10]

In view of Ms. Gscheidle's position as the director of one of the nation's major metropolitan public libraries, one might wonder how a person with such restrictive attitudes toward freedom of expression managed to fulfill her professional obligation to provide free and unrestricted library services to Chicago citizens. Although Ms. Gscheidle's ideas about works of art suggested a narrow outlook, apparently they reflected the attitudes of other Midwestern librarians toward freedom of expression. Busha's study of the opinions of Midwestern public librarians toward censorship revealed that "a marked disparity exists between the attitudes of many librarians toward intellectual freedom as a concept and toward censorship as an activity."[11] Busha has also reminded librarians that the removal of materials from library collections, including visual material accepted for exhibit, "because someone feels that certain works are obscene, obnoxious, immoral, depraved, or seditious is contrary to the idea of freedom of choice."[12]

GOVERNMENT REPRESSION OF VISUAL ART

Suppression of the fine arts by government officials on purely political and propagandistic grounds has been particularly characteristic of the twentieth century. Censorship of the visual arts has been sanctioned directly or indirectly and to varying degrees by almost all nations; however, as explained previously, this chapter will be limited to a discussion of freedom of the visual arts in Russia, Nazi Germany, and the United States. Within this context, similarities or differences in ideologies of the three countries and the effects of censorship on artists and their audiences are delineated. Incidents presented here are designed to demonstrate abridgments of "artistic freedom." In 1954, the American Federation of Arts spoke out about artistic freedom as follows:

Freedom of artistic expression in a visual work of art, like freedom of speech and press, is fundamental in our democracy.[13]

Soviet Art Censorship

The Russian Revolution of 1917 initially provided Soviet artists with new creative freedoms and placed them in the forefront of the development of modern art. In order to better understand later artistic repressions by the Soviet government, a brief discussion of revolutionary artistic ideas is in order. Prior to 1917, Russian artists had maintained close relationships with established European art centers, principally Paris and Munich. But revolutionary inspiration led them to experiment with newer European art developments and to discover innovative visual realities. Three new art styles were developed by Russian artists: Suprematism, Rayonism, and Constructivism. Suprematism was an attempt to express pure feeling rather than to only depict subject matter; it is embodied in Malevich's "Suprematist Composition: White on White," a tilted white square on white paper, which attempted to express the "sensation of flight" or the feeling of a mystic "wave" from "outer space."[14] Rayonism, an offshoot of Cubism, was developed by Larionov, whose painting "Blue Rayonism" visually depicted the new concepts of time and space expressed by physicists and mathematicians such as Felix Klein, Ernst Mach, and Albert Einstein. Constructivism, a more uniquely Russian art development, was a significant new concept which has influenced much of twentieth century sculpture. The truly constructive principles of this development allow the building of sculpture with elements of wood, metal, glass, plastic, or other materials, and the primary emphasis of the constructivist school is on sculptural space rather than the sculptural mass that has characterized traditional sculpture. Instead of taking away from a mass, as in wood or stone carving, and rather than building up from the mass, as in clay modeling, constructed sculptures utilize space, motion and environment, as well as non-traditional materials.[15]

Among the most innovative and influential of the Russian artists whose artistic experiments were permitted between 1917 and 1920 were Vasily Kandinsky, Eleazar Lissitsky, Vladimir Tatlin, Naum Gabo, and Anton Pevsner. With the return of relatively more stable conditions to Russia by 1920, old academic standards combined with new technological ideas were placed in the service of communist philosophy. Artists were encouraged to turn their energies from pure experimentation and to serve the revolution by generating practical ideas for industrial, engineering, or product design. Those who disagreed with the new Soviet philosophy set forth their ideas in the *Realistic Manifesto*, published in Moscow on August 5, 1920. These artists called for a new great style in art and underlined their conviction that recent experiments in abstract painting and constructions constituted the development of a new reality. But the revolutionary government prevailed, so many artists emigrated to Europe and to the United States so that they could continue to develop and express their individual artistic ideas.[16] One consequence of the emigration of Russian artists was the establishment in Germany of the Bauhaus, an art school to which many Russians contributed talent and ideas. As the prescriptive curtain of Soviet interference was drawn, the visual arts became stagnant.

Leon Trotsky's *Literature and Revolution* (1924) further strengthened and defined the place of art in a revolutionary society. Trotsky's concern was with the Marxist concept of the objective social dependence and social utility of art, so he naturally visualized art as a service to the revolutionary state. The narrow, restrictive doctrine of Socialist Realism thus permitted artists to create in an atmosphere of relative freedom under "watchful revolutionary censorship."[17] Hence, Russian artists continued to labor within the strict framework of the Socialist Realism mode of expression. Subject matter was restricted primarily to the depiction of scenes of industry, construction, and collective farm work in an effort to portray the new Soviet man and society. Even landscapes were not exempted from prescribed limits; they were accepted only if the changed Soviet landscape was depicted by the inclusion of such subject matter as dams or electric power plants, or farmers using mechanized equipment.[18]

Russian authorities have at times been remiss in maintaining controls on art, however. Josef Stalin, in 1939, redefined the artist's role in Soviet Russia as active participation "in the political guidance of the country." Stalin viewed the artist as "an engineer of men's souls," so Russian artists were expected to become their own censors in the interest of the state and to insure the creation of an art "national in form and socialist in content."[19] Stalin was vigorous in his persecution of all artists who attempted to express their individuality by creating works in violation of Soviet standards of artistic expression. Uncooperative artists often vanished suddenly; many were never heard of again, having been either exiled or executed. Given the severity of intimidation of artists in the Soviet Union, there has understandably been a powerful, leveling effect on Russian visual arts.

The restrictiveness of artistic expression in Russia has been reiterated on several occasions, although the Soviets have claimed that they merely attempted to prevent the possibility of decadent, capitalistic art from influencing the purity of revolutionary art. In reality, Soviet reminders about the purpose of art have denied art for art's sake and have repeated the concept of art for Marx's sake. Russian artists have been told what and how to paint, i.e., realistically, since realistic art is considered to be in the best service of the people. Considered "ideologically sound and cheerful,"[20] realism is the only officially approved style.

Repressive attitudes and actions toward the fine arts were extended by the Russians after World War II to new territory acquired by the Soviet Union. An example of the strict reorganization of a nation's visual arts into the standardized Soviet mold is the case of the German Democratic Republic. A public lecture delivered by Lieutenant-Colonel Dymschitz in the Soviet Haus der Kultur in Berlin outlined the direction which East German art was expected to take. In the lecture entitled "Soviet Art and Its Relation to Bourgeois Art," Dymschitz stated that Soviet culture was "open to every worthwhile artistic effort anywhere in the world—provided only that it was genuinely democratic and truly socialistic."[21] He repeated Stalin's preference for art that was simple enough to be readily understood by everyone, so that the message of social progress could be carried to the people.[22] Thus, the only form of art considered acceptable by Soviet officials was that which was realistic in style and content; all other art forms, especially surrealism and abstract art, were judged as worthless. Art that did not conform to government standards was often labeled as "individualistic, capitalistic, bourgeois, snobbish, and decadent."[23]

Immediately following World War II, the Soviets encouraged the development of art in East Germany by devoting prompt attention and by giving assistance to art schools and by granting certain artists official recognition as well as preferential financial support. But artistic freedom in the Eastern Zone of Germany lasted only one year. The real motives underlying the Soviets' encouragement of the arts soon became clear when Dymschitz delivered his lecture. Thereafter, art and artists were to be enlisted in a totalitarian political program,[24] and basically, the position of art in Soviet-controlled East Germany has not changed from its status under the Nazis.

Art under Communist Domination

To exercise more effective control over artists in Russia, the Union of Soviet Artists was formed in 1939. Members included painters, sculptors, graphic artists, theater and film actors, and art critics, and its official approval of a movement or an organization in the Soviet Union was necessary if artists, performers, or critics were to achieve favorable public attention, which in turn would improve their economic positions. By 1941, over 3,700 Russian artists had joined the Union of Soviet Artists.[25] Personal and imaginative artistic statements continued to be produced sporadically by independent Soviet artists; however, nonconformity in the arts was often described by Soviet authorities as "subjective anarchy." Artists who expressed individualism by using the style of "hideous and revolting" modernism were in danger of being expelled from art guilds and unions. Professor Vladimir Kemenov, director of Moscow's Tretjakov Gallery, vigorously criticized modern art as "decadent, antihumanist, and pathological."[26]

Exhibitions of art works in any style other than Socialist Realism were virtually unknown in Russia until 1953, when the collection of the Museum of Modern Western Art was placed on view in Moscow's Pushkin Museum. Despite the official judgment of these works as distortions filled with "bourgeois formalism, and international cosmopolitanism" with "no direct relation to Communist ideology," the opening of the collection was a major artistic event.[27] Then in 1957, the work of Ilya Glazunov was placed on exhibit in the Central House of Art Workers in Moscow. Representative of the icon style of the fourteenth and fifteenth centuries, Glazunov's exhibit was vigorously attacked by Boris V. Ologanson, president of the Academy of Arts. Artist Glazunov had produced works outside the prescribed official limits; he was denounced as an "art student who had the conceit to declare himself a newly discovered genius" through the organization of a personal show.[28] At the same time, Nikita Khrushchev, the Communist Party secretary, restated the Party line:

> Literature and Art are organic parts of the general struggle of the people for Communism; the Russian people want works of art that mirror the pathos of labor and which they can understand; Soviet artists and sculptors continue to be worthy sons of their Socialist homeland by using all their energies and their talents to glorify the heroic feats of our great people, the builders of Communist Society.[29]

In 1962, Sergei Smirnov, a Russian playwright and champion of lost causes, claimed in a *Literaturnaya Gazeta* article that Ilya Glazunov had been refused full membership in the Soviet Artists Union because his style of art did not conform to official tastes. Smirnov accused the Artists Union of preventing innovations by young artists; he also claimed that artistic talent should be regarded as national property.[30] That same year a semi-private art show by students of Eli Belyutin was permitted to be exhibited for a few hours, the paintings being executed in

abstract or semi-abstract styles. Also included in the exhibit were works by Ernst
Neizvestny, who had been described as a "notorious, officially condemned, decadent, and 'unpatriotic' sculptor."[31] The paranoia to which many Russians fell
victim was demonstrated by official regulation of attendance at the exhibition to
Western correspondents, Soviet cultural officials, and several hundred carefully
chosen Russian citizens.[32] The abstract art exhibit was closed to the general public.
Further evidence of artistic repression in Russia was demonstrated by the Soviets'
refusal to allow the Salon for the Sale of Art Objects to accept from abroad any
applications for the purchase of Neizvestny's sculptures.

Other exhibits of modern art were planned and organized during 1962; one
was mysteriously postponed only a few hours before its scheduled opening.
Another exhibit entitled "Thirty Years of Moscow Art" inspired a proclamation
from Khrushchev that the displayed paintings and sculpture were "anti-Soviet"
and "amoral."[33] *Pravda*, the official state newspaper, took note of Khrushchev's
words and reaffirmed Leninist art policies in an editorial entitled "Art Belongs to
the People." The editorial claimed that art should be characterized by "party-
mindedness." It also condemned artists who strayed from the style of Socialist
Realism by adhering to individual styles and visions.[34]

Glazunov again attempted to exhibit his works in Moscow in 1964, and,
although the Artists Union objected, the exhibit was sanctioned by the USSR
Culture Ministry. But the one-man show was quickly banned when Soviet
officials became aware of, and angered by, a nude portrait of the artist's wife.[35]

All countries under Russian influence are generally expected to follow the
guidelines for artistic expression that were established by early revolutionary
leaders. However, during a trip to Poland in 1959-1960, art historian Herschel Chipp
reported that he discovered free artistic expression to be a reality rather than just a
goal.[36] Polish artists had rebelled against Socialist Realism in the mid-fifties; they
were subsequently allowed to explore all styles and media and to exhibit their work
and to sell it in cooperative galleries or to send it abroad.[37] Poland has thus been
the only nation among the Communist satellites to permit artists the freedom
necessary for the production of innovative, original works.

Noy has pointed out that "the gift of artistic creativity as an enduring personal trait is dependent on at least two different factors . . . an urge, drive, or
motivation to create something new and . . . talent to carry out and materialize this
creative urge."[38] These two factors presently exist within the Soviet Union, as
evidenced by recent unauthorized presentations of art works, such as the non-
conformist art displayed in 1974 at an open-air exhibit in Moscow's Smenovskoye
suburb. The exhibit angered Soviet authorities to the extent that bulldozers, dump
trucks, and water-spraying trucks manned by "volunteer workers" were employed
to disrupt the show and to turn the vacant lot in which the exhibit had been set
up into a cultural park. In the process of clearing the field, workers upset the
exhibited paintings and churned them into the mud with bulldozers. In addition,
a group of approximately 500 spectators, including foreign correspondents and
diplomats, were menaced, spectators being chased by trucks and having steel sewer
pipes rolled toward them. These actions were taken with the tacit approval of
uniformed militiamen and secret police agents, who observed the disturbance but
took no action to prevent it. The event was given wide coverage by foreign news
media; thus, a minor act of dissent was turned into an embarrassing political incident of large proportions.[39] Some exhibit organizers complained to the Communist

Party Politburo, protesting the "lawlessness, arbitrary misuse of force, and violation of guaranteed constitutional rights." They further demanded an investigation of the incident, the return of their property, and the punishment of persons responsible for the destruction.[40] Although no official reaction was forthcoming to the international adverse publicity and to artists' protests, permission was granted for another exhibit to be held at an alternate site. Consequently, two weeks after the abortive exhibition, a crowd of more than 5,000 spectators viewed the first outdoor exhibit of unofficial art in the Soviet Union since the short-lived, liberal years which followed the 1917 revolution. On the other hand, the exhibit was allowed to be on display only four hours. When asked for comments about the exhibit, Russian poet Yevtushenko stated that the displayed art works were uneven in quality but that "the most important fact is that they are here in the first place."[41] Artists were enthusiastic about the exhibit and anticipated similar shows, yet many observers and artists feared that the unofficial exhibit was a one-time event.

Alexander Melamid and Vitaly Komar, two of the artists who exhibited works in the unofficial, outdoor show, described their style of painting as "sock art" or socialist pop art. Russian sock artists attempt to portray the excesses of ideology by which they are surrounded, as opposed to Western pop art which they feel represents an excess of "things" (e.g., soupcans or Jell-O boxes). Instead of franchised stores and restaurants with distinctive features and signs, such as golden arches, giant bells, buckets of chicken, etc., Russian citizens are surrounded by posters and billboards about maternity, or portraits of Solzhenitsyn as a dog with fangs, or pictures of Moshe Dayan with a swastika for an eye patch.[42] These, then, are the factors that have influenced the development of sock art in the Soviet Union.

Leningrad artist Yevgeny Rukhin noted that although official artists had been warned by the Artists Union to stay away, six official artists and fifty-five unofficial artists participated in the outdoor exhibit. Rukhin also said that artists whose works had been in the disrupted exhibit preferred to consider the episode as "an unfortunate misunderstanding."[43] Oboler has written that "one of the major mechanisms for regulating the moral ideas of men has always been control over what man has thought, heard, seen, written, and read."[44] These mechanisms are not confined to the control of moral ideas; political ideologies are also protected by the same control, which is evident in the strict regulation of artistic expression in the Soviet Union.

Artists under the Nazis

Prior to World War I, official regulations of art works in Germany were concerned mainly with the portrayal of the Emperor or other government officials in a satirical or derogatory manner or with art containing socially conscious material. The case of "The Weavers," a set of six poignant etchings by Kathe Kollwitz, is an example of the latter kind of control. The Kollwitz prints, inspired by Gerhart Hauptmann's drama about an 1840 textile strike, required four years for completion and were considered worthy of a Gold Medal by art judges. Kaiser Wilhelm II labeled the etchings "gutter art" and denied Kollwitz the medal.[45]

By 1927, the Reichstag had passed a morality law to protect young people under the age of eighteen from indecent prints and pictures which they might encounter in art shows and in other performances or exhibitions. German officials feared that objectionable works could taint morals and purvey "moral dirt."[46]

Although German artists objected vigorously to the law and claimed that the statute contained "immeasurable damage for intellectual freedom of the German Republic, and might occasion tremendous damage to genuine works of art,"[47] the law was deemed "necessary to guard the innocent."[48] To enforce the law, police were given considerable power to meddle in the private lives of German citizens. For example, law enforcement officers were allowed to supervise dancing in homes, to enter into private homes, and to protect children from parents[49] —all in the name of morality.

A powerful influence on the development of Nazi esthetics and the concept of "degenerate art" was a book by the well-known architect Schultze-Naumberg. Published in 1928 and entitled *Art and Race*, the book outlined the architect's theories about "hereditary determinism" in art. Schultze-Naumberg attempted to prove that "the artist cannot help but reproduce his own racial type in his creations."[50] The idea of racial influence on creativity was further expanded and strengthened by Alfred Rosenberg, Nazi leader and writer. Rosenberg's *Myth of the Twentieth Century* became the "accepted Bible of Nazi ideology" and was devoted primarily to the Nazi doctrine of art.[51] These writings probably stimulated the already obsessive Nazi preoccupation with race. In addition, they undoubtedly inspired the Lebensborn (Fountain of Life) program, which was begun in 1935 as an attempt to make the Germans a super-race through the process of selective breeding. Under the Lebensborn program, the racially and politically elite were encouraged to reproduce, and thousands of foreign children who met Nazi qualifications were kidnapped and sent to Germany to expand the nation's breeding stock and to hasten the increase of the super-race.[52]

Expressionism was considered to be the most offensive of art styles by German leaders in the early part of the twentieth century, for they were displeased by the Expressionists' abandonment of the naturalism of Impressionism in favor of a more simplified style which could convey greater emotional impact by means of exaggerations and distortions of line and color. Subject matter became less concerned with beauty and often dealt with the harshest of human conditions, such as Barlach's "Have Pity!," a sculptured portrayal of an old beggar woman. Expressionism was stimulated by the paintings of van Gogh, and while artists in several countries created in that style, and while Expressionism was considered to be distasteful to German officials, the movement's greatest exponents were found in Germany, where several Munich artists formed a group in 1911 called the Blaue Reiter. By 1933, when the National Socialists came to power, modern art was banned, and leaders of the Expressionist movement were exiled or forbidden to work in Germany. Adolph Hitler considered the works of Expressionist artists to be "an expression of a mankind subnormal from the racial point of view."[53] Hitler's overall art policy was to forbid "any work of art which does not render an object faithfully or which derides such Nazi ideals as War and Women." Paradoxically, the Nazi art policy approved of explicit nudes but found modern art completely unacceptable.[54] In addition, Schultze-Naumberg, who was appointed director of the Weimar Art School, declared that "anyone who found aesthetic pleasure in Expressionism was not a German."[55]

Even the Bauhaus, the influential German art school founded by Walter Gropius in 1919, was not free from restrictive controls under the Nazis. The basic premise of the school's founder was the need for unity among architects, artists, and craftsmen and the importance of empirical experience, so that all artists and architects could become competent craftsmen as well as creative designers. The stimulating atmosphere at the Bauhaus attracted many important European artists as instructors, among whom were Paul Klee, Vasily Kandinsky, Joseph Albers, Johannes Itten, Laszlo Moholy-Nagy, and several dissident Russian artists who moved to Germany seeking artistic freedom to create what had been forbidden by the Soviet government in the early 1920s. The Bauhaus was dissolved in the mid-1930s by the Dessau City Council, which labeled the school "one of the most prominent centers of the Jewish-Marxist art program."[56] Many of the dispossessed artists emigrated first to other areas in Europe and then to the United States, where they stimulated the development of improved functional designs and encouraged greater participation in the advancement of modern art. In 1937, Moholy-Nagy founded and directed the New Bauhaus in Chicago, which later became the Institute of Design of the Illinois Institute of Technology. According to art historian Arnason, Moholy-Nagy's

> teaching of the implications of abstract painting and sculpture for industrial design, graphic design, architecture, and the total environment of man have affected an entire generation of artists, architects, designers, and consumers everywhere.[57]

When World War II ended in Germany and the country was divided into two distinct national areas, Colonel Dymschitz outlined the Soviet policy for East German art. Thus, Nazi policies for artistic expression were replaced with Soviet policies, but the exchange of one political system for another—Communism for Nazism—brought few surprises. Artists realized the problems under which they had to work; they either managed to escape or they remained to create within the guidelines set by officially imposed restrictions.

Artistic Expression in America

Let us turn now to an examination of how artistic freedom has been officially treated in the United States. Until the 1840s, interference in the intellectual freedom of artists in the United States was based primarily on societal, unofficial pressures at the local level, as well as pressure by peers and the artist's own definition of artistic "decency." However, the enactment by Congress of the Tariff Law of 1842 produced a federal obscenity law concerned with visual art alone, rather than with books and related materials which utilized the printed word.[58] Outraged public response toward the importation of "indecent" prints, paintings, and sculpture prompted Congress to include in the Tariff Law of 1842 the section declaring that "the importation of all indecent and obscene prints, paintings, lithographs, engravings, and transparencies is hereby prohibited."[59] Congress then gave the power to enforce the law to Customs officers, who were authorized to confiscate all visual material they considered to be "obscene or immoral" and to initiate court proceedings to destroy objectionable material.[60]

Within a year after the enactment of the Tariff Act of 1842, the law had been applied in the seizure of nine indecent paintings, each attached to the false bottoms of snuff boxes imported from Germany and declared to be of "so very obscene a character that they were unfit to be produced in court, and only one of them was exhibited, having been first defaced with ink to hide its obscenity." Although the objectionable snuff boxes represented only a small part of the entire shipment and the importers were unaware of the type of painting decorating the boxes, the jury ruled in favor of the government; thus, the entire shipment was confiscated.[61]

However, art works deemed to be obscene, such as copies of ancient Greek nude statues, continued to be imported. In 1857, the Tariff Law of 1842 was amended to "more effectually accomplish the purpose for which the provision was enacted."[62] In addition to the earlier banned items, images and figures were included so that the importation of sculpture, as well as indecent daguerreotypes and photographs, could be controlled.[63] However, one must bear in mind that, throughout the years, governmental banning of famous art works was not limited to the United States. For instance, a poster that advertised Palmolive soap with a picture of the "Venus de Milo" could not be displayed in Montreal because of local censorship regulations. To remedy the situation, one Canadian merchant placed a white patch over the female figure's breast in 1927.[64] In addition, in Budapest, Hungary, police prevented the displaying of a photograph of the "Venus de Milo" in a shop window.[65] These are but two examples among hundreds which could be used to demonstrate that people who support censorship and other repressive activities are usually not concerned with the quality, beauty, or importance of art works; usually they are primarily concerned with imposing their own restrictive viewpoints.

In addition to the increased powers granted to the Customs Department by the amended Tariff Law, a second federal agency was empowered in the United States to restrict the flow of obscene or indecent material, this through the passage in 1865 of the nation's first postal obscenity law. Need for the law was said to have been prompted, at least in part, by "complaints about the reading materials mailed to many soldiers who served in the Civil War," including Cleland's *Memoirs of a Woman of Pleasure.*[66] The new postal law barred obscene books and pictures from the United States mails and made the mailing of these materials a criminal offense "punishable by a fine of not more than $500 or imprisonment for not more than one year or both."[67]

The efforts of the U.S. Customs and Postal Departments to maintain public decency and morals were strongly encouraged and aided by Anthony Comstock, a zealot of conventional morals whose influence on the restriction of artistic freedom in the visual arts began over one hundred years ago. Comstock was a co-founder and secretary of the New York Society for the Suppression of Vice, which was organized in 1873. By a special act of the New York Legislature, the New York Society for the Suppression of Vice was given a monopoly in eliminating vice, and its agents were endowed with "the rights of search, seizure, and arrest," an authority that had been previously reserved exclusively for publicly constituted police authority.[68] The founding of the Watch and Ward Society in Boston was also inspired by the flamboyant anti-smut crusader. Nevertheless, Comstock's greatest triumph in his lifelong struggle "to improve the morals of other people by rendering obscene literature and photographs inaccessible"[69] was the success of his lobbyist activities in Congress. With less than a total of one hour of debate, for example, the Comstock Act was passed by Congress as Section 1461, Title 18, *United States Code.*[70] A decisive factor in the enactment of the Comstock Act was the distribution of so-called "obscene" pictures, not objectionable books.[71] The bill, signed by President Ullyses S. Grant on June 8, 1873, strengthened the 1865 law by allowing more severe penalties to offenders and by incorporating controls on information about contraceptives.[72] Comstock's persistent activities to prod passage of the law, as well as his many well-publicized attacks on "obscene" material, resulted in the use of the term "comstockery" as "a convenient synonym for prudery, Puritanism, and officious meddling."[73]

Comstock's influence was sufficiently powerful to assure the puritanical crusader's appointment as a special postal agent, so that the law could be applied more thoroughly and obscenity could be suppressed more directly.[74] In the two-year period between 1872 and 1874, Comstock, the "Roundsman of the Lord," was able to seize and to destroy 194,000 obscene pictures and photographs. He boasted of his repressive accomplishments, claiming that "in the guise of art the foe to moral purity comes in its most insidious, fascinating, and seductive form."[75] As a matter of record, Comstock was proud of his four decades of suppression; he claimed to have destroyed "more than fifty tons of indecent books, 28,425 pounds of plates for the printing of such books, almost four million obscene pictures, and 16,900 negatives for such pictures."[76]

Comstock based his censorship activities on the premise that nude art was not in its "proper place" when exhibited "before the eyes of the uncultivated and inexperienced."[77] This concept was not new; pictured nudity and pornography had been considered for many years the special province of wealthy, educated people. An assumption was made that these people were better qualified to understand and to cope with erotica than were the poorer classes. Therefore, Comstock did not singlehandedly fight obscenity and moral impropriety; his power was increased because he had the solid backing of many citizens. Comstock's record speaks for itself, and a few examples will suffice to demonstrate the crusader's attempts to maintain public morality. One of the most notorious instances was the repression of "September Morn," a rather romantic and insipid painting by Paul Chabas which depicts a nude, young girl demurely bathing on the shore of a lake. The painting received critical acclaim when first shown at an exhibit in Paris in 1912, and a reproduction of the work was published in the magazine *Town and Country*.[78] Widespread dissemination of reproductions of the painting brought about objections and caused censorship problems despite critics' protests of the work's undeserved persecution. A well-known Chicago politician, Alderman "Bath House John" Coughlin, passed a ruling preventing the display of "September Morn" anywhere in the city. A subsequent jury trial regarding the morality of the painting resulted in a "not guilty" verdict, despite claims by Vice Commissioner W. W. Hallam that the picture's subject matter was lewd. One art critic present at the trial maintained that the young woman depicted in the painting should be considered "nude, not naked."[79]

The reality of the "nude" or the "naked" in all art works was difficult for the public to accept, even in classical works such as Greek or Roman statues and especially in etchings, serigraphs, or lithographs which could be mass-produced and made available to middle-class Americans at reasonable prices. One had to be daring and avant-garde in the first quarter of the twentieth century to display a painting or statue of a nude figure in one's home where it might catch the eye of a casual visitor. In his discussion of the "nude versus naked" concept, art historian Kenneth Clark made the distinction that the word "nude" implies "a balanced, prosperous, confident body" as opposed to the term "naked" which conjures up an image of a "huddled and defenseless" body deprived of clothes.[80] Clark further proposed that "the nude is not the subject of art, but a form of art" that was invented and perfected by the Greeks in the fifth century and has survived through the centuries as our "chief link with the classic disciplines."[81] We have also been reminded by

Clark that artistic use of an unclothed body demonstrates the wish to perpetuate ourselves. According to Clark:

> ... no nude, however abstract, should fail to arouse in the spectator some vestige of erotic feeling, even though it be only the faintest shadow—and if it does not do so, it is bad art and false morals.[82]

Regardless of faulty conceptualizations, the moral side of the nudity issue enraged vice societies and Anthony Comstock, the foremost guardian of public morals. Comstock's role in the "September Morn" controversy was manipulated and encouraged by Harry Reichenbach, the owner of the painting and a master promoter. Reichenbach realized that an investigation by Comstock of a nude painting, even one as innocent as "September Morn," would ensure worldwide publicity. Having purchased the painting, Reichenbach displayed it in the window of Braun and Company in New York City and hired a small group of urchins to congregate before the window to point, grimace, and whisper. Comstock was lured to the site by an anonymous phone call. After viewing the painting, the portly vice fighter declared that "September Morn" was "salacious," and he stated: "There's too little morning and too much maid in that picture." Comstock realized, however, that on an obscene or immoral basis no legal action could be taken.[83] Newspaper publicity regarding Comstock's visit to the storefront and the zealot's subsequent remarks stimulated public discussion about the relationship of nudity, art, and morality. Thus, Comstock's behavior encouraged the beginning of a gradual relaxation of standards and the expansion of artistic freedom. Publicity also served to increase sales of reproductions of "September Morn" to an estimated 7,000,000 copies. In addition, the nude bather appeared on dolls, statues, calendars, umbrella and cane handles, and sailors' tatoos. Chabas' innocuous painting has been rivalled in popularity only by the works of Maxfield Parrish and von Gogh's "Sunflowers."[84]

The prudish moral standards held by Comstock were eventually weakened by adverse publicity, by technological changes which brought about an increased tempo in modern life, and by the appearance of "modern art" on the American scene, with the opening in 1913 of the International Exhibition of Modern Art at New York City's 69th Regiment Armory. The Armory Show collection contained contemporary art and included works important in the development of European painting from the last quarter of the nineteenth century. European art works, which comprised approximately one-third of the show, highlighted the provincialism of American art and shocked critics, artists, and the general public with their strong primitive elements. Decided antagonism was exhibited toward new visual forms displayed in the Armory Show, though works included in the collection had been created by such artists as Duchamp, Matisse, Picabia, Brancusi, and Picasso. Duchamp's "Nude Descending a Staircase" was especially controversial; as was the case with many other of the paintings, the design did not coincide with the visual reality of the title. The controversy preceded the exhibition when it was moved to Chicago's Art Institute, where the gallery was crowded by 125,000 more visitors than attended the New York exhibition. Encouraged by faculty members, conservative students from the Art Institute burned Matisse and Brancusi in effigy. In Boston, reaction to the exhibit was considerably less violent. Art of a controversial nature in the U.S. had been previously related to pictorial subject matter, particularly nudity. After the Armory Show, however, *styles* of painting were being condemned as obscene. While changes incorporating new styles of expression did not immediately appear in American art works, the Armory Show had an unquestionable impact on subsequent trends in American art.[85]

The U.S. Customs Department played a major role in the dispersion of modern art by its controls on imports and by declarations that certain works were "merchandise" rather than art. Sculptures, particularly, were sometimes not classified as art and were denied duty-free admission as art objects. For example, in 1927 the sale of eight sculptures by Brancusi in the United States for about $10,000 was subject to government tariffs of $4,000. The Customs ruling was strengthened by the unanimous opinion of some art experts who declared that Brancusi's sculpture was not art because it "left too much to the imagination."[86]

An important legal case which challenged the power of the Customs Department to classify art works as utilitarian merchandise centered around Brancusi's bronze sculpture "Bird in Space"—popularly known as "Bird in Flight"—which was imported in 1928. The Treasury Department's restrictive definition of sculpture as imitations of natural objects in true proportions of length, breadth, and thickness was applied to Brancusi's work. Using the restrictive, official definition, Customs agents classified "Bird in Space" as a mere "manufacture of metal" and placed the work in the hardware category along with kitchen utensils and hospital supplies. Expert witnesses were called upon to support Brancusi's claim that the sculpture was indeed art, including Edward Steichen, the noted photographer who purchased the sculpture; sculptor Jacob Epstein; Frank Crowinshield, editor of *Vanity Fair*; Forbes Watson, editor of *The Arts*; Henry McBride, critic; and William Fox, Director of the Brooklyn Museum. The vigorous arguments of these recognized experts eventually convinced Judge Waite to declare that while the sculpture was characterized as a bird, it had "neither head nor feet nor feathers," yet "it is beautiful and symmetrical in outline . . . pleasing to look at and highly ornamental" and should be entitled to duty-free entry. Although the decision strengthened the acceptance of modern art in the United States, the academic, imitative standards by which sculpture had been customarily judged prevailed for another 30 years.[87]

Prior to the Armory exhibit, a group of American artists, variously called "The Eight" or "The Black Gang," endeavored to develop a style of art in keeping with the American experience. Everyday objects and humble experiences provided subject material for the group's artistic efforts, which were rendered in a realistic style. The controversial products of these innovative artists resulted in the use of the label "Ash Can School." The Eight, all of whom were in revolt against "the exclusiveness and privilege of the academies and against rules and regulations in general," included Robert Henri, John Sloan, William Glackens, George Luks, Everett Sloan, James Preston, Edward Davis, Charles Redfield, and A. Stirling Calder.[88] Despite their liberal and progressive social views, art produced by artists in the Ash Can School remained conservative, but it contained "a feeling for humanity in all its possible conditions."[89] However, native American artistic innovation and creativity were largely unnoticed. In 1925, when an official invitation was extended to the American government to send representative art to be exhibited at the Exposition des Arts Decoratifs in Paris, President Calvin Coolige responded with the following incredible statement: "America has no art to send."[90]

Censorship powers invested in the Customs Department were eventually eroded by the Smoots Amendment of 1930, which placed final arbitrations about obscenity in literature and art in the hands of district courts. Whenever a Customs' seizure was contested, a regular federal district court, with a jury trial, became the authority to decide whether questionable material was obscene or immoral.[91] Nudity remained the primary issue in these cases, and according to law, all pictured nudity was indecent. Therefore, in the early 1930s—despite a weakening of power— the Customs Bureau in New York easily banned a postcard containing a reproduction of a Sistine Chapel fresco by Michelangelo.[92]

The decade of the 1930s was a period of ferment for artists in many countries. While Russia and Germany were tightening controls on intellectual and artistic freedoms, artists in England and the United States were demanding even greater freedoms for artistic experimentation and further breaks with past traditions. As repression became more unbearable in communist and fascist countries, many European artists emigrated to the United States, where they often encouraged and stimulated native American artists to greater accomplishments. Less than 25 years after the burning in effigy of Matisse and Brancusi in Chicago, Moholy-Nagy was able to establish the New Bauhaus in the queen city of the Midwest. Modern art had at last arrived in the United States, although its continued progress was not without obstacles, and ironically, some of these restraints were created by the same government that had provided asylum for refugee artists.

During the Great Depression of the 1930s, the WPA Federal Art Project supported numerous American artists by funding the creation of 2,500 murals, 18,000 sculptures, and 100,000 paintings, all of which were used to decorate government buildings. Art which displayed un-American symbols—symbols related, however remotely, to communist ideology—was banned through the efforts of private individuals or government officials. Many offensive murals eventually disappeared under layers of whitewash or paint.

Private funds were used at times for the embellishment of public buildings; an example was Mexican artist Diego Rivera's mural on the wall of the Great Hall facing the doors in the RCA Building at Rockefeller Center. Nelson Rockefeller objected to a small head of Lenin which was depicted near the center of the Rivera fresco. Rockefeller had understood that Abraham Lincoln was the great leader who would be portrayed in the mural. When Rivera painted Lenin, Rockefeller wrote the artist as follows: "As much as I dislike to do so, I'm afraid we must ask you to substitute the face of some unknown man where Lenin's face now appears." Rivera refused to comply with the request, offering to balance the depiction of Lenin with a portrait of Lincoln. But this solution was unsatisfactory to Rockefeller, who promptly paid Rivera his full fee and fired him. Rivera's mural was then chipped off the wall and replaced by a painting which featured Lincoln and Thomas Edison. The new mural was executed in a more conventional manner by artist José Marie Sert.[93]

World War II and its aftermath increased the sensitivity of Americans to communist influences—both real and imaginary—and brought the U.S. State Department under attack for its part in the development of better cultural relations with foreign nations through the Cultural Cooperation Program. State Department difficulties arose when two exhibits entitled "Advancing American Art," which had been sent on tour for a five-year period to Europe and Latin America, aroused conservative art groups because of the "esthetically radical character" of the paintings.[94] Press and radio were used by these conservative art organizations to vigorously protest the exhibits, and adverse publicity about the Cultural Cooperation Program resulted in a flood of critical letters to congressmen. People complained about the use of public funds for art that was considered to be "Communist propaganda." Even President Truman expressed a negative opinion upon viewing one of Yasuo Kuniyoshi's works in the exhibit, entitled "Circus Girl," stating "If that is art, I'm a Hottentot." Influenced by criticism from Congress at appropriations bill hearings for the State Department, Secretary of State George Marshall and other federal officials expressed their doubts about the value of the traveling American art exhibits and finally recalled them. Paintings from the exhibits were eventually sold at a loss of approximately $44,000 and as war surplus to public institutions such as colleges, high schools, museums, and libraries.[95]

Politics entered into art in earnest via the efforts of U.S. Congressman George A. Dondero, a Republican representative from Michigan. Although Dondero had been active in closing the "Advancing American Art" exhibits, he became much more well known in 1949 for his censorship activities. Congressman Dondero prevented the continued showing of paintings in the "Gallery on Wheels," an exhibit assembled by Mr. and Mrs. Carroll Aumont "for the pleasure and therapeutic benefit of paraplegics at St. Alban's Naval Hospital on Long Island." Dondero attacked artists whose works were displayed in the exhibit, claiming that they were radicals who had taken advantage of "a great opportunity not only to spread propaganda, but to engage in espionage."[96] Dondero continued to assault modern art in speeches that were recorded in the *Congressional Record*. He even attacked such prestigious established museums as the New York Museum of Modern Art, the Art Institute of Chicago, the Fogg Art Museum at Harvard University, and national professional art organizations, such as Artists Equity Association. Dondero asserted that they displayed degenerate modern art.[97] He forcefully urged that the National Academy of Design, the American Artists Professional League, the Allied Artists of America, the Illustrators Society, and the American Watercolor Society expel members who belonged to the Communist Party. The crusading congressman also advocated that talented, patriotic members of these organizations be rewarded for their advocacy of academic art.[98]

Congressman Dondero's speeches in the *Congressional Record* bore titles such as: "Modern Art as Communist Heresy," "Communism in the Heart of American Art—What To Do About It," and "Modern Art Shackled to Communism." These speeches contained complaints that 17 of the 28 artists who loaned paintings for the "Gallery on Wheels" were mentioned by Martin Dies's House Committee on Un-American Activities as being subversive, that the Armory Show of 1913 was a Communist plot, and that various styles of art were vehicles for the destruction of America's cultural heritage. As a whole, Dondero's speeches expressed a "traditional hatred of modern art . . . harnessed to fear of Soviet aggression."[99] The following statements are examples of Dondero's repressive ideas:

Cubism aims to destroy by designed disorder.
Futurism aims to destroy by the machine myth.
Dadaism aims to destroy by ridicule.
Expressionism aims to destroy by aping the primitive and insane.
Abstractionism aims to destroy by the creation of brainstorms.
Surrealism aims to destroy by the denial of reason.[100]

In an interview with art critic Emily Genauer, Dondero further enlarged his ideas about art:

> Modern art is communistic because it is distorted and ugly, because it does not glorify our beautiful country, our cheerful and smiling people, our great material progress. Art which does not portray our beautiful country in plain, simple terms that everyone can understand breeds dissatisfaction. It is therefore opposed to our government, and those who create and promote it are our enemies.[101]

Objections to Dondero's attacks which were published by art editors and museum directors were summed up by Alfred Frankfurter in *Art News*:

> Only a great, generous, muddling democracy like ours could afford the simultaneous paradox of a congressman who tries to attack Communism by demanding the very rules which Communists enforce wherever they are in power, and a handful of artists who enroll idealistically in movements sympathetic to Soviet Russia while they go on painting pictures that would land them in jail under a Communist government.[102]

Citizens' anger over artistic works that were perceived as a mockery of traditional American views or that hinted at communist ideology and symbols was expressed through various conservative organizations, including the Veterans of Foreign Wars, American Legion, Sailors' Union, and Daughters of the American Revolution. Some of the objections of these organizations concerned the use of the color red in paintings. A letter to a California congressman written by C. E. Plant, Commander of a San Francisco American Legion Post, suggested that questionable murals be removed from San Francisco's Rincon Annex Post Office Building. Painted by Anton Refregier, the murals depicted California history in a manner deemed derogatory by "patriotic" citizens. Congressman Richard Nixon drafted a reply to Plant on July 18, 1949. Nixon's response stated, in part:

> I realize that some very objectionable art of a subversive nature has been allowed to go into Federal buildings in many parts of the country ... At such time as we may have a change in the administration and in the majority of Congress, I believe a committee should make a thorough investigation of this type of art in Government buildings with the view to obtaining removal of all that is found to be inconsistent with American ideals and principles.[103]

Unfortunately, Nixon's viewpoint reflected the thinking of the majority of Congress; Dondero found that few of his peers disapproved of his attacks on modern art. But one notable opponent was Senator Jacob Javits of New York, who said:

> The very point which distinguishes our form of free expression from Communism is the fact that modern art can live and flourish here without state authority or censorship and be accepted by Americans who think well of it.[104]

By 1953, a resolution to remove post office murals painted by Refregier was introduced in the House of Representatives by Herbert Scudder, Republican from Sebastopol, California. The resolution prompted a hearing by the House Committee on Public Works, which was chaired by Dondero. With enthusiastic backing from several patriotic and civic organizations, Congressman Scudder charged that paintings on the lobby walls of the 208-foot Rincon Post Office Annex were "artistically offensive and historically inaccurate" and that they reflected ignominiously on the character of the pioneers and the history of California.[105] The most controversial panels depicted the anti-Chinese riots of the 1870s, the Mooney case, the San Francisco waterfront strike of 1934, and the founding of the United Nations. In reaction to criticisms of the murals, vigorous public protests were lodged. The protests, which contained expressions of both dismay and disgust over the proposed destruction of the entire Refregier mural, came from private groups and societies and from professional organizations, including the three major San Francisco museums as well as the Museum of Modern Art in New York, the American Federation of Arts, and Artists' Equity. Some foreign art journals and the London *Times* even published protests. One German art journal noted:

> In a country which on paper has the best constitution in the world, today
> it is becoming difficult to live, to think, and to act according to the
> constitution.[106]

Determined, unified objections to Congressman Scudder's ideas from so many concerned persons and organizations led to the eventual shelving of the resolution and to the preservation of Refregier's murals. The struggle was a major victory for intellectual and artistic freedom.

Repeated attacks and repressive measures against modern art considered to be radical and subversive led the Museum of Modern Art in New York City to issue a *Manifesto on Modern Art*, which was endorsed by the Whitney Museum of American Art, and the Institute of Contemporary Art. The *Manifesto* affirmed the belief in freedom of expression in the arts and pointed out that:

> Almost all the art of the past one hundred and fifty years now generally
> accepted as good was originally misunderstood, neglected, or ridiculed
> not only by the public, but by many artists, critics, and museum
> officials.

The *Manifesto on Modern Art* also deplored "the reckless and ignorant use of political and moral terms in attacking modern art" and proclaimed that diversity in modern art was "a sign of vitality and freedom of expression inherent in a democratic society." According to the declaration of artistic freedom, freedom of expression for artists is absolutely necessary so that "art may grow, change, and serve the human spirit."[107]

Vigilance in matters relating to artistic freedom was especially important during the McCarthy decade, when politics of hate ran rampant and anti-communist hysteria was at its peak. The American Committee for Intellectual Freedom, founded in 1951, even considered cultural freedom "as whatever best served the interests of the United States government."[108] In addition, the federal government conducted a security check on artists before granting federal commissions for painting and sculpture to be placed in public buildings. In 1953, at the height of McCarthy's demagoguery, A. H. Berding, a chief spokesman for the United States Information Agency, declared that "our government should not sponsor examples of our creative energy which are non-representational." McCarthy's success at manipulating the fears of government officials were evident in Congressman Dondero's repressive activities against the arts, as discussed earlier, and in the activities of private individuals who were instrumental in arranging the cancellation of traveling exhibits sponsored by the United States Information Agency. One exhibit, entitled "Sports in Art," was organized by the American Federation of Arts and sponsored by *Sports Illustrated* magazine in May 1956. The show was well received and heavily attended in several cities before it arrived in Dallas, Texas, where opposition to works by artists perceived as pro-communist was sufficiently intense to obtain a cancellation of the show.[109] By the end of June 1956, the U.S.I.A. had cancelled another exhibit, entitled "100 American Artists of the Twentieth Century," because of charges that some of the artists were politically unacceptable and pro-communist. Despite President Dwight Eisenhower's declaration that "Freedom of the arts is a basic freedom, one of the pillars of liberty in our land . . . ," even tighter and more restrictive governmental control over government-sponsored traveling art exhibits was exercised. Oil paintings completed after 1917 were banned from the exhibits because of the possibility that modern artists might be communists or sympathetic to communist causes.[110]

Visual art of a traditional and representational nature was acceptable, while modern art was immediately vilified; artists were either suspected of communist leanings or of possessing a desire to corrupt viewers in one way or another. In *Painting in the Twentieth Century*, Haftmann explains this controversial position of modern art as:

... an entirely natural accompaniment of the painful processes by which a system of reference which has long been valid and has splendid achievements to its credit is being dissolved and replaced by a new and entirely different system of reference.[111]

Haftmann further remarks that the bitterness of the controversy "proves that the issues at stake are truly fundamental to our being."[112] Official acceptance of modern art may be found in a new, liberalized definition of creative works used by Customs Department agents in order to permit free duty for all fine art objects made of any material and in any form. Changes in the 1930 Tariff Act were instituted by Jacob K. Javits, Republican from New York, and by Frank Thompson, Jr., Democrat from New Jersey, who introduced identical bills in the United States Senate and House of Representatives.[113] President Eisenhower signed Public Law 86-262 as an amendment to paragraph 1629 of the Tariff Act of 1930, thereby making possible the importation of art designed for exhibitions on a duty-free basis. This change in the law helped to eliminate embarrassing court cases involving abstract sculptures, collages, lithographs, and primitive carvings that were not adequately covered by the outmoded guidelines previously used by the Customs Department.[114]

* * *

With the gradual acceptance of modern art and the reduction of hysteria about communist activities, attention turned once again to art works of an erotic nature. Definitions of the term "erotic" vary from one individual to another; Larry Rivers has stated "that if the individual is aroused by something, it's erotic,"[115] Dr. Alfred C. Kinsey, founder of the Institute for Sex Research, used the term in a broad context to designate an "evocation more or less related to sexual interest in the subject matter."[116] Sidney Janis explained that "while eroticism may be titillating, it has esthetic interest first and foremost."[117] Although the scope of this chapter does not include a discussion of the erotic in art, except where government action is concerned, two controversial exhibits are worthy of mention. One exhibit, organized and shown at the Sidney Janis Gallery in New York City, was called "Erotic Art '66." Advance publicity was designed to establish the show as a *cause célèbre* in anticipation of censorship, but, as critic John Canaday commented, the show failed in its purpose as it was "neither erotic nor art." Canaday further declared that the art works displayed had the same relationship with the erotic impulse as "a photograph of an airplane has to do with the principles of flight."[118]

The second major show was the "International Exhibit of Erotic Art" organized by Phyllis and Eberhard Kronhausen and shown first in Denmark and Sweden. The Kronhausens sent ten explicit paintings from Europe to Baltimore, Maryland, to test the reaction of federal authorities to interstate transportation of erotic works before the entire exhibit of 200 works was sent to New York City for display. Some of the artists whose works were sent in the trial run included Rembrandt, Grosz, Picasso, Chagall, Belman, and artists from Japan, China, and India. The United States Justice Department claimed that the ten paintings were obscene and requested permission to destroy them. The Baltimore Customs Department excluded the works from entry in November 1969. Despite these actions, Judge Frank A. Kaufman ruled in March 1970 that the paintings had "redeeming social value" and therefore could not be kept out of the country.[119]

During this same period, the President's Commission on Obscenity and Pornography spent nearly two million dollars to determine the effects of obscenity and pornography and to investigate accepted standards of decency in the United States. The study was accomplished through research by staff members of the Commission and by 40 federal contracts for investigations conducted in a variety of geographic areas—on the UCLA campus, in pornography book stores of Denmark, at colleges, in hospitals, and in prisons.[120] Data from the research and subsequent conclusions were presented on September 30, 1970, in a final, public report. The majority of the 18-member Commission advocated the repeal of 114 state and federal laws that forbade the importation, sale, or display of pornography to adults. The President's Commission on Obscenity and Pornography claimed:

> The laws are ineffective, are not supported by public opinion, and conflict with the right of each individual to determine for himself what books he wishes to read and what pictures or films he wishes to see.[121]

Former President Nixon, whose personal moral and ethical standards were subsequently revealed in the sordid Watergate case, promptly issued a statement rejecting the recommendations of the Commission as "morally bankrupt." Furthermore, Nixon urged each state to ban pornography.[122]

Widespread book censorship in the United States appears to be on the decline. While a few books do provoke restrictive actions in certain communities, most published works are generally either accepted or ignored by the public at large. However, pictured material treating the same topics discussed in printed works have not been accorded the same latitude of freedom. Several court cases have resulted because of public outrage over graphically illustrated pornography. On May 3, 1971, the U.S. Supreme Court reinforced controls on the importation of obscene material destined for commercial use. The Court declared that its 1969 decision that permitted importation of these materials for private use did not preclude governmental power "to remove obscene materials from the channels of commerce."[123] The "Nixon Court," more responsive and sympathetic toward complaints of Middle America, handed down decisions in five obscenity cases on June 21, 1973; those decisions affirmed the rights of states to regulate commerce in obscene materials and established revised guidelines for determining obscenity. Chief Justice Warren Burger noted that the development of national standards for obscene material is "an exercise in futility" and that the identification of local standards is equally frustrating. In the past, the prosecution had to prove the worthlessness of obscene material; now the *defendant* "has the responsibility to prove through expert testimony that the controversial work does have redeeming social value."[124] Although the climate of opinion toward erotica appears to be more tolerant than in the days of Comstockery, other incidents could be cited as examples of community censorship since the Supreme Court decision of 1973. It is obvious, therefore, that local government interference in the visual arts will continue. But artists must have the freedom to explore and display a variety of art styles and means of artistic expression. According to Oboler, "To deny the artist his audience on the ground that his work must be limited to outdated standards and moralities, which are neither standard nor moral, is itself immoral."[125]

SUMMARY AND CONCLUSIONS

Despite a decrease in restrictions on artists in recent decades, eternal vigilance is still necessary to prevent the erosion of freedoms that man has struggled to achieve through the years. Misfortunes of artists who attempt to create a personal, original view of reality in totalitarian states must be kept in mind so that similar problems can be prevented in a democratic society. Restrictive attitudes and practices of various organizations and individuals in the United States have demonstrated that totalitarian governments do not have a monopoly on the repression and censorship of the arts. An example is the violent, suspicious feelings that have from time to time been engendered by modern art in both the Soviet Union and in the United States. Both countries have labeled modern art as decadent—one called it "capitalistic" and the other called it "communistic."

Under totalitarianism, however, the government is the major purchaser of art—but only that art reflecting the accepted political ideology. In other words, the slogan "art for propaganda's sake" rather than "art for man's sake" has prevailed in anti-democratic societies. Artists who have managed to leave the Soviet Union in the last few years are not very optimistic about the future of non-conformist art in Russia. They feel that "official Russian propaganda has created a hate toward any art that might be called reactionary."[126] While changes in artistic expression have often developed slowly in the United States, they have eventually occurred. Controversies about modern art demonstrate how little some attitudes have changed since Plato recognized the influence of the fine arts.

From the preceding discussion of contemporary restrictions on art, it might be said that those persons who cannot appreciate a work of art often tend to label it as unacceptable, unpatriotic, or even obscene. Such restrictive attitudes have not allowed a full realization of the dimensions and intricacies of feeling that twentieth century works of art are capable of eliciting. Since much of modern art is abstract in style, a new dimension of expression has been added: each viewer is able to interpret new forms, colors, and shapes in the light of personal experiences, and he must "give more of himself" to many of these works of art. Philosopher Suzanne Langer has pointed out that the arts make us aware of subjective reality, feeling, and emotion, and that "every generation has its styles of feeling which are determined by many social causes, but *shaped* by artists." Through the arts, inward experiences are given form. Self-knowledge and insight into all phases of life and mind are increased by art because 1) art makes feeling apparent, objectively given so it may be reflected upon and understood; 2) practice and knowledge of any art provide outlets for human feelings, as language provides forms for sensory experiences and factual observation, and 3) art educates the senses to see nature in expressive form. In this way, the real world becomes symbolic of feeling and more personally significant.[127]

On the other hand, Langer reminds us that bad art is a corruption of feeling, which is a large factor in the irrationalism that dictators and demagogues exploit.[128] Thus, in order to become more autonomous beings, individuals must have unrestricted outlets for the expression of feelings. While some express themselves with the printed word, others prefer music, the dance, or the visual arts. Freedom of expression in all these modes of communication is essential if society is to benefit from the fruits of liberty.

FOOTNOTES

[1] Aniela Jaffe, "Symbolism in the Visual Arts," in Carl G. Jung, *Man and His Symbols* (London: Aldus Books, 1964), pp. 258-59.

[2] E. H. Gombrich, *The Story of Art*, 12th ed. (London: Phaidon Press, 1972), pp. 29-30.

[3] Suzanne Langer, *Philosophy in a New Key* (New York: New American Library, 1951), p. 135.

[4] Ralph Adams Cram, *The Catholic Church and Art* (New York: Macmillan, 1930), pp. 60-61.

[5] Clarence Crane Brinton, *A History of Western Morals* (New York: Harcourt Brace, 1959), pp. 226-27.

[6] Germain Bazin, *The Avant-Garde in Painting* (New York: Simon and Schuster, 1969), pp. 144-45.

[7] Richard Larter, "Police Action in Australia," *Studio* 179 (February 1970): 45.

[8] *New York Times*, 6 July 1949, sec. II, p. 19.

[9] Ralph Edward McCoy, "The ABC's of Illinois Censorship, 1965," *Illinois Libraries* 48 (May 1966): 372-77.

[10] "Chicago Public Library Bans Art Again," *Library Journal* 92 (1 May 1967): 1783.

[11] Charles H. Busha, *Freedom versus Suppression and Censorship* (Littleton, Colo.: Libraries Unlimited, 1972), p. 147.

[12] *Ibid.*, p. 76.

[13] American Federation of Arts, *Statement on Artistic Freedom*, adopted 22 October 1954.

[14] H. H. Arnason, *History of Modern Art* (New York: Abrams, 1968). p. 220.

[15] *Ibid.*, p. 222.

[16] *Ibid.*, p. 224.

[17] Herschel B. Chipp, comp., *Theories of Modern Art* (Berkeley: University of California Press, 1967), p. 457.

[18] Paul Sjoklocha and Igor Mead, *Unofficial Art in the Soviet Union* (Berkeley: University of California Press, 1967), pp. 44-45.

[19] *Ibid.*

[20] Eric Newton, "Art for Marx's Sake in Russia," *New York Times*, 19 October 1947, sec. VI, p. 8.

[21] Hellmut Lehmann-Haupt, "German Art Behind the Iron Curtain," *Magazine of Art* 44 (March 1951): 83.

[22] *Ibid.*

[23] *Ibid.*

[24] *Ibid.*, p. 84.

[25] Sjoklocha, *Unofficial Art*, p. 51.

[26] Chipp, *Theories of Modern Art*, pp. 457-59.

[27] *Art News* 53 (May 1954): 17.

[28] *New York Times*, 8 July 1962, p. 1.

[29] N. S. Khrushchev, "Khrushchev Lays Down the Line on the Arts," *New York Times Magazine*, 29 September 1957, p. 18.

[30] *New York Times*, 8 July 1962, p. 1.

[31] John Berger, *Art and Revolution* (New York: Pantheon, 1969), p. 19.

[32] Priscilla Johnson, *Khrushchev and the Arts: The Politics of Soviet Culture, 1962-1964* (Cambridge, Mass.: M.I.T. Press, 1970), p. 7.

[33] Sjoklocha, *Unofficial Art*, pp. 93-95.

[34] *Ibid.*, p. 96.

[35] *Censorship Today* 2 (October/November 1969): 54.

[36] Chipp, *Theories of Modern Art*, p. 460.

[37] *Ibid.*

[38] Pinchas Noy, "About Art and Artistic Talent," *International Journal of Psychoanalysis* 53 (1972): 243.

[39] "Art versus Politics," *Time*, 30 September 1974, p. 54.

[40] "Soviet Authorities Disrupt Outdoor Art Show," *Tampa Tribune*, 16 September 1974, sec. A, p. 9.

[41] "5,000 Visit Rare Russian Art Exhibit," *Sarasota Herald-Tribune*, 30 September 1974, sec. A, p. 8.

[42] Herbert Gold, "In Russian, 'To Be Silent' Is an Active Verb," *Playboy* 21 (October 1974), pp. 196, 200.

[43] *Ibid.*

[44] Eli M. Oboler, "Everything You Always Wanted To Know About Censorship," *American Libraries* 2 (February 1971): 194.

[45] Ralph E. Shikes, *The Indignant Eye; the Artist as Social Critic in Prints and Drawings, from the Fifteenth Century to Picasso* (Boston: Beacon Press, 1969), p. 255.

[46] Paul S. Boyer, *Purity in Print; the Vice-Society Movement and Book Censorship in America* (New York: Scribner's, 1968), p. 266.

[47] *New York Times*, 26 November 1926, p. 7.

[48] *New York Times*, 18 May 1927, p. 8.

[49] *New York Times*, 3 January 1927, p. 8.

[50] *The Contemporary Scene; A Symposium, March 28-30, 1952* (New York: Metropolitan Museum of Art, 1954), p. 52.

[51] *Ibid.*

[52] "Himmler's Fountain," *Time*, 28 October 1974, p. 33.

[53] Adolf Hitler, *Mein Kampf* (New York: Reynal and Hitchcock, 1939), pp. 352-62.

[54] "Forbidden Lehmbruck, 'Kneeling Woman'," *Life* 7 (October 1939): 55.

[55] Hitler, *Mein Kampf*, pp. 352-62.

[56] Donald Drew Egbert, *Social Radicalism and the Arts* (New York: Knopf, 1970), p. 658.

[57] Arnason, *History of Modern Art*, p. 318.

[58] Harold L. Nelson, *Freedom of the Press from Hamilton to the Warren Court* (Indianapolis: Bobbs-Merrill, 1967), p. ii.

[59] Morris Leopold Ernst, *Censorship: The Search for the Obscene* (New York: Macmillan, 1964), pp. 19-20.

[60] James C. N. Paul and Murray L. Schwartz, *Federal Censorship; Obscenity in the Mail* (Glencoe, Ill.: Free Press, 1961), p. 12.

[61] *Ibid.*, p. 341.

[62] Heywood Broun and Margaret Leech, *Anthony Comstock, Roundsman of the Lord* (New York: Boni, 1927), p. 79.

[63] Ernst, *Censorship*, p. 21.

[64] "The Art Forum: Letter from Louis Muhlstock," *Canadian Art* 4 (May 1947): 134.

[65] *New York Times*, 5 March 1927, p. 12.

[66] Harold L. Nelson, *Law of Mass Communications: Freedom and Control of Print and Broadcast Media* (Mineola, N.Y.: Foundation Press, 1969), p. 327.

[67] Terence J. Murphy, *Censorship: Government and Obscenity* (Baltimore, Md.: Helicon Press, 1963), p. 75.

[68] Morris Leopold Ernst, *To the Pure . . . A Study of Obscenity and the Censor* (New York: Viking, 1928), pp. 10-11.

[69] Robert W. Haney, *Comstockery in America; Patterns of Censorship and Control* (Boston: Beacon Press, 1960), p. 20.

[70] Hartford Montgomery Hyde, *A History of Pornography* (New York: Farrar, 1965), p. 191.

[71] Morris Leopold Ernst, *The Censor Marches On: Recent Milestones in the Administration of the Obscenity Law in the United States* (New York: Doubleday, 1940), p. 134.

[72] Anthony Comstock, *Traps for the Young*, edited by Robert Bremner (Cambridge: Belknap Press of Harvard University, 1967), p. xii.

[73] Broun, *Anthony Comstock*, p. 122.

[74] Haney, *Comstockery in America*, p. 20.

[75] Broun, *Anthony Comstock*, p. 224.

[76] Haney, *Comstockery in America*, p. 20.

[77] Anthony Comstock, "Morals versus Art," *People's Library* 12, No. 406 (New York: Ogilvie Co., 1888), p. 62.

[78] "One Hundred Years of *Town and Country*," *Life* 21 (December 1946): 90.

[79] Giselle d' Unger, "Censorship, U.S.," *American Art News* 11 (March 1913): 10.

[80] Kenneth Clark, *The Nude; A Study in Ideal Form* (Princeton, N.J.: Princeton University Press, 1956), p. 3.

[81] *Ibid.*, pp. 4-5.

[82] *Ibid.*, p. 8.

[83] "Newsworthy Nude; 'September Morn'," *American Artist* 21 (November 1957): 6.

[84] Curtis Daniel MacDougall, *Hoaxes*, 2nd ed. (New York: Dover, 1958), pp. 252-53.

[85] Harold Rosenberg, *The Anxious Object; Art Today and Its Audience* (New York: New American Library, 1966), pp. 150-57.

[86] *New York Times*, 24 February 1927, p. 23.

[87] Laurie Adams, *Art on Trial* (New York: Walker and Company, 1976), pp. 35-58.

[88] Barbara Rose, *American Art since 1900; A Critical History* (New York: Praeger, 1967), p. 12.

[89] *Ibid.*, p. 16.

[90] Edgar P. Richardson, *Painting in America* (New York: Crowell, 1965), p. 393.

[91] Paul Blanshard, *The Right to Read; The Battle Against Censorship* (Boston: Beacon Press, 1955), p. 46.

[92] Edwin A. Roberts, *The Smut Rakers; A Report in Depth on Obscenity and the Censors* (Silver Springs, Md.: National Observer, 1966), p. 73.

[93] *Time* magazine, *Time Capsule* (New York: Time-Life Books, 1933), pp. 186-87.

[94] Ralph Purcell, *Government and Art: A Study of American Experience* (Washington, D.C.: Public Affairs Press, 1956), pp. 84-85.

[95] *New York Times*, 18 May 1947, p. 53.

[96] Emily Genauer, "Still Life with Red Herring," *Harper's* 199 (September 1949), pp. 88-89.

[97] *New York Times*, 18 March 1952, p. 24.

[98] Carey McWilliams, *Witch Hunt: The Revival of Heresy* (New York: Little, Brown, 1950), pp. 121-33.

[99] "Dondero on the Left," *Newsweek* 33 (June 1949): 84.

[100] William Hauptmann, "The Suppression of Art in the McCarthy Decade," *Artforum* (8 October 1973): 48.

[101] Genauer, "Still Life," p. 89.

[102] Hauptmann, "Suppression of Art," p. 48.

[103] Matthew Josephson, "Vandals Are Here," *Nation* 177 (26 September 1953): 247.

[104] Hauptmann, "Suppression of Art," p. 48.

[105] Corliss Lamont, *Freedom Is As Freedom Does; Civil Liberties Today* (New York: Horizon, 1963), p. 197.

[106] Hauptmann, "Suppression of Art," p. 52.

[107] *Americana Annual* (New York: Americana Corp., 1951), p. 521.

[108] Barton J. Bernstein, ed., *Towards a New Past: Dissenting Essays in American History* (New York: Vintage Books, 1968), p. 339.

[109] Hauptmann, "Suppression of Art," p. 50.

[110] Charlotte Devree, "The United States Government Vetoes Living Art," *Art News* 55 (September 1956): 34-35.

[111] Werner Haftmann, *Painting in the Twentieth Century* (New York: Praeger, 1965), p. 15.

[112] *Ibid.*

[113] *New York Times*, 27 May 1958, p. 33.

[114] *Americana Annual*, 1960, p. 574.

[115] Phyllis Kronhausen and Eberhard Kronhausen, *Erotic Art* (New York: Bell, 1968), p. 41.

[116] Wardell B. Pomeroy, *Dr. Kinsey and the Institute for Sex Research* (New York: Harper and Row, 1972), p. 199.

[117] "Eros in Polyester; Show at Sidney Janis Gallery Called Erotic Art '66," *Newsweek* 68 (10 October 1966): 102.

[118] John Canaday, *Culture Gulch; Notes on Art and Its Public in the 1960s* (New York: Farrar, 1969), pp. 34-35.

[119] *Newsletter on Intellectual Freedom* (May 1970), p. 40.

[120] *Los Angeles Times*, 23 March 1970, p. 1.

[121] *Los Angeles Times*, 1 October 1970, p. 23.

[122] *Los Angeles Times*, 25 October 1970, sec. A, p. 1.

[123] *Los Angeles Times*, 4 May 1971, p. 1.

[124] Richard A. Blake, "Will Fig Leaves Blossom Again?" *America* (18 August 1973): 82-84.

[125] Eli M. Oboler, *The Fear of the Word: Censorship and Sex* (Metuchen, N.J.: Scarecrow, 1974), p. 121.

[126] Paul Gardner, "Art and Politics in Russia," *Art News* 73 (December 1974): 46.

[127] Suzanne Langer, *Problems of Art* (New York: Scribner's Sons, 1957), pp. 71-74.

[128] Suzanne Langer, *Philosophical Sketches* (Baltimore, Md.: Johns Hopkins Press, 1962), p. 84.

BIBLIOGRAPHICAL CONTROL OF EROTICA

Rebecca Dixon

Increasing attention is focused on problems of bibliographical control as libraries in the Western world attempt to acquire the publications of developing nations. Widely recognized is the fact that even so-called "national" bibliographies frequently fail to record all items published in any given country. Some publications issued by societies, institutions, and government agencies—works not distributed through traditional book-trade channels—are not regularly listed upon publication in bibliographies, if they are, in fact, ever recorded. The uncertainty of whether any one bibliography actually reflects the total publishing output of a given country is of great concern.

Franz Kaltwasser has discussed some of the formidable difficulties faced by librarians and bibliographers in their attempts to achieve bibliographical control; he defined universal bibliographical control as "the systematic handling of bibliographical data from the time a book is printed anywhere in the world until its cataloging by libraries in many places. . . . "[1] Kaltwasser outlined some of the problems in this systematic handling, including the sources of information, the standardization of the bibliographic form to permit the exchange of information, and the organization required to permit as rapid an exchange as possible.[2] Efforts are underway to bring some of these problems under control. Such projects as the Library of Congress's experiment with cataloging-in-publication and the standardization of bibliographic elements to permit the exchange of cataloging and bibliographic information in machine-readable form are preliminary to the achievement of a larger bibliographic goal. Although much remains to be accomplished in relation to maintaining records of the output of publications, some groups have also directed their efforts to similar bibliographic problems with non-print materials.

Contemporary efforts in the quest for elusive universal bibliographical control notwithstanding, there is at least one body of material which has so far evaded many of these efforts and will, perhaps, always do so. This body of material is one which can be labeled "erotica." While definitions of the term "erotica" may vary—and while the classification of individual items in this subject category is rather subjective—for the purpose of this discussion, erotica is defined as that body of material produced for the purpose of arousing sexual response and which some scholars and much of the general public refer to as "pornography." The Kronhausens have distinguished between "pornography" and "erotic realism" in their book *Pornography and the Law.*[3] While such distinctions could be useful, in terms of bibliographical control many publications that could be categorized as erotic realism have historically been grouped with erotica for censorship purposes and must be considered similarly in reference to bibliographical control.

As defined here, erotica encompasses a wide range of material. Besides the sexually explicit literature which can be labeled as "erotic realism," there are publications which have been produced *sub rosa* over the centuries for the amusement and titillation of readers who could gain access to it. The contemporary erotic pulp market includes 1) many reprints of these earlier works, 2) translations of titles from other languages, and 3) modern versions of similar sexual themes.

Photographic processes have had a significant influence on the production of contemporary erotica. While many of the earlier erotic novels were illustrated by artists of some competence, photographs of sexual activity are increasingly being used to illustrate contemporary publications (described on covers occasionally as "Illustrated from Life"), even though the illustrations often have little relevance to the text. Photography has further contributed to an increase in the number of magazines and books devoted strictly to pictures of nude females and males and to sexual activity. These graphic materials, along with sexually explicit films, have been the chief objects of many censorship efforts. Thus, the scope of erotica extends beyond printed material; attempts to achieve bibliographical control of it involve efforts with non-print media as well.

The problem of achieving bibliographical control of erotica is complex; many persons are far more concerned about the control of erotica in ways other than bibliographically. However, in recognition of the fact that erotica is indeed produced, the concerns of some librarians are related to recording what has been published or produced and to the standardization of bibliographic elements so that this information can be transmitted. Employing Kaltwasser's definition of bibliographical control, the first matter to be considered is the systematic recording of erotic publications at their *sources*. To consider this matter, one must first be aware of the circumstances under which erotica has been produced and the nature of its bibliographic elements which must be recorded. Secondly, problems relating to the cataloging of erotica in libraries must be recognized.

The history of erotica's bibliographical control is inseparable from the reluctance on the part of most librarians to collect sexually oriented literature. Attempts to compile a comprehensive retrospective or current bibliography of erotic literature using standard bibliographic sources such as national bibliographies and catalogs of major libraries usually produce only some of the better known classics of erotica such as Apuleius Madaurensis' *The Golden Ass*, Ovid's *Art of Love*, and Aretino's *Sonnets*. These catalogs and bibliographies do not include much of the erotic literature produced, especially that which was published in the eighteenth, nineteenth, and twentieth centuries. Such is the case because most of this material has been published *sub rosa*. In addition, librarians in *publicly* supported institutions have apparently avoided the collection of erotic literature. Moreover, they have often denied having erotica when they have been reluctant recipients of it as gifts. Another factor to take into account is that when erotic literature is published *sub rosa*, publishers disguise themselves, printing their publications privately for distribution to a small group of consumers. In turn, consumers have access to underground sources only because they seek them. Consequently, erotic literature has been collected primarily by private persons. However, some scholars are grateful that at least a few bibliophiles were interested in recording their private holdings of erotica, because relatively few collections have remained intact after the deaths of owners. Heirs to such collections occasionally burn the embarrassing evidence of what might be considered a "perverted" interest. More frequently, collections of erotica are sold at auction to other private collectors or scattered by other methods. Though a few of these collections of erotica have found their way into libraries, not all recipient libraries have been willing to acknowledge such holdings or to devote the time needed to catalog them.

Several bibliographies of erotic literature appeared in the latter part of the nineteenth century; they provide a record for the contemporary world of what existed at that time. The first such work, appearing in 1861, was Jules Gay's *Bibliographie des ouvrages relatifs à l'amour, aux femmes, au mariage, indiquant les auteurs de ces ouvrages, leurs éditions, leur valeur et les prohibitions ou condamnations dont certains d'entre eux ont été l'objet* (Paris: Chez Jules Gay, éditeur). Three more editions of this bibliography were published, the last work appearing after the death of the editor. For the most part, the descriptive information contained in Gay's bibliography is minimal, and the work's accuracy and scholarship have also been questioned. However, Gay's work represents the only nineteenth-century record of French-language erotica.

In 1875, the first German bibliography of erotic literature was published. It was Hugo Nay's *Bibliotheca Germanorum Erotica* (Leipzig: Privatdruck). Two years later, the initial volume of the first English bibliography of erotica appeared: Pisanus Fraxi's *Index Librorum Prohibitorum: Being Notes Bio-Biblio-Icono-graphical and Critical, on Curious and Uncommon Books* (London: Privately printed). Pisanus Fraxi was a pseudonym used by Henry Spencer Ashbee, a collector of erotic literature. The second volume of Ashbee's bibliography, *Centuria Librorum Absconditorum*, was issued in 1879; the third, *Catena Librorum Tacendorum*, appeared in 1885. These three works comprise the most comprehensive bibliography of erotic literature available today. The contemporary significance of Ashbee's bibliographies was reaffirmed by the reprinting of these volumes in 1962. The original volumes were issued only in limited numbers (*Bibliography of Prohibited Books*, by Pisanus Fraxi, Introduction by G. Legman. New York: Jack Brussel, Publisher). Each volume of this bibliography is indexed separately, critical notes in the work are profuse, and Ashbee delighted in quoting from the original texts, no matter what the language. The bibliography includes erotic literature published in several languages, as well as in various editions and translations of different titles. For ease of use, the bibliography leaves much to be desired. In a subject area in which complete bibliographical control is nearly impossible, Ashbee's bibliography of erotica stands out as one of the most comprehensive reference tools.[4]

The first volume of the fourth edition of Jules Gay's *Bibliographie des ouvrages relatifs à l'amour, aux femmes, au mariage* . . . was published in 1894 (Paris: K. Lemonnyer, éditeur; Chez Gilliet, Libraire); the second volume appeared in 1897; the third was published in 1899; and the fourth was issued in 1900. This final volume (Lille: Stephane Bécour, Libraire) consists of an alphabetical list (by both author and title) of anonymous works arranged in sections according to the original language of publication. These bibliographies, issued in the late nineteenth century, constitute a record for erotica published up to the turn of the century. Virtually non-existent are bibliographies with extensive listings of works published in the twentieth century. In 1913, a complete catalogue of the Enfer collection of the Bibliothèque Nationale was issued (*L'Enfer de la Bibliothèque Nationale.* Paris: Bibliothèque des Curieux). Compiled by Guillaume Apollinaire, Fernand Fleuret, and Louis Perceau, it contained 930 entries. In 1930, Louis Perceau alone compiled a two-volume work, *Bibliographie du roman érotique au XIXe siècle* . . . (Paris: Georges Fourdrinier, éditeur), which includes prose writings chiefly in French, published from the nineteenth century through 1929.

In 1912, the first volume of *Bibliotheca Germanorum Erotica and Curiosa* (München: Verlegt bei Georg Müller) was issued in Munich. It was edited by Hugo Nay and Alfred N. Gotendorf. The eighth volume was completed in 1914, and a ninth supplementary volume, edited by Paul Englisch, was issued in 1929. This third edition of Hugo Nay's bibliography is the most comprehensive available bibliography of German erotica.

The *Registrum Librorum Eroticorum* . . . , compiled by Alfred Rose under the pseudonym Rolf S. Reade, was published in 1936 (London: Privately printed for subscribers). As Alfred Rose died before his compilation was published, the final bibliography was edited by W. J. Stanislas. It contains 5,061 entries, many of which are works listed in Ashbee's work and in other bibliographies; however, it does record erotica supposedly contained in the collection of the British Museum.

In the work *Catalogi Librorum Eroticorum: A Critical Bibliography of Erotic Bibliographies and Book Catalogues* (London: Cecil & Amelia Woolf, 1964), Terence J. Deakin lists and briefly describes 78 bibliographies of erotic literature. The catalog is unique in that it provides an indication of the location of listed works. Only one of the listed bibliographies indicates coverage of contemporary literature, but it has not yet been published. According to Deakin, Alan Hull Walton's *Bibliographia sexualis* was to have been published in 1963, covering in three volumes erotic literature and scientific works related to sex from antiquity to the present day. The Institute for Sex Research Library at Indiana University has identified in its collection 44 of the bibliographies listed by Deakin and a few others as well, even though Deakin indicates that only three titles are included in the Institute's collection.

As most of the books listed in these bibliographies were not included in institutional libraries at the time the lists were compiled, the bibliographers must have been able to prepare their catalogs by virtue of physical access to private collections—their own or those of other collectors. Although the bibliographers probably had seen most of the books they listed, they did occasionally refer to editions of which they had merely heard, thus lending some degree of inaccuracy to the reporting. An unfortunate degree of repetition of error is contained in some bibliographies and histories of erotica; consequently, contemporary scholarship relating to such literature is made more difficult.

There is no certainty as to the comprehensiveness of these bibliographies relative to the extent of publishing of their day. Scholars will probably never know how much erotic literature has been lost forever. Censorship records show that at least some erotic works have been purposely destroyed. Some editions of works listed in these bibliographies apparently do not exist today. Fortunately, Ashbee willed his collection of approximately 15,000 titles to the British Museum. (Although the British Museum reportedly was reluctant to accept the Ashbee erotica collection, it apparently did so because a substantial portion of Ashbee's collection consisted of all the editions and translations of *Don Quixote*.) A further complication involves editions of erotic works extant which are not recorded in any existing bibliographies. Some of these can be identified in extant catalogs of the few publishers and printers. However, these bring up the topic of the circumstances surrounding the publication of erotica, the methods by which bibliophiles acquired their works, and the identification of the bibliographic elements needed to provide bibliographical control in this field.

Steven Marcus comments as follows in *The Other Victorians*:

> Pornography is, for example, the most disorderly kind of writing; not
> only are the contents of pornographic writing "disorderly," but the
> entire field, from the volumes themselves through all the circumstances
> of publication and collection, amounts to a veritable model of disorgan-
> ization and absence of control—it is, to be sure, a "dirty" and chaotic
> state of affairs.[5]

Compilers of some bibliographies of erotica did not use their actual names on
title pages of their publications. For instance, Hugo Nay used the name Hugo Hayn;
Jules Gay listed himself as M. Le C. D.'I***; and Ashbee, as already noted, identified himself as Pisanus Fraxi. This is a noteworthy characteristic of the literature
itself. For obvious reasons, the authors of many of these works did not wish to be
identified. This attitude was also prevalent among publishers and printers of erotic
material, so sexually oriented works were often privately printed, sometimes by
publishers or printers of more acceptable publications. These persons deliberately
disguised their identities by using false imprints, pseudonyms, false places of publication, and false publishing dates. A title with a Brussels, 1778, imprint could very
well have been published in London in 1860.

Some publishers were so involved in the publication of erotica and had such a
substantial output that one can often tentatively identify their products as being
from a single firm, even though the actual publisher cannot be verified by
imprints. In fact, one of the challenging aspects of cataloging erotic literature
involves deciphering a coding system, the key to which has been lost and may never
be retrieved. Scholars who deal with erotic literature, as well as analytical bibliographers, learn to recognize subtleties in typefaces, printing plates, and various decora-
tive treatments of the title pages which were customarily used by certain printers.
In the case of retrospective or historical materials, it has also been possible at times
to identify the various imprints associated with one individual. Rarely did a publisher or printer openly acknowledge association with such publications, and since
works were not copyrighted, there was also a high degree of theft among publishers.
Printing plates were at times stolen or sold, and new editions were published that
can scarcely be distinguished from earlier ones. In other cases, texts of some stories
were stolen and titles changed so that earlier works could be reissued by a different
printer. This practice resulted in a variety of editions of essentially the same work;
thus, variant editions of such works comprise the bulk of eighteenth and nineteenth
century extant erotica. Identification of such instances, however, requires not just
a simple recording of the bibliographic elements on the title page but a careful reading of the text itself.

Publishers' and dealers' catalogs are sometimes useful as bibliographic records
for the verification of variant editions of erotic works. In the 1880s, H. S. Nichols,
who identified himself as a "second-hand and new bookseller" at the Gladstone
Buildings, Church Street, Sheffield, issued monthly catalogs of books for sale.
Among these were erotic novels and the pseudo-scientific sex works issued during
the latter part of the nineteenth century. Some works were identified by Nichols
as parts of private collections which he was disseminating; many were editions of
classical erotica. In the early twentieth century, Nichols was identified as a publisher
who issued publications in New York. The circumstances of Nichols' move to the

United States are not clear; however, books bearing his imprint and a 1938 catalog of his publications are available. One can only speculate that Nichols was a printer for some of the erotic works that he sold in the 1880s. Nichols is believed to have also printed Ashbee's bibliography.

Publishers who printed erotic works occasionally included titles of perennially issued works in lists that appeared at the end of regularly issued publications. One such firm that followed this practice was J. Lemonnyer of Rouen, publisher of the first volume of the fourth edition of Jules Gay's bibliography. The works listed in these catalogs appended to books are rarely among the most erotic ever written, but nevertheless, they are titles which, at the time of their publication, would usually be classified with erotic literature because of their general subject matter.

In 1887, Isidore Liseux, a Paris publisher, issued his *Catalogue Annoté des éditions publiées par Isidore Liseux du Ier Février 1875 au 31 Mars 1887*. He listed 118 titles, many of which are classics of erotic literature such as Aretino's *Sonnets*. Three series are represented among these titles: Petite Collection Elzévirienne, Musée secret du Bibliophile, and Nouvelle Collection Elzévirienne. In this catalog and on the publications themselves, Liseux departed from the tradition somewhat by identifying himself as a publisher of erotica.

One of the more prolific publishers of erotica at the turn of the century was Charles Carrington. His publishing enterprise flourished primarily in Paris from the 1890s until about 1915, issuing works written both in English and in French. His publications included reprints of classic erotica, pseudo-scientific sex studies, and novels with sado-masochistic themes. Charles Carrington, who used at least two pseudonyms, has been tentatively identified as the author of several of the latter. Documentation exists of his publications in the form of a compilation of advertising brochures, descriptive title pages, and catalogs of Carrington publications entitled *Bibliotheca Carringtoniensis*, a collection put together in the 1930s by a collector or dealer. Carrington used at least two other imprints, but a number of his works were issued with the Carrington imprint. Title pages of many of his publications are distinctive and can be easily recognized even though the Carrington imprint might have been omitted.

In the 1920s, "Bulletin Périodique des Publications Nouvelles" was issued by the Bibliothèque des Curieux, 4 Rue de Furstenberg, Paris. The publisher was Georges Briffaut, who also published several series, including Les Maitres de l'Amour, Le Coffret du Bibliophile, and Les Chroniques Libertines.

Publishers of some of the pseudo-scientific sex studies which flourished in the early twentieth century were less hesitant to advertise their works. A number of catalogs of these publishers have survived, and some of the titles listed in them are also recorded in various published library catalogs, such as those of the Library of Congress. The authors of these works, however, were frequently disguised; in fact, several different writers appear to have used the same pseudonym (e.g., Jacobus X . . .).

The circumstances under which erotica collectors and bibliophiles of yesterday acquired their collections is not precisely known. Undoubtedly, an underground information system existed among collectors, as is the case today. That erotic manuscripts were circulated privately among collectors is a well-established fact. Though some manuscripts may later have been published, many never found their way into print and have quite possibly been lost altogether. Furthermore, some booksellers issued catalogs which included erotica under the headings *Facetiae* or

Curiosa. These headings also included pseudo-scientific sex studies and curious anthropological works.

While much information relating to authors and publishers of erotica will never be known, several sources provide limited facts about the history of erotica publishing. Histories of pornography and records of censorship cases reveal some information on the subject. But the most detailed information is contained in the *Bilderlexikon der Erotik*, Volume 2 (Wein: Verlag für Kulturforschung, 1928-31), which deals with art and literature, and in two books by Paul Englisch: *Geschichte der erotischen Literatur* (Stuttgart und Berlin: Julius Puttman, 1927) and *Irrgarten der Erotik* (Leipzig: Lykeion, Kulturwissenschaftliche Verlagsgesellschaft, mbH, 1931). Although these works are not limited to German erotica, they add considerable knowledge about the publication in Germany of many erotic titles issued in other languages. These works are neither indexed nor organized in a manner which facilitates ease of use. However, persons with a reading knowledge of German and a bit of perseverance will find them very useful for scholarship in this field.

Insofar as bibliographical control is concerned, scholars and other persons are dependent on the few collectors and bibliophiles who had an interest in compiling a list of their own holdings of erotic materials. There has been no systematic handling of bibliographic information for erotica, as measured against Kaltwasser's definition of bibliographical control—from the time a book was printed anywhere in the world until it is cataloged in many places. Furthermore, records for what has been published since 1930 are extremely sketchy. Most of the collections are still in private hands. The Ashbees of the contemporary world may be at work, but they have yet to produce a comprehensive erotica bibliography.

From the 1930s to the early 1960s, a number of brochures and small catalogs appeared which advertised new erotic titles and reprints of older works. These catalogs were issued from firms such as Falstaff Books, Book Awards, Book Gems, and Arrowhead Books. Scholars in the field have associated these publishers and at least 40 others with Samuel Roth, the subject of a 1957 U.S. Supreme Court case [Roth-Alberts], which provided legal guidelines for the identification of obscene works for many years (i.e., whether the dominant theme of the material, taken as a whole, appeals to prurient interests in the average person in light of contemporary community standards). Among Roth's publications is the *American Aphrodite: A Quarterly for the Fancy Free*, which first appeared in 1951 and continued to be published for at least 20 issues. This publication was advertised as America's first privately published magazine. The Golden Hind Press of New York, tentatively identified with Samuel Roth, advertised 31 books for sale in one of its catalogs. During the same period, Falstaff Press of New York (not to be confused with Falstaff Books mentioned earlier), advertised a sizeable number of titles, among them pseudo-anthropological works similar to earlier pseudo-medical books.

The Miller Brothers, a publisher or a distributor of books in New York in the 1930s, is also identified with the name Golden Hind Press. The Millers were not actually brothers, nor was the name Miller. The true identity of the publisher is not positively known, but the firm produced pirated editions of *The Perfumed Garden*, *White Stains*, and *The Town Bull.* Its editions were poorly printed and often poorly bound. The Miller Brothers firm reportedly went out of business after its owner was sentenced to federal prison. Another publisher of this period, who used the name Percy Shostac, apparently worked with the Miller Brothers for a time, during which the quality of the latter's printing improved. Shostac separately published editions of *Grushenka* and *The Prodigal Virgin.*

But much of the erotica of the 1930s existed in the form of manuscripts commissioned by wealthy individuals through booksellers or dealers. Many of these manuscripts are reported to have been written by now-famous authors such as Henry Miller and Anaïs Nin, although that fact is now denied by these authors. Copies were made of these manuscripts, which some booksellers or dealers then sold to special customers. Thus the tradition of the underground market remained strong in the 1930s. Too, some erotic manuscripts have undoubtedly been published under different titles in subsequent years.

The Olympia Press, a Paris publishing house, produced a large number of erotic novels in English under various trade names in the 1950s and 1960s. Under the directorship of Maurice Girodias, The Olympia Press published the Traveller's Companion series, Ophelia Press, Mediterranean Press, and others. Girodias followed the tradition of his father, Jack Kahane, who published under the firm name Obelisk Press in the 1930s, and, initially, Girodias's novels were brought illegally into the United States. The authors of some of the Olympia novels are now well-known writers, most notably, Henry Miller and Vladimir Nabokov. Girodias had a crew of writers in his employ who collaboratively produced many additional titles under a variety of pseudonyms. The accurate identification of the true authors of some of the titles issued in these series is almost impossible, but a record of The Olympia Press's publications does exist in a series of catalogs issued during the 1950s and into the early 1960s. In addition, copies of these novels are contained in some library collections, and they will probably be cataloged, eventually. Girodias is reported to have collaborated with Jean Jacques Pauvert in his early days; Pauvert continued to publish in the 1970s in France.

In the 1960s, Ralph Ginzburg advertised an erotic novel, *The Housewife's Handbook on Selective Promiscuity*, and a magazine entitled *Eros.* Ginzburg mailed his advertisements from locations that had names with sexual connotations, and he was eventually arrested and charged with pandering (defined as the appeal to prurient interests through advertising—a new concept in terms of obscenity rulings).

The liberalization of opinions and attitudes which has taken place in the last decade or so has resulted in an increased degree of bibliographical control for some erotic literature. Literature which might be classified as "erotic realism," such as the novel *Portnoy's Complaint*, is currently being published by well-established firms. Furthermore, major publishers have begun to reprint paperback editions of erotic classics such as *Memoirs of a Woman of Pleasure* (Putnam, 1963). These titles are copyrighted, discussed in traditional library book review media, purchased by a number of libraries, cataloged by the Library of Congress, and thus recorded bibliographically in a relatively systematic fashion.

Emphasis on the Supreme Court's criteria for what can be excluded from the obscenity category (works of "socially redeeming value" and of "scientific, artistic, or literary merit") has resulted in an increase in the publication of pseudo-scientific sex studies, purported histories of censorship and erotica, and other thinly disguised pieces which facilitate the production of sexually explicit literature and/or graphic materials. Such works as *Sex, Censorship and Pornography* by Donald H. Gilmore (San Diego, Calif.: Greenleaf Classics, 1968) usually bear a copyright date and are therefore deposited in the Library of Congress. (The Library of Congress has made available printed catalog cards for some of these titles.) These works are not substantially different from the pseudo-scientific titles which flourished at the turn of the century and were listed under the subject heading *Curiosa* along with other erotica of the day. Some of these contemporary works are advertised in *Publishers Weekly*, listed in *Books in Print*, and undoubtedly purchased by a number of libraries. The zenith in such publishing was probably reached in the production by Greenleaf Classics of *The Illustrated Presidential Report of the Commission on Obscenity and Pornography*, for which illustrations were neither authorized nor contemplated by the Commission, which was unaware of Greenleaf's publication plan. In 1974, the U.S. Supreme Court upheld a lower court's conviction of William Hamling and others for mailing 55,000 copies of a brochure advertising the *Illustrated Presidential Report* . . . . The Court held that the brochure was obscene because it contained pictures portraying heterosexual and homosexual intercourse, sodomy, and a variety of deviate sexual acts.

Some major paperback publishers (Ace, Bantam, etc.) have begun to produce sex-oriented materials of a pseudo-biographical nature (e.g., *The Happy Hooker* by Xaviera Hollander). Though seldom well-written or well-documented, these works provide the only information available on some rather esoteric aspects of contemporary sexuality. Publishers such as Ace, Bantam, and Avon advertise their books in *Publishers Weekly*; consequently, some of these contemporary sex-oriented works are being documented in national bibliographical tools. In regard to the use of pseudonyms and to methods of distribution, these sexually oriented publications share characteristics of typical erotica despite their legitimization. However, acquisition of some of these works through regular book-trade channels poses a rather difficult problem for libraries. Publishers do not respond well to single-copy orders; they are better organized to supply books to distributors of sex-oriented materials.

In recent years the types of erotica available to consumers have changed in form. As for the forms still subject to legal reprisals, detection of what is being produced and by whom is extremely difficult. Erotica publishing has become a minor industry, but a second one also exists, and it deals predominantly in sex-oriented materials distributed through channels different from those used by the major industry. Products of the secondary publishing industry often are not dated, so that they can remain on the market for as long as sales warrant. The predominant format of books produced by these publishers is the soft-cover "pulp," which was initially described as "soft-core pornography." This term was used because works of fiction, though dominated by a sexual theme, stopped short of deliberate, explicit description of sexual activity; use of common "four-letter" words was also avoided. Since about 1967, however, "soft-core pornography" has been replaced in the erotica market by "hard-core pornography," which devotes exclusive attention to explicit descriptions of sexual activities. In earlier periods, such material would have been distributed underground rather than through commercial channels.

Publishers of this secondary industry distribute their works through several channels; some become their own distributors, often using the direct-mail outlet. Other publishers deal with a small number of distributors who handle sex-oriented materials exclusively. A few publishers supply major book distributors, who handle only a small percentage of sex-oriented publications. The retail outlet for these distributors is generally the "adult" bookstore, where admission is usually limited to persons over eighteen years of age. Retail stores that specialize in pornography usually acquire shipments of materials with a guarantee that unsold items can be returned. Publishers then sell unsold works as remainders, often through dealers employing direct-mail outlets.

Some of the publishers which comprise this secondary industry organized themselves as the American Publishers and Distributors Association in the late 1960s to provide support and legal expertise to members involved in censorship legislation and obscenity cases. In 1970, the Association began to publish the *APDA Newsletter*, "to champion the causes of our industry."

Some of the publications of the secondary industry contain copyright information; however, most of them are not copyrighted and not routinely deposited in the Library of Congress. Those that are deposited are not cataloged and are quite likely destroyed. Furthermore, other libraries probably do not collect them.[6] *Publishers Weekly* and *Paperbound Books in Print* regularly list the pseudo-scientific publications of major trade-book publishers. The location of bibliographic information about these publications or the addresses for representatives of the secondary industry, though, have often been impossible to obtain until recently. Some of the publishers in the secondary erotica industry, such as Brandon House, Holloway House, Grove Press, Greenleaf Classics, and a few others that have operated for a reasonably long time, now list some of their publications in book-trade bibliographies. The more recent publishers, many of which enter and go out of business rather rapidly, do not presently record their works in this manner. Few of these publishers issue catalogs of in-print titles.

The 1973 *Publishers' Trade List Annual* (PTLA) contained catalogs of the publications of Brandon House, Barclay House, Academy Press, Sexcope Press, Socio-Library Books (all subsidiaries of Parliament News in Los Angeles), Grove Press, and a few listings for Holloway House. But many other producers of erotica were not listed, including Surrey House (San Diego), Aquarius 7 (North Hollywood), Orpheus Classics (a subsidiary of Carlyle Communications in New York), Star Distributors (New York), Eros Publishing (Wilmington), and Greenleaf (San Diego). Works published by Carlyle Communications are advertised in *Publishers Weekly* and are listed in *Books in Print*, as are publications from Greenleaf in San Diego, a subsidiary of Reed Enterprises. Olympia Press, which has been publishing the Traveller's Companion series in the United States, is also not listed in *Publishers' Trade List Annual*. Even those publishers whose erotic works are included in *PTLA* do not appear to maintain extensive records of what they have published; some of them have been known to deny knowledge of the existence of titles bearing their imprint within two years of the date of publication.

Publishers of erotic pulps often include lists of in-print titles at the end of the novels themselves, but these firms obviously do not submit such lists to *PTLA*. Furthermore, one can conclude that, even if these firms were to be solicited for listings to be included in *Books in Print* or other bibliographic tools, many publishers would be unable to cooperate because of lack of staff, lack of records, and the uncertainty of continuation in business. A visit by this writer to several "adult" bookstores resulted in a list of new publishers which produced works in 1974, firms not previously listed in *PTLA*. Among them were Valley Circle Publishing Company (North Hollywood), as well as Windsor Library Press and Chelsea Library Press of Manchester Publications (San Diego), all of which could be new firms as of 1974—or they may be firms that have changed names for existing operations. (Illustrating the instability in this publishing area, the Institute for Sex Research Library once received a phone call from a person who was seeking assistance in locating a publisher for his manuscript. He had written to all the publishers of works included in a local "adult" bookstore but had found that all of them had gone out of business. However, the local erotica outlet had no 1974 publications in stock when the writer checked that year.)

In its study of the erotica industry, the Commission on Obscenity and Pornography surveyed secondary industry publishers, and with about a 50 percent return from the survey, the Commission was able to determine that 2,750 new titles were issued in one year from 50 percent of the publishers.[7] Generalizing these statistics to the entire industry (if there are indeed 5,500 titles being published each year in this secondary erotica industry), only a relatively small percentage of the titles produced are being recorded or systematically recorded from their date of publication. It also follows that they are certainly not being cataloged by libraries in many places.

Contemporary publishers of erotica appear to advertise their products to a greater degree than their predecessors, although this observation would be difficult to prove. Relatively few persons or libraries save or collect advertising materials; however, the Institute for Sex Research Library not only keeps the advertising which it receives, but it also accepts donations of collections of catalogs and ads acquired and donated by individuals. Some of the advertising in the Institute's collection dates back to the earlier periods of publishing. A large amount of contemporary advertising for erotica originates from distributors rather than from the publishers themselves, and the distributors deal in a variety of wares. These wares may include paperback novels, occasional hardbound novels, "girlie" magazines, nudist publications, pseudo-nudist magazines, male nudist magazines, stag films, and pseudo-medical sex aids. A large mail-order business which offers a wide variety of such sex merchandise has flourished in Los Angeles and in New York for several years. The first to note perhaps is that of David S. Alberts, defendant in the previously mentioned Roth-Alberts case. Alberts has operated as the Male Merchandise Mart as well as with other names. He was selling "obscene" books and photographs when arrested for a violation of the California penal code.[8]

Parliament News, publisher of Brandon Books and others, has been a major distributor for "girlie" magazines and nudist magazines for a number of years. Parliament News is located in the Los Angeles area. Another major distributor of these magazines is John Amslow & Assoc. Even though this is not his true name, "Amslow" and his like-named associates have subsidiaries that use an even wider variety of names. The connection is apparent when one compares the physical appearance of the advertising and notes the use of identical addresses, even though the latter can be confusing, since published addresses change back and forth from street locations to post office box numbers.

New York distributors of erotica operate under such auspicious names as Educational Books, Inc., Social Research Corp., Medi-Date, Inc., and Bob Anthony Studio. The latter, the reader might be interested to learn, accepts both Bank-Americard and Master Charge. Currently, and in compliance with many laws, these mail-order firms require buyers to declare that they are at least 21 years of age, a practice which proved futile in earlier decades. While most of these distributors of erotica occasionally sell reprints of classics or remainders of legitimate studies or pseudo-scientific works, their merchandise is not incorporated, for the most part, into major bibliographical tools.

In terms of bibliographical control, sex-oriented magazines pose an even greater problem than erotic novels. Graphic materials have always been of greater concern to censors than written works, because the impact of such works appears to be more immediate. For example, relatively innocuous forms of nudity in contemporary art are still sometimes subject to attempts at censorship. Semi-erotic humor magazines such as *Capt. Billy's Whiz Bang*, which was popular in the 1920s, were the forerunners to contemporary "girlie" magazines. Drawings of women which revealed the daringly-exposed ankle were used to illustrate some magazines primarily devoted to jokes and other written material. In the 1930s, written material gave way somewhat to a heavier concentration of drawings of females, including those of famous women of the era, such as Mae West, on the cover of *Ballyhoo*. Replacement of many drawings with photographs occurred in the 1940s, and the institution of "cheesecake" photos also appeared during that period. The 1950s saw an increase in the production of such magazines, sometimes referred to as men's sophisticates or barbershop magazines. Such titles as *Adam*, *Caper*, and *Rogue* began to appear regularly in some newsstands. *Playboy* began as one of these in 1953. Photographs of scantily clad females posed in seductive postures and settings were featured, and the industry appeared to impose some degree of self-censorship in this regard.

Appearing alongside the men's magazines were publications such as *The American Sunbather*, which was distributed by a nudist organization. These nudist publications contained photographs of nude persons at play in the great outdoors. Pubic hair was carefully air-brushed in the newsstand editions of nudist magazines as a protection against obscenity charges. Nudist magazine publishers eventually won the right to show pubic hair and ceased to produce separate newsstand and membership editions of their publications; however, the "girlie" magazine continued their restrictions. The apparent liberalization of social and moral conventions during the 1960s was also reflected in these popular publications. First, a number of pseudo-nudist periodicals appeared which, unlike the genuine nudist magazines, emphasized sexuality. Gradually, "girlie" magazines became more daring and showed pubic hair as well as more explicitly erotic photographic depictions, including photographs of males and females in simulated coital activity. In addition, a number of new titles appeared, and the textual content of sex magazines was minimized in favor of photographs.

While these magazines appeared quite regularly on newsstands, subscriptions were usually impossible. *Playboy* was the exception to the rule. Many of the titles, names of publishers, and addresses of publishers changed frequently. *Playboy* separated itself from that tradition and moved into a class by itself. Though it led the way in its earlier days, *Playboy* remained more conservative than its imitators. Editors of *Playboy* devoted substantial attention to the fantasies, sexual and nonsexual, of the sophisticated man of the world—advertising directed at the man who has everything—and to the writings of young, talented novelists and essayists.

By 1970, the influence of Danish and Swedish sex periodicals was visible in "girlie" magazines published in the United States. An explosion of new titles, each labeled volume 1, number 1, often with no date and no publisher's imprint, appeared in adult bookstores rather than on newsstands. Essentially, the same practices hold true for the publication of magazines featuring male nudes, homosexual activity, and female impersonation. Graphic materials are currently subjected to greater legal repressions than are erotic novels; publishers of these magazines appear to be more apprehensive about the content of magazines than of novels. Therefore, greater care is exercised in disguising source information. In an effort to avoid legal repercussions, publishers of sex magazines occasionally provide accompanying text of a pseudo-scientific nature, apparently in an attempt to legitimatize their graphic erotica. A number of so-called sex manuals (e.g., *Sense and Sex in Marriage*) have been issued with pseudo-scientific content and format; they are heavily illustrated with photographs suggesting, if not actually showing, sexual activity.

Among the distributors of adult materials, Connoisseur Publications of Cleveland, Ohio, issued catalog number 655 in the mid-1960s. The catalog featured soft-core pornography; pseudo-scientific titles; hard-cover adult titles; sado-masochistic pulp; nudist magazines; male nudist magazines; imported English "girlie" magazines; and photo sets. Some of Connoisseur Publications' hard-cover editions included Grove Press publications; one of their offerings was a paper edition of *The Wolfenden Report*.

In the late 1960s, Collector's Publications, under the direction of Marvin Miller, claimed to be the largest West Coast publisher of erotic books. In February 1969, Miller addressed a catalog to librarians in which he reprinted, with permission, an article by Robert S. Bravard from *Choice* entitled "In the Balance: A Librarian's Guide to Black Literature" [5 (1968: 915-21)]. Several hundred in-print titles of Collector's Publications were contained in this catalog. Miller is somewhat unique in that he identified himself openly with his erotica publishing efforts. He subsequently encountered legal difficulty, and Collector's Publications now appears to have gone out of business.

Publishers of strictly sado-masochistic works have also advertised their products. Irving Klaw issued a series of bulletins in the 1950s advertising photo sets, films, and magazines that depicted various sado-masochistic activities. Other publishers and producers of similar material have issued catalogs which featured photo sets, sex devices, and a few publications. Catalogs of Kaysey Sales Co., Inc., and Tana Louise appear to be those of the Burmel Publishing Co., which also issued catalogs. Although these catalogs were numbered consecutively, imprints varied for some issues. The attainment of anything close to bibliographical control would be nearly impossible for the works of these distributors and publishers.

Obviously, bibliographical control of erotica is presently inadequate. Whether it is possible to attain bibliographic access in this area depends largely on publishers of erotica and on libraries that collect erotica. Factors affecting both of these groups are complex and fluctuating. Erotica has always been available to those persons who have the interest, money, and the ability to acquire it. Prices of such material have been within the reach of many consumers for a number of years, although current costs of sexually oriented magazines generally range from $3.50 to $18.50 per issue. The existence of erotica cannot be denied; as such, it becomes resource material for social historians or scientists. In recent years, erotica has proven useful to behavioral scientists as stimulus material for controlled experiments in varied psychological and physiological research. Growing numbers of scholars are beginning to study elements of popular culture; many of them will eventually need these materials. Scholars such as Morse Peckham have explored the resources and have developed highly philosophical treatises on the genre itself. An example is Peckham's *Pornography; An Experiment in Explanation* (New York: Basic Books, 1969). If erotica were available to researchers, its potential uses can scarcely be imagined; all available research collections are repeatedly mined by scholars in new and unexpected ways. However, libraries are subject to some of the same pressures that affect publishing, and, questions of censorship aside, most library budgets are already strained by the mass of publications needed in other, perhaps more acceptable, subject areas.

The previously mentioned *Choice* article by Bravard advocated the establishment of erotica collections in libraries as resource material for social historians. As Bravard so accurately reports, ephemeral resource material for these scholars is all too frequently discarded shortly after having been issued and read. Among Bravard's recommendations for library acquisitions are contemporary paperback reprints of the erotic classics and selected titles from the newly written novels. One cannot be certain, however, how many librarians have accepted this recommendation. A 1969 letter by LeRoy C. Merritt in the ALA *Newsletter on Intellectual Freedom* indicated a negative response by librarians to Bravard's contention that such material should be preserved for the benefit of future researchers.[9] Nonetheless, other librarians have also offered justification for the purchase of erotica based upon the idea of the maintenance of intellectual freedom.[10] The ALA *Newsletter on Intellectual Freedom* documents cases in which librarians have defended this freedom in reference to the collection of underground press and avant garde publications.

Should librarians suddenly recognize the need for the preservation of such material and should they attempt to collect erotica, the difficulties encountered would be staggering. For example, there is the problem of selection. Traditional book-reviewing media upon which librarians depend for the selection of materials are of little help in the acquisition of erotica. As mentioned previously, *Publishers Weekly* provides evaluations of only a small portion of available erotic publications. The sex tabloids such as *SCREW* also review erotic pulp works, but conditions that work against the purchase of erotic pulps by libraries also essentially preclude obtaining subscriptions to sex tabloids. Therefore, librarians who attempt to establish or to expand the scope of erotic literature collections will need to rely on evaluative and selection media in which objective, critical reviews are uncommon and which lack adequate order information such as price and address of publisher. Although works of an erotic nature might be reviewed frequently in these selection aids, usually only partial bibliographic information is included.

Assuming that a librarian wants to purchase a current erotic publication, the problem of the work's actual acquisition remains to be solved. Since most of the secondary industry publishers do not provide lists of their publications to the R. R. Bowker Company or to any other agency concerned with contemporary bibliography, order information such as prices or publishers' addresses may be impossible to locate. Furthermore, publishers whose works are listed in *Books in Print* are usually not interested in single-copy orders; this is generally also the case with most paperback publishers. As an alternative to systematic selection using reviewing tools or other bibliographic aids, librarians can purchase randomly on the retail market—i.e., from "adult" bookstores or in response to direct-mail advertising. However, direct-mail distributors of erotica have not always been reliable as a source for material. Checks in payment of ordered merchandise have been cashed, but ordered materials have sometimes not been delivered.

Bookstores specializing in sex-oriented literature are usually stocked by distributors. Owners of these establishments seldom know what will be received, what the store has in stock, or who the publishers are. While "adult" bookstores may be good sources for a sample of contemporary erotic publications, they are neither adequate sources for systematic acquisition nor outlets for obtaining specific titles.

Furthermore, two of the four "adult" bookstores visited by the author of this chapter were selling some merchandise that was as much as seven years old; virtually none of the publications was published in 1974. One of these bookstores displayed all merchandise sealed in cellophane, a practice which does not facilitate selection; however, in other similar outlets this practice is often limited to illustrated materials.

Assuming librarians have acquired erotic literature, the question arises as to how it should be cataloged. While some of the past practices which made cataloging quite difficult and time-consuming have been discontinued, problems still remain. The use of pseudonyms on erotic literature is still the rule rather than the exception, although a small group called the Dirty Writers of America came out of their closets in 1971 to picket The Olympia Press for unpaid royalties.[11] Sex tabloids do occasionally reveal the true identity of some of the authors of reviewed books. In addition, imprint information varies insofar as availability and accuracy are concerned.

Of 22 titles purchased in 1974 by the writer in "adult" bookstores, twelve contained a traditional imprint, six contained partial information such as series titles and dates, and four did not contain any bibliographic information. However, other titles observed but not purchased confirmed the suspicion that the omission of bibliographic information is still common. While dates of publication are probably accurate when given, most erotic works contain no date. The practice of omitting dates apparently allows works to remain on the market for a longer time period. As the Library of Congress does not catalog most of these titles, the individual librarian will be responsible for a considerable amount of original, descriptive cataloging for most erotic publications. On the other hand, descriptive cataloging does not require much time if little bibliographic information is available. The publications of Reed Enterprises, of which Greenleaf Classics is a subsidiary, and the materials of Parliament News, of which Brandon Books is only one branch, are available in "adult" bookstores. Very little detective work is necessary to identify the relationship of subsidiaries with parent organizations. A greater number of erotic publications now appear to be providing imprint information that is fictitious and nearly impossible to verify. Traditional library bibliographic resources are of little help in this respect.

If librarians were to attempt a subclassification of erotica by theme (a fairly logical means of organizing it and one frequently used by the "adult" bookstores), titles of works would pose a problem. Quite often, titles have no relationship to the contents of publications; they are often merely sensational devices to attract customers in search of greater novelty. This is particularly true in the case of some of the pseudo-scientific materials. While some pseudo-scientific works have been given titles that imply a research emphasis, others have titles similar to novel titles. Some titles of erotic works are indicative of case histories of one kind or another. Works with titles that imply that the contents are based upon research are usually separately shelved in bookstores, but they are often intershelved with fiction according to the subject area of interests to which they might appeal. Of course, these materials are all fiction and can be classified as such. But the classification of erotica by titles alone is not of much use in libraries where persons often search for information under selected subject headings in card catalogs.

Efforts of librarians to select, acquire, and organize erotica would be useful beyond the purpose of preserving research material for the future. Librarians can help to bring bibliographical control to the subject area of erotica. While the nature of the secondary publishing industry currently precludes systematic bibliographical listings when materials are first published, the recording of cataloging information in library catalogs and the exchange of bibliographical information make a significant contribution to the goal of universal bibliographical control as described by Kaltwasser.

While most libraries have traditionally neither collected nor organized erotica, the Institute for Sex Research, founded by Alfred C. Kinsey, has assembled a unique collection of erotic literature, erotic art, sexual ephemera, and social and behavioral materials relevant to the understanding of human sexual behavior. In his book *Dr. Kinsey and the Institute*, Wardell B. Pomeroy, who was one of Kinsey's colleagues, comments on the collection:

> The library and archives stand as an enduring monument to Kinsey's lifetime of devotion to his work. . . . State and grant money have not been used to build up either the library or the archives. Instead the Institute has spent its own funds, saved from book royalties and fees, and it also depends heavily on donors, as it did when Kinsey was alive. Fortunately, donations of money or materials to the Institute are tax deductible. . . . Anything that is relevant to human sexuality in any way merits consideration for possible inclusion. In addition to virtually all scientific works on human sex research, numerous specialized fields are strongly represented, including physiology, abortion, sex law, prostitution, psychology, marriage counseling and many other related topics. Nonscientific published materials, such as popular books and articles, are included. The Institute has a large collection of fiction, poetry, art books, girlie magazines, nudist magazines and the publications of various sexual (and antisexual) organizations. Included is the largest collection of erotic literature assembled in any one place. A considerable number of Institute books are the only copies extant, as far as anyone knows. One reason is that sexual literature is particularly subject to destruction, either intentionally or through wear, and it is seldom protected in a library.[12]

Research activities at the Institute for Sex Research continue under the direction of Dr. Paul H. Gebhard. As presently constituted, however, the Institute's primary focus is not on the development of the library's collections. Funds to organize the library's collection adequately have never been available. In addition, there is presently only limited access to erotica contained in the Institute's library. Hopefully, a catalog of the Institute's erotica collection can be published in the future, as was its social and behavioral sciences catalog (G. K. Hall, 1975). Presently, the erotica collection of the Institute for Sex Research is available only to certified scholars engaged in *bona fide* research projects who can travel to Bloomington, Indiana. Criteria for use of the library are outlined in a 1957 customs case before a United States District Court, which permits the Institute for Sex Research to import and to maintain erotica under security conditions for the purpose of supporting scientific research.[13] Thus, the Institute's library appears to be the only one in the United States which is protected against fluctuation in public and governmental attitudes toward erotica.

Unfortunately, Institute funds for the acquiring of publications and other media for the library's collections are precarious. Austerity has dictated a passive acquisition policy toward erotica; active purchasing has been directed to the more critical needs in the social and behavioral science collections of the library. The result is a less-than-comprehensive contemporary erotica collection. Gift collections of erotica have been a major source of new acquisitions; however, there is no certainty that future gifts will provide an adequate representation of contemporary materials. This situation seems most unfortunate in view of the protected position of the Institute for Sex Research *vis-à-vis* the collection of erotica. In addition, the lack of a concerted effort on the part of other agencies and institutions to extend and to improve the level of bibliographical control of erotica places the library of the Institute for Sex Research in an advantageous position to make substantial efforts toward that goal.

FOOTNOTES

[1] Franz Georg Kaltwasser, "The Quest for Universal Bibliographical Control: Beyond Man's Reach?," *Wilson Library Bulletin* 46 (June 1972): 895.

[2] Kaltwasser, p. 895.

[3] Eberhard and Phyllis Kronhausen, *Pornography and the Law; The Psychology of Erotic Realism and Pornography*, rev. ed. (New York: Ballantine Books, 1964).

[4] Steven Marcus discusses Ashbee and his bibliographies at length in *The Other Victorians: A Study of Sexuality and Pornography in Mid-Nineteenth Century England* (New York: Basic Books, 1966).

[5] Marcus, p. 54.

[6] Marjorie Fiske, *Book Selection and Censorship* (Berkeley: University of California Press, 1959); Charles H. Busha, *Freedom versus Suppression and Censorship* (Littleton, Colo.: Libraries Unlimited, 1972); Michael Pope, *Sex and the Undecided Librarian* (Metuchen, N.J.: Scarecrow Press, 1974).

[7] Technical Report of the Commission on Obscenity and Pornography, v. 3, *The Marketplace: The Industry* (Washington, D.C.: U.S. Government Printing Office, 1971), p. 98.

[8] James Jackson Kilpatrick, *The Smut Peddlers* (Garden City, N.Y.: Doubleday, 1960), p. 86.

[9] LeRoy Charles Merritt (letter), *Newsletter on Intellectual Freedom* 18 (January 1969): 12.

[10] Bill Katz, "The Pornography Collection," *Library Journal* 96 (December 15, 1971): 4060-66.

[11] *SCREW*, No. 123 (1971), p. 19.

[12] Wardell B. Pomeroy, *Dr. Kinsey and the Institute for Sex Research* (New York: Harper & Row, 1972), pp. 458-59.

[13] United States of America, Libellant, against 31 photographs. Admiralty 189-50. October 31, 1957. United States District Court, Southern District of New York. Edmund L. Palmieri, Judge.

SELECTED BIBLIOGRAPHY

Though much of the material contained in this chapter is based on the author's observations while working with a collection that includes erotica, the following works offer additional information on the subject.

Foxon, David. *Libertine Literature in England, 1660-1745*. New Hyde Park, N.Y.: University Books, 1965.

Fryer, Peter. *Private Case–Public Scandal*. London: Secker & Warburg, 1966.

Hyde, H. Montgomery. *A History of Pornography*. New York: Farrar, Straus and Giroux, 1964.

Kaltwasser, Franz Georg. "The Quest for Universal Bibliographical Control: Beyond Man's Reach?," *Wilson Library Bulletin* 46 (June 1972): 894-901.

Katz, Bill. "The Pornography Collection," *Library Journal* 96 (December 15, 1971): 4060-66.

Kilpatrick, James J. *The Smut Peddlers*. Garden City, N.Y.: Doubleday, 1960.

Kronhausen, Eberhard, and Phyllis Kronhausen. *Pornography and the Law; The Psychology of Erotic Realism and Pornography*. New York: Ballantine Books, 1964. Rev. ed.

Legman, G. *The Horn Book; Studies in Erotic Folklore and Bibliography*. New Hyde Park, N.Y.: University Books, 1964.

Loth, David. *The Erotic in Literature; A Historical Survey of Pornography As Delightful As It Is Indiscreet*. New York: Julian Messner, Inc., 1961.

Marcus, Steven. *The Other Victorians: A Study of Sexuality and Pornography in Mid-Nineteenth Century England*. New York: Basic Books, 1966.

Matta, Seoud. "Bowker's Books In Print: A Critique and a Response by the R. R. Bowker Co.," *Library Journal* 98 (July 1973): 2048-51.

Technical Report of the Commission on Obscenity and Pornography, v. 3. *The Marketplace: The Industry*. Washington, D.C.: U.S. Government Printing Office, 1971.

CENSORSHIP AND THE PERFORMING ARTS:
A Review of the Issues

Barbara Connally Kaplan

     Music, theatre, and dance, in retrospect and in present practice, have constituted the "lively arts." These art forms, by virtue of their performance aspects, possess a vitality of breath and movement that distinguishes them from the more tangible and capturable qualities of painting, sculpture, architecture, graphics, and literature, all of which are characterized by different kinds of movement and vitality. Lively aspects of the visual and verbal arts are achieved because of the direct liaison between the artist and the respondent, viewer, or reader, while those of the performing arts pass through an interpreter—the musician, actor, dancer—whatever his specialty may be.

     Cinema and television also are encompassed in the performing arts, and film has, in fact, been termed the "liveliest art." However, like the visual arts, film is treated as a separate subject in another essay of this book. Moreover, the cinema is among the capturable arts—the live aspects, recorded for the lifetime of the preserving medium, are produced in advance of exhibition to the public. Television has the same capability of prior preparation through the videotape, but unpredictable moments of performance are still possible in live television. Some of these moments are comparable to the life of music, theatre, or dance prior to recordings of any of these arts; therefore, it seems reasonable to consider this quality of the "performing moment" as a unique problem with respect to freedom of expression—primarily in relation to music, dance, theatre, and live television in their multiple forms.

     Although censorship has been approached from the standpoint of the creator, the courts, and the society,[1] comparatively few attempts have been made to survey or to analyze the peculiar problems of performance, except in terms of the performer's rights.[2] Performers have been confronted by censorship problems in professional situations and in school activities; in the formal contexts of concert companies, solo appearances, opera, and symphony; and in the less formal categories of street performance, burlesque house, televised comedy, and rock music festivals. Court decisions related to restraints on the arts have dealt with general issues, such as artistic and social values, performers' rights, and regulatory powers; or with more specific issues, including politics, nudity, obscenity, religion, race, nuisance, dress, non-verbal expression, symbolic speech, and the needs and rights of children. The fields of entertainment and the performing arts, as means of communication, fall under the free speech guarantees of the First Amendment; actors, dancers, singers and comedians have their rights of communication with their audiences protected by the nation's basic laws.

ARTISTIC AND SOCIAL VALUES

Concern with artistic value and aesthetic doctrine as related to the idea and ideal of freedom—particularly the first freedom—has not been confined to the twentieth century, although new technologies and changing moral standards have spawned increasing instances of censorship in the performing arts. Plato argued that the artist should enlarge men's feelings rather than regulating them.[3] Santayana pursued this ideal of enlarging human capacity, maintaining that such enlargement has no tendency to constitute a single standard of beauty, and that to awaken and marshal perceptions for the many kinds of beauty, we must turn to the man who combines the greatest range of diverse perceptive habits with the greatest endowment in each particular—the lover of *all* kinds of beauty.[4] The whole question of artistic value is of primary importance to the creative and recreative artist, while social values may be secondary or irrelevant; however, for the observer-participant-respondent, social concerns may be uppermost. The basis of artistic value as a liberating factor in the life of man, according to Horace Kallen, is in its new use of nature, which

> liberates the spirit, if for an instant only, from the coercions and constraints which beset it. Whatever other relations a thing may have, we are disposed to attribute beauty to it if it consummates this liberation, and we tend to realize its beauty as a relation between ourselves and the liberating power. Let the power be pattern and good order, let it be disorder and confusing, if it be liberating, we call it beautiful.[5]

The phrase "social value" is encountered frequently throughout decisions on the censorship of performance, as delineated in the *United States Code*, but social value is often determined specifically in relation to literary, artistic, political, or scientific values.[6] In the case of *People v. Adler*, 1972, expert testimony that the films in question had no artistic merit, no story, no relationship that changed, no dialogue or communication, nor any psychological value, had the effect of establishing the conclusion that such material was utterly without redeeming *social* importance even though those specific words were not used.[7] The importance of considering a theatrical production as a complete entity in order to determine such social value was emphasized in the decisions of *Southeastern Promotions, Inc. v. Conrad*. The lower court held that the United States Supreme Court does not permit judging only selected parts of a theatrical production in order to detect obscenity (for purposes of determining rights of freedom of speech); rather, the production must be judged as a whole and will be granted protection of the First Amendment unless, judged as a whole, it is "utterly without redeeming social value."[8] These decisions seem to assert that artistic merit is related to the social functions of art and that artistic value becomes social value as well. In the past, such an opinion has not been universally held, particularly as men tend to reveal their commitments to specific points of view. Such commitment can lead all too easily to censorship because of convictions by some that they have perceived the only real truth about life,[9] and such "truth" must be perpetuated. No wonder, then, that both philosophers and politicians have often regarded the liberating power of the artist as a danger to the particular concept of society that they espouse.

RIGHTS OF THE PERFORMING ARTIST

The performing artist in theatre has been aptly described by Walter Kerr as being kept up to pitch by a "kind of optimum tension, a certain necessary insecurity," a state that undoubtedly contributes to the liveliness of theatre. Kerr suggests that theatre is a total insecurity, extending from pre-curtain nervousness and backstage mechanical risk to the audience itself. The profession itself holds "brilliance and breakdown in the same frightened breath," yet performers for centuries have risked established careers or secure positions to attempt some new challenge that will lead to even greater future risks.[10] An understanding of the performing artist's apparent imperviousness to danger is essential to any consideration of protest arising from the impact on an audience of a live performance.

With the changes in the economics of entertainment that have been accentuated by television, for example, there have been concomitant legal developments that have led courts to protect the person who contributes ideas or services simply because of the daily proof of their economic importance, over and above artistic merit.[11] Silverberg has drawn comparisons between authors and performers that may be valid as well for the problems of censorship, although his treatment of the rights of authors and performers is concerned primarily with the question of "authorship." In cases involving a controversy between two film cowboys, Roy Rogers and Gene Autrey,[12] the Ninth Circuit Court held that the terms "acts, poses, plays and appearance" did not mean the same thing as "name, voice and likeness"; therefore, the former referred to activities in motion pictures while the latter had reference to non-motion picture reproduction of characteristics of a performer.

> In considering legal protection of authors and performers, a distinction must be made between the two groups because legal protection of each of the two groups rests on a different foundation. Authors' rights (even including those of directors) may be based either on the Copyright Act or on the common-law, whereas performers must rely entirely on common-law protection, notably the theories of unfair competition, common-law literary rights and in some cases, the right of privacy or the right of publicity. . . . In any small or financially weak . . . industry, the talent groups may discover that even though the law grants them perfect protection . . . the first time they endeavor to take advantage of or efface those agreements the unstable nature of the industry renders them powerless.[13]

Distinction between the rights of the listener and of the performer, in terms of the "broadcaster" specifically, have been drawn in the case of the *Columbia Broadcasting System v. the Democratic National Committee.*[14] Because the broadcast media utilize a valuable and limited public resource, it was held that there is also present an unusual order of values under this amendment; although the broadcaster is not without protection, the right of the viewers and listeners is paramount. Furthermore, distinctions between the actual broadcaster and the stage performer were delineated in *National Lampoon, Inc. v. American Broadcasting Companies, Inc.* Here the court maintained that under the First Amendment the rights of licensed broadcasters are subject to more limitations than those of performers on the stage or publishers.[15]

THE COMMUNITY AND THE REGULATION OF PERFORMANCE

The increasing mobility of the population during the post World War II decades and the broadening scope of the subject matter of live television have brought a more general tolerance, if not acceptance, of previous targets for censorship in the performing arts. While pockets of active, local community protest still persist insofar as publications and performances are concerned, the use of the word "community" in determining standards of decency or obscenity meant until 1973 not the local area involved but a national standard. The test of whether material was obscene consisted of determining whether to the average person, applying contemporary community standards, the dominant theme of the material taken as a whole appeals to prurient interest. Therefore, with a broader concept of the term "community" governing standards and with the even broader "freedom to receive information and ideas regardless of their social worth,"[17] performers in the United States were accorded considerable latitude in their freedom of expression. Now, however, with the *Miller v. California* decision of 1973, the Supreme Court narrowed once again the concept of "community" from national to local standards. This has raised serious questions as to the actual application of anti-obscenity ordinances, but the court has yet to clarify its ruling to anyone's satisfaction.

While *Miller* and numerous other decisions having broad applications under the First Amendment will present problems of censorship in the future for performing artists as well, the issues that have risen from specific controversies present a panorama of past problems as colorful and varied as the stage itself.

POLITICAL RESTRAINTS

The right of the performer to practice his profession free from political oppression has never been more poignantly illustrated than in the years of increasing exchange performances and cultural détente, both between the United States and Russia and between the United States and China. The artist-intellectual, concerned with artistic tradition and knowledgeable about the symbolic system relating to his national ideology, often develops an interest in politics, sometimes because he has been excluded from political decision-making.[18] In March 1975, the *Washington Post* published the text of a letter to *Le Monde* from Mstislav Rostropovich, who had been permitted to come to the United States as a direct result of Senator Edward Kennedy's comment in Russia that many people in the United States would like to hear the eminent cellist. Leonard Bernstein, among others, had also requested that Rostropovich be allowed to resume concert performances in the West. Answering charges made by Igor Shafarevich against Russian cultural figures who had voluntarily left Russia, Rostropovich's letter described the conflicts with the Soviet ruling system that led him to come to the West:

being a musician, I have never been a politician. My life, was dictated by my heart and my conscience. . . . I had never signed pre-fabricated letters. . . . I had never participated in the officially organized campaigns against composers, writers, artists, scientists, and as is well known, I gave shelter to my friend Alexander Solzhenitsyn in my country house. All these are my "crimes."

How do you imagine my creative life was in my motherland if as an artist, I was deprived of the possibility of self-expression? What can one do if the art of the performer-musician gets older and dies together with him? Only on records (although it is not good enough) one could leave a "print" which could even survive the artist himself—but what if the recording simply is stopped by somebody's order, literally on half-a-word, and you practically get kicked out of the studio, as it once happened when my wife[19] was recording Puccini's *Tosca* with me as conductor, at the Bolshoi Theatre? . . .

How long could I be treated, in the planning of my concerts abroad, as a marionette in the hands of the state organization "Gosconcert"? Only they could say . . . where I could go and where I could not, which parts I could play and which ones not.[20] I never refused to perform in the most remote parts of Siberia, Chukotka and the Far East. When I had no piano, I played an accordion. But for me as a musician and an artist— for my professional growth, it is necessary to do the more important projects. . . .

I am only 47 and in my prime. How much I could do for my country, had I been given just "musical freedom" without being regulated or tripped up, without someone trying to destroy me as a person and as a musician, just to prove that even a talented man can be destroyed if he is not obedient, that such a man can be replaced with a mediocrity, obeying the bosses like a slave and blindly walking the narrow and often stupid official line.

It must be possible for one's hope and belief to come true. A musician cannot close himself up in four walls and create for himself: he must pass his art on to the people. Otherwise his art, not finding an outlet, destroys the artist. . . .

. . . being abroad is not an escape from Russia, but the only way to realize our musical dreams, by which we express our love for Russia and our great people.[21]

Rostropovich's letter will surely take its place with Beethoven's Heiligenstadt Testament as one of the unforgettable documents of the history of music performance and composition. Each is a romantic expression of the artist's innermost feelings about both the profession by which he is impelled and the restrictions designed to compel him to follow a course that is contrary to his entire being.

Russia has a special pride in her "Bolshoi" Opera (so named because it is bigger than any other company in the country), for the Bolshoi serves as a repository for all the great Russian classic works. According to Kiril Molchanov, the director who has taken his place as an operatic composer beside Tchaikovsky and Prokofiev in the Bolshoi's repertoire, the absence of Wagnerian literature from the Bolshoi repertoire was not a matter of discrimination, but rather due to Wagner's failure to be acceptable to the public through the war years. It will not be restored until it is prepared in Russian, although the visiting Stockholm Opera has performed the *Ring* in Swedish for the Moscow public.[22] Both Prokofiev's *War and Peace* and Modeste Moussorgsky's *Boris Godunow* were written and rewritten, revised and amended, rather more than one might anticipate, in accordance with advice from governmental sources. In the 1870s, Moussorgsky had to contend with a St. Petersburg censor who thought that the first version of *Boris*, without the Polish scene and a principal female performer, was unsatisfactory. In 1942, one of Prokofiev's hurdles was the demand of the Committee of the Arts for the addition of more choral material to emphasize the plight of Mother Russia before they would approve the first eleven scenes of *War and Peace.*

Another significant instance of censorship was the decision of the Central Committee of the Communist Party of 10 February, 1948. This censure of "comrades Shostakovich, Prokofiev, Khachaturian, Shebalin, Popov, Miaskovsky, and others" (Muradeli, Shaporin and, originally, Kabalevsky were also under discussion) resulted in many problematic side-effects: the loss of jobs, cancellation of performances, delays in productions, and the removal of the names of these stellar composer-performers from programs because they were in political trouble stemming from their "formalistic distortions and anti-democratic tendencies which are alien to the Soviet People and its artistic taste."[23] In 1948, the definition of formalism as the "cult of atonality, dissonance and disharmony, the rejection of melody and the involvement with confused neuro-pathological combinations that transform music into cacophony . . . branded such music as decayed bourgeois culture and the total negation of musical art."[24] The philosophy that allowed the censure of Russian musical giants of the 1940s, '50s and '60s originated in the work of Anatol Lunacharsky, to whom Lenin, in 1917, entrusted the task of developing artistic continuity and ideological reforms through the office of the People's Commission of Public Education. Lunacharsky was able to rule through persuasion rather than dogmatism, to reconcile the diverse needs and demands of artists, audiences and politicians, and to succeed in this three-fold task of educating an uninstructed public, winning the confidence of the artistic community, and convincing political leaders of the importance of supporting the arts for the purposes of mass education— all highly desirable aims. The extreme position of the 1948 statement was somewhat softened a decade later, yet even the performance of Shostakovich's Symphony No. 13 in 1963 was marked with controversy because it contained choral singing of verses from Yevgeny Yevtushenko's poem "Babi Yar," a complaint that there was no memorial to the thousands of Jews slain by the Nazis in Kiev. This was considered by some to mean that Soviet anti-Semitism was to blame for the lack of a memorial, although Yevtushenko denied the interpretation; nonetheless, Shostakovich was forced to reword the chorus.[25] Full official recognition of Shostakovich's genius did not come until 1966, during celebrations marking his sixtieth birthday.

The ballet choreographer in the Soviet Union today faces the political require-ment of *sovremennost*, or "contemporaneity," defined as the embodiment and reflection of contemporary life.[26] Pyotr Gusev, a ballet star of the 1930s and a prominent teacher today, has appealed to the younger generation to return to subjects dealing with this issue, although he admits that such ballets have failed artistically in the past. On the other hand, Yuri Grigorovich, the artistic director and choreographer for the Bolshoi Ballet, contends that, although a contemporary subject is not necessarily contemporary in essence, Soviet ballet cannot isolate itself from the people, echoing the 1963 insistence of the dance historian-librettist, Yuri Slonimsky, that "realism" selects from life that which is most important, that which moves man and humanity. This depiction of reality as it "should" be from the viewpoint of Soviet authorities has led to a crisis in Soviet choreography. Grigorovich criticizes the use of movement in ballet as the concrete definition of an image rather than as poetic metaphor.[27]

In 1918, a decree by Lenin initiated *Glavlit—Glavnoye upravlenie po delam literatury i pechati* (the Central Board for Literature and Press Affairs). At that time, its purpose was to temporarily restrict freedom of the press; through Leonid Vladimirov's appraisal,[28] it is clear that Glavlit in 1973, for all practical purposes, was essentially the same, with every aspect of the communications and publishing media institutionalized and controlled, with the assistance of several auxiliary censorship boards.

The cutting edge of censorship in the United States may not butcher the artists' rights as in the case of Rostropovich, but it is just as effective in severing the completeness of the audience's "freedom to listen, regardless of social worth." The Performing Arts Troupe of China, a group of 60 musicians, singers and dancers from various parts of the country (including some of China's most prominent artists), was to have toured the United States, commencing in March 1975. The month-long tour was cancelled because the program included a song expressing determination of the People's Republic of China to liberate Taiwan.

> People of Taiwan, our own brothers
> Day and night you are in our heart
> We are determined to liberate Taiwan
> And let the light of the sun shine on the island.

The Chinese insisted that the words of the songs be printed in Chinese and English for performances of the tour. The United States State Department requested that the song be dropped from the repertory due, in the words of a department press officer, to its "high political content for a cultural presentation." (Obviously the officer must have known little about the origin of Mozart's *Marriage of Figaro*.) The episode was not considered significant enough to affect the trend toward improved relations with the People's Republic of China and was justified on the basis of "avoiding the kind of controversy that the inclusion of this kind of song would have created."[29] China later accused the United States of interference in her internal affairs, and branded the U.S. objection as a violation of a communiqué signed in Shanghai by Richard Nixon and Chou-En-Lai. China asserted that, in the communi-qué, the U.S. Government had agreed that there is but one China and that Taiwan is part of China.[30] The tour was indefinitely postponed. Still another instance of attempted censorship of the performing arts occurred with the warning of the government of the People's Republic of China that the United States should not allow a Tibetan song and dance troup to tour the country in October 1975. Again, this was termed a violation of the 1972 Shanghai agreement.

The centuries-old tradition of Peking Opera, a phenomenal oral tradition originating in the Yuan Dynasty, has endured musically, although there have been drastic changes in content and in outer appearance. The theme of "contemporaneity" evident in Soviet ballet is making its mark upon Peking opera (and ballet as well) as performed in the People's Republic of China. *The Strategy of Taking Tiger Mountain*, a "modern revolutionary opera," uses Western instruments, colloquial language, modern dress and properties, but maintains traditional techniques of singing, mime, acrobatics, swordplay, and even make-up. Some Chinese opera enthusiasts consider the change in the rigid conventions an enhancement of the form of Chinese opera but others think that the changes are unfortunate. The fact that large audiences now understand the form and are now attending Peking Opera as popular theatre[31] recalls the Lunacharsky ideal of making the arts palatable for a vast uneducated public. It is entirely possible that characters in Chinese opera may fall victim to the same campaign of innuendo and historical criticism that was the fate of the classic fourteenth century novel, *The Water Margin*, long a favorite of Chairman Mao Tse-Tung. The Robin Hood story of peasant heroes battling corrupt court officials has now been denounced in articles in authoritative Chinese publications because Sung Chiang, the peasant leader, ultimately surrenders to the Emperor; thus the book espouses "capitulationism." The criticism has thus far been confined to ideology, without focusing on anyone in power.[32]

On the international scene, the appearance of a new cantata entitled "To Posterity," composed by Gottfried von Einem of Austria, became an issue at the United Nations in late 1975.[33] Political overtones involved the omission of the verse "He that keepeth Israel shall neither slumber nor sleep" from the cantata's text which was based in part on Psalm 121. The absence of the verse caused Israeli delegates to comment that after listening to the consistent distortion of history during United Nations sessions, even the effort to "amend the Bible" was no surprise. Meanwhile, the composer defended his position by explaining that he had worked from a 1781 German Bible and had not realized that the work was an abridged version. United Nations officials were considering the possibility of eliminating the numbers of the verses from the program, since the numbering had first called attention to the omission of the fourth verse.

Hilton Kramer, in reviewing the 1975 exhibition of "Master Paintings from the Hermitage and the State Russian Museum, Leningrad"[34] held in New York City, commented on the significance of the exhibition as a statement on the fate of Soviet culture. The "unofficial" artists who are attempting to keep alive the idea of free and independent artistic life can scarcely expect to have their paintings chosen for exhibitions under the present cultural ministry, and yet many future "détente" art displays are planned. Since the language of diplomacy has never been famous for its moral rigor, Kramer predicts that the art in which the Western mind has made its deepest avowal of feeling in this century will not be accorded the slightest sign of acknowledgment.[35] The performing arts, to some degree, have escaped the total anonymity which Kramer suggests has been the fate of politically unacceptable Soviet painters, but the tensions and career disruptions have been as evident in performance as in literature and the visual arts. The question then posed is a delineation of the line of demarcation between achieving international political understanding and sacrificing the basic tenet of artistic life—the freedom of expression. Strangely enough, the international understanding that exists in the artistic community has proven often to be a bridge to political understanding; the artist is left with the impression that political powers espouse a superficial détente in lieu of nurturing the entente that is already a reality.

OBSCENITY

The performing arts, like the verbal and visual media, eventually must grapple with the specific issue of obscenity, although Eric Larrabee wrote, in 1955, that sex censorship arises, not from what is done but from what is said, written, seen, heard, thought, or felt.[36] The statement, made in relation to sexual behavior specifically forbidden by the law, apparently did not take into consideration the limitations which might be stipulated for the performer's spontaneous movement or gesture in the transient moments of live performance. What was actually *done* has, in the decades since 1955, been very much an issue not only in sex censorship, but in other facets of the obscenity question as well.

In determining what is obscene, the addition, in 1962, of the standard of "patent offensiveness" for the purpose of protecting worthwhile works in literature, science, or art to the criterion of "appealing to prurient interest," allows the community as well as the court to exercise the element of judgment desired by Mr. Justice Harlan.[37] On one hand, charges of obscenity in performance revolve around considerations of sex and nudity, and on the other they are directed at sarcasm, satire, and impropriety. Albert Goldman describes the persecution of the comedian Lenny Bruce who, after searing British Prime Minister Harold MacMillan, the Queen, commercialized religion, African nationalism, Beaverbrook journalism, semantic philosophy, and Old Vic Shakespeare in England, was bounced from Vancouver by the morality squad, then made his way to Sydney where:

> . . . he walked out on the stage that had been set up in the dingy dining room of the hotel . . . confronting an audience of beat-looking cats, who were his only Australian fans, he started bitching about the lighting and the sound system. For . . . nearly fifteen minutes, he complained until the crowd began to feel restless and guilty. Finally he settled down and began doing his material. The show was full of dynamics: he slammed into one highly charged topic after another—"niggers," divorce, Adolf Eichmann, religion, sex, the whole bag. In a sophisticated nightclub in New York or San Francisco it would have been a heavy dose—in Australia it was pure insanity. The audience gasped and tittered with nervousness, four women got up at various points and walked out. The laughter was of that strangled variety that denotes anything but merriment. By the time the show ended, Lenny had kicked an enormous hole in the local proprieties. . . .[38]

Called sick by some, an attention-grabber by others, Bruce retorted "I'm not a comedian, and I'm not sick. The world is sick and I'm the doctor. I'm a surgeon with a scalpel for false values. I don't have an act. I'm just Lenny Bruce. . . . "

Bruce contended that "obscenity was in the ear of the beholder." His show had elicited stunned silence, but also laughter and applause. Some condemned the performance as "obscene," while others felt that the comedian was "a true iconoclast who breaks through the barrier of laughter to the horizon beyond where the truth has its sanctuary."

More than a specific performance by a comedian, the issue in the Bruce trial was the surge of moral license throughout the contemporary arts. Richard Kuh, the chief prosecutor, saw Bruce's trial not as retaliation for political or religious irreverence, but as a reflex action at the effort to push too far too fast and at sexual imagery that stripped privacy from sex and made it ugly in words and gestures.[39] Bruce's biographer, Albert Goldman, portrays the comedian in as moralistic and conservative a light as that of the judge and district attorney; he calls Bruce

> an alienated conservative . . . a typical satirist seeking revenge for out-raged moral idealism through techniques of shock and obscenity as old as Aristophanes. . . .
>
> Satirists are the last men in the world with whom the avant-garde should consort. . . . What they have to express is not a passion for change and improvement . . . but an endless reiteration of the follies and sins of human kind.[40]

Allen Ginsberg, concerned with what he believed to be a city-wide crackdown on the arts in New York, circulated a petition in June 1964, to "protest the use of the New York obscenity law in the harassment of the social satirist, Lenny Bruce." Signed by luminaries like Theodore Bikel, Merce Cunningham, Bob Dylan, Lillian Hellman, LeRoi Jones, Max Lerner, Norman Mailer, Reinhold Niebuhr, Paul Newman, Norman Podhoretz, Robert Rauschenberg, Susan Sontag, Lionel Trilling, Louis Untemeyer, Rudy Vallee, and dozens of other equally potent personalities, the petition effected an immediate public protest; however, several endorsements, notably those of Niebuhr and Trilling, were made without first-hand knowledge of Bruce's performances. Ginsberg had compared Bruce to Swift, Rabelais and Mark Twain, but during the trial, Kuh argued that Bruce's perform-ances were obscene in substance, not just in language; that they were prurient even if they were not erotic because "prurience" as a legal term embraced not only "erotically stimulating" but "filthy and disgusting material"; and that Bruce's performance represented not a meaningful whole but a collection of bits that dealt with a hundred different topics.[41] Ultimately found guilty as charged, Lenny Bruce drew a statement in legal form in support of a temporary restraining order and preliminary injunction against Judge Murtagh, and he also attempted to show that he was exempt from prosecution under the provisions of New York Statute 1140-A as amended. The case was never appealed in the proper form, although with the liberalizing decisions made in other cases during the trial period,[42] the chances of exoneration appeared to be strong.

SEX AND NUDITY IN THEATRE

Another facet of obscenity is sex, often the central issue in cases concerned with whole or partial nudity, obscenity in dance, or obscenity in music. The debates over obscenity have engendered some confusion in the performing arts because attention has often been focused on the question of artistic merit, although a performer could hardly acquiesce in Larrabee's opinion that such a question is a "near-irrelevancy."[43] Standards have seemed to vary widely with the explosion of new technological and new expressive media, upholding the contention that the older or more established the medium, the greater the freedom from attack.[44] New forms in art and entertainment seem to engender new outlets for expressions that could be considered "obscene." (Obscenity decisions relating to theatrical performance, dance, and phonograph records as well as the visual arts and motion pictures were selectively summarized by Judge William Ringel in a 1970 publication;[45] however, a number of significant cases have come before the courts in more recent litigations.)

In music, several court cases have revolved around the innovative and controversial musical production *Hair*, which startled even New Yorkers with its extensive use of nudity in performances. In the case of *Southeastern Promotions, Limited v. City of Mobile, Alabama, Hair* was considered to be speech and therefore entitled to protection under the First Amendment,[46] again incorporating the performing arts under the protection of the free speech guarantees of the First Amendment. A 1973 Tennessee legal judgment on *Hair* held that it was not error to consider obscene conduct independently from "speech"; but, whether the production's speech and conduct were considered separately or they were joined, the musical was deemed to be obscene.[47] An earlier judgment, also in Tennessee, had maintained that a theatrical production which is otherwise obscene is not protected from regulation by mere fact that it is performed before a consenting audience. The same judgment held that obscenity, as it relates to theatrical productions, can consist of either speech or conduct, or a combination of both. In addition, the Court stated that conduct, when not in the form of symbolic speech or so closely related to speech as to be illustrative thereof, is not speech, and hence, does not fall within the freedom of speech guarantee.[48] Yet in a 1973 Arkansas controversy,[49] the arrest of female performers without prior adversary hearing, after they had danced on stage clad only in "briefs" covering the lower part of their bodies, was not viewed as prior restraint on the exercise of freedom of expression; a decision was also made that the painting of the female performers' breasts by a male participant using fluorescent paint added nothing to "freedom of expression."

In March, 1975, the United States Supreme Court ruled on the constitutionality of a Chattanooga ban on *Hair*, maintaining that live theatre may not be censored in advance unless the government adheres to strict procedural safeguards for the protection of First Amendment rights.[50] The legal principle involved was the preference of a free society for punishing the few who abuse rights of speech after they break the law rather than throttling them and all others beforehand. For the first time, the Court ruled that live drama enjoys the same legal protections against prior restraint that the justices have accorded to books, movies, and other forms of expression; however, it did not guarantee that the rock musical *Hair* would not be considered obscene in a criminal prosecution of the show, the producers, and the actors. By a 5-4 vote, the Court held that Chattanooga could deny the use of a municipal theatre prior to opening night only by specific procedures, such as taking the initiative in going to court for a prompt judicial hearing, with the city bearing the burden of proving that the production was obscene.

Among the dissenters, Justice William O. Douglas disagreed with any legal action against the musical. He complained about the application of "procedural band-aids" and emphasized that the Constitution forbids all forms of content screening. Justices Rehnquist, Burger and White dissented on other bases; Justice Blackmun commented that live drama might have an added measure of protection in a court hearing held in advance of production; the city and the courts could not be sure that they knew precisely the extent of nudity or simulated sex in the performance, unlike the situation with books and films.

SEX AND NUDITY IN DANCE

While nudity in dance is not confined to the burlesque production or the striptease routine, the comparative conservatism of those forms of expression in the earlier decades of the twentieth century has been superseded, although not completely supplanted, by the topless-bottomless go-go dance since 1964. Aldridge's brief history of the striptease, from its possible origins in the Spanish Golden Age through the first Parisian performance of the act in 1893 and Little Egypt's belly dance at the Chicago World's Fair in the same year, to contemporary practices in the United States and abroad, reviews a line of major stars like Ann Corio, Josephine Baker, Sally Rand, and Gypsy Rose Lee.[51] In 1975, *The Serena Technique of Belly Dancing*, found on many bookstands, represented for the housewife or sedentary career girl a "fun way to keep fit, feel relaxed and expand creativity." "Serena" distinguishes between the belly dance which she terms "sensual," requiring skill and artistry, and the "sexy" dance—"random flesh-peddling, with distorted dance steps resulting in a coarse and common expression of sex and biological display."[52]

Decisions relating to nudity and obscenity in dance cover a wider range of circumstances than those relating to theatrical production, even including instances relating to the privacy of a residence. An ordinance of the city of Madison, Wisconsin, making it unlawful for any person to participate in an obscene dance at any place, at any time, and under any circumstances—including one's own home—was judged constitutionally over-broad for its failure to limit offensive conduct to a situation in which children are exposed to obscenity or in which sensibilities of unwilling adults are assaulted.[53] In this judgment, the definition of obscenity in the Madison ordinance conformed to the most recent (at that time, 1970) definition by the Supreme Court of the United States. The controversy over "topless" dancing continues to find its way into the newspapers of communities throughout the country, either in terms of performance as self-expression, or on the basis of "mixing and mingling." A 1972 decision in a topless dancing case held that dancing, even topless dancing, is a type of expression entitled to protection under the First Amendment and under the guarantee of the Fourteenth Amendment.[54] This decision was confirmed in the 1973 case of *Salem Inn v. Frank*,[55] which also branded a town ordinance prohibiting across-the-board non-obscene conduct (in the form of topless dancing in a public place) as constitutionally invalid because it represented an infringement upon the freedom, under the First Amendment, of bar operators to provide entertainment for their customers. An Arizona case confined the "protective mantle" of the First Amendment only to nudity which has become part of a form of expression, such as a dance or a play.[56] In another "topless" case, in Nebraska, a court held that the communicative elements present in topless go-go dance were incidental, if not accidental, to the activity; therefore, dance was not viewed as encompassed by protections of the First Amendment.[57] Enactment of local and state regulations attempting to restrict or eliminate live sex entertainment was stimulated by a 1972 decision of the U.S. Supreme Court in *California v. LaRue*, which upheld a state regulation controlling such activities in establishments holding liquor licenses.[58] In a thorough review of the case and its implications, Diane Diel and Robert Salinger caution against the wholesale application of *LaRue* as a blanket endorsement of all restrictive regulations or the summary enforcement of them, recalling Justice Felix Frankfurter's warning that the transfer of a set of generalizations developed for one set of situations to seemingly analogous, yet essentially different, situations is a treacherous tendency in legal reasoning.[59]

SATIRE AND NUISANCE ASPECTS OF ROCK MUSIC

The interlocking relationships of words and music and the power of song to achieve extra-musical ends are incontrovertible but hotly discussed questions in music. It is a well-known fact that many nursery rhymes originated in political satire and that monarchs like Henry VIII and Elizabeth I were careful to control ballads and broadsides opposing their political regimes or personal characteristics. In the folksong revival of the twentieth century, one frequent target of criticism has been Bob Dylan, folk-singer-turned-rock-artist, who was first censored by some media for his song "Talking John Birch Society." Later he was criticized by his audience as being a "sell-out" to the detrimental effects of censorship on his career. Invited to appear on the Ed Sullivan show in May 1962, he auditioned successfully for Sullivan and the producer, who were delighted with the song. Hours before the show, Dylan was told that he could not perform the song because CBS network officials feared possible libel charges; although they sympathized with the viewpoint of the producers, they could not "take the subject into entertainment."[60] Dylan later was attacked by former admirers because he allowed the omission of the song from the actual recording by Columbia Records, although it had been scheduled for inclusion in his second album. The censorship incident and its repercussions had far-reaching effects not only on Dylan's life but on his style of performance as well.

In the world of rock, one of the early cases of radio station censorship limited the sales of the 1956 rock 'n roll hit by Nervous Norvus entitled "Transfusion," a novelty song describing a man who kept getting in car wrecks; each verse ended with the sound effects of a wreck as the victim screamed for a doctor with lines like "shoot the juice to me, Bruce."[61] Twelve years later, "Street Fight Man" was banned during the 1968 National Democratic Convention as a potential riot-causer by several radio stations. A product of the ability and collaboration of Mick Jagger and Keith Richard, the song as performed by the Rolling Stones was an underground and FM rock radio sensation, although it achieved the ranking of only Number 48 in popularity.[62] Announcing the need for revolution, the lyrics paradoxically characterize rock not as revolutionary, but rather as an opiate for the masses.

The Woodstock Music and Art Fair of August, 1969, proclaimed by its organizers as the arrival of the long-awaited generation-state called "Woodstock Nation," was denounced by some critics as an outrageous episode, although it was later praised by others as the declaration of independence of a life style. Woodstock served as a showcase for a dozen giants of the rock world of the 1960s. The three-day festival at Bethel, New York, easily the most famous of the rock festivals of the late '60s and early '70s, has been analyzed in terms of significance, of diverse reactions to the holdings of festivals, and of the dangers they pose. Presenting problems of health and sanitation, crowd control, crime, drug abuse, traffic control, property rights, unscrupulous promoters, and of cultural security, such festivals have encountered frequent repressive or censorship attempts on the part of local municipal or county authorities.[63] Some of the hastily enacted, but constitutionally defective ordinances, have led to efforts to develop reasonable standards for rock festivals, and several specific legal decisions relating to First Amendment freedoms have centered around rock concert performances. After a riot at a rock concert which was to consist principally of "music dealing with social, political and national issues of importance," the Chicago Park District cancelled some rock concerts in 1970. The decision held that such cancellation did not violate the rights of the plaintiff corporation, where there was nothing in the corporation's permit application to indicate that the corporation was seeking a platform for anything but a "rock music concert" and where issuance of the permit indicated that the Park District had no existing policy to interfere with the form of expression represented by a rock concert. The cancellation was considered to be a "good-faith exercise of the police power by a public body."[64]

Besides the political and obscenity issues related to rock music performance, the question of "nuisance" has been yet another consideration for the courts under the headings of breach of peace, noise, disorderly conduct, and related, still more specific, categories such as "sound-trucks." The high decibel level of rock music has long been a source of complaint on the part of non-proponents of this form of expression, while rock enthusiasts maintain that the amplification must be extreme to produce the real rock sound. A decision in the case *Grayned v. City of Rockford, Ill.* determined that government may turn down over-amplified speakers if they "assault the citizenry" and that such restraints do not violate the right of free expression.[65] Another legal decision relating to the regulation of sound amplifying equipment held that the ability of technology to produce sounds more raucous than those of human voices justifies restrictions on sound level, as well as on hours and places of use of sound trucks—so long as restrictions are reasonable and applied without discrimination.[66] Both of these cases concern sound trucks rather than live performance by a rock group, although the basis of complaint is similar. Litigation over rock concert and rock festival performance as a public nuisance has been linked rather with the allegation that the scheduled festival will violate either licensing laws, zoning laws, or both.[67] Among the leading cases have been *Walpack v. Ratcliffe,*[68] the Powder Ridge Festival,[69] and *Preble v. Song Mountain, Inc.*[70]

In *Walpack*, the festival was prevented on grounds that promoters' plans were too sketchy for the limited facilities of the township, and were therefore insufficient to prevent a nuisance in view of the selected location and the zoning ordinances. The site of the Powder Ridge Festival was found adequate, and the festival was not considered a nuisance "in and of itself"; however, the festival was enjoined because the defendants had not met the requirement of proving that their plans for a "limited" attendance would prevent a traffic jam. In the third case, the festival was enjoined on the basis that the potential for harm to the community and public far outweighed any good that might be derived from the performance or the entire event. The circumstances of these three cases seem to indicate that what has often been decried as "censorship" or banning of performance *per se* is actually a consideration of the needs of a larger community than those of persons who actually attend rock performances.

In addition to rock performances and festivals, other actions have come under fire on the basis of "nuisance." For example, a student who led the after-midnight singing of chants on the lawn of a state college president was adjudged to have engaged in conduct permissible under the First Amendment; he was therefore entitled to the benefit of doubt, making his suspension by the college improper. The chants in themselves were not considered as a non-peaceful activity, and demonstrations of a non-peaceful nature had not accompanied the singing.[71]

Further censorship of performance on the premise of nuisance or breach of peace was the action of a Board of Education in Nassau County in barring a folk singer from giving a scheduled concert in a school auditorium, this on the basis that he was a highly controversial figure whose presence might provoke a disturbance. The singer had been engaged by the community concert association, and the court ruled that the fact that the date for the concert had passed gave no justification for declining to review the constitutional issue as to whether the school board had the right to prevent the performance.[72]

A comical incident occurred in November, 1974, with the revival of a 1919 ordinance against public dancing in Rush Springs, Oklahoma. The ordinance was expanded to include private dancing by a 266-181 vote. This meant that the high school class of 1975 would be breaking the law with their junior-senior prom, but that was deemed more advisable than legalizing hoedowns or sock hops. The city judge, the police chief, and the mayor all agreed that they would look the other direction on the night of the dance.[73]

The issue of censorship of rock music surfaced during December, 1975, in two blacklists of popular music by the South Korean Art and Culture Ethics Committee of the South Korean Federation of Cultural Organizations. This private organization, which derives part of its budget from the Korean government, began a purge of what it called "decadent" foreign musical influences by banning 261 songs which it considered politically and morally harmful to the youth of South Korea. Radio stations, record makers, and singers were affected by the action, and those who attempted to defy the prohibition risked forfeiting rights to entertain or to produce records. In the "revolutionary, subversive and anti-social" category were songs by Joan Baez, John Lennon and Yoko Ono, Bob Dylan, and all records by The Fugs; in addition to being "subversive," Alice Cooper was also termed "decadent, obscene and freaky." Among specific songs and recordings banned were "Never on Sunday," "Delila" (Tom Jones), "We Shall Overcome," "Blowin' in the Wind" (Dylan), "Dona, Dona, Dona" (Baez), "Tom Dooley" (Kingston Trio), "Sometime in New York City" (Lennon and Ono), "One on the right is on the left" (Johnny Cash), a number of songs by Elvis Presley, and several selections from *Hair*. The committee has been censoring Korean songs since 1966, but this was the first time that foreign music had been scrutinized so closely. The campaign against protest music apparently originated in the work of three Korean linguists who translated about 3,700 songs to analyze whether they contained any political or obscene messages. Cho Yon Hyon, the chairman of the committee, explained the measures as a protective action for the cultural climate of South Korean society and urged that they should not be considered anti-foreign, anti-American or chauvinistic.[74]

RELIGION AND THE PERFORMING ARTS

Religious-based censorship of the performing arts has had a long history both in America and in Europe. Music in the Hellenistic cults had a variety of functions: the accompaniment of sacrifices and worship, apotropaic protection from evil gods, epiclesis, catharsis, and sorcery. The association of music with pagan practices undoubtedly led to strictures imposed by the early Christian church, reflecting distrust of instrumental accompaniment in religious ceremonies.[75] The Greek aulos, or flute, carried the Dionysian connotation. Music in early American churches often consisted of a leader who "lined out" the melody for the congregation to follow, while instruments were frowned upon because of the connotation of "ceremonial" worship. Contrary to popular opinion, the Puritans did not pass laws forbidding the use of specific instruments. There were instances when music and dancing figured in court proceedings; however, music was usually incidental to the considerations of disorderly conduct and drunkenness, as in the 1653 case of Salem citizen Thomas Wheeler, who was fined for "profane and foolish dancing, singing and wanton speeches, probably being drunk."[76]

A musical comedy entitled "Two Sides of Heaven," written for the local Bicentennial Commission in Wallingford, Connecticut, was the center of a storm of controversy in 1975 because it dealt with a controversial Perfectionist commune which had existed in the community 100 years previously. The protest resulted from a belief that the show presented the church in a bad light, although the story bears some resemblance to the long-hailed ballet *Appalachian Spring*, written by Aaron Copland for Martha Graham. Editorial support for the bicentennial production maintained that an artistic presentation based on a unique chapter in the community's history should give no offense, and the threat of actual censorship subsided.[77] In contrast, a significant departure from the tradition of removing secular theatre from religious worship occurred in the 1975 use of portions of Gounod's *Faust* in the National Presbyterian Church in Washington, D.C.[78] With the wealth of religious material contained in opera, the existence of an informal censorship has now been counteracted by the efforts of an American University Seminar student, echoing a doctrine of the freedom of art as separate from the freedom of the state and of the church.

CHILDREN

Yet another "community" whose needs, rights, and protection present a specific area for concern is the community of children. Jerry McNeely, an award-winning author of television plays, commented in 1967 that television would never match the theatre or motion pictures in its presentation of "shocking" material because of its accessibility to children.[79] Today with "parental guidance" warnings, there are few limitations on the use of avant-garde or shocking material on television—live or pre-taped. A *Washington Post* reader concerned with censorship of the Johnny Carson show was answered by another reader who asserted that:

> NBC is not trying to protect the audience; it's trying to protect itself. Some subjects still shock late night talk show viewers—mainly sex—and the networks would rather offend those of us who don't want a moral baby sitter at midnight than the various people who fire off letters to sponsors alleging "dirty talk" and other improprieties. Complainers like that don't change channels; they just get indignant.[80]

Concern about "obscene" dance, even in a private residence, in the presence of children was mentioned earlier,[81] and it has been held in the case of *Cinecom Theatres Midwest States, Inc. v. City of Fort Wayne*, that a city may restrict a child's exposure to nudity of an obscene nature and may define obscenity as it relates only to children. The case in question applied to cinema.[82] However, in the case of a theatrical production, a contention was not upheld that a city civic center was an "image" for presentation of "family-type entertainment" and would suffer financial harm if it did not conform to this image. The decision in *Southeastern Promotions, Ltd. v. The City of Atlanta* held that the civic center's image did not justify the director's ban on a theatrical performance in which the theme was the exposure of hypocrisy and pretense of the contemporary middle-age "establishment." In this production, members of the cast appeared nude under subdued lighting for a period of less than 35 seconds, and one actor was draped in an American flag.[83] Censorship was avoided, although the directors of the center were characterized as acting with the best of intentions in their effort to maintain a family image.

SYMBOLIC SPEECH

Symbolic speech is closely related to theatrical or musical expression by virtue of its many non-verbal variants: the significance of costume and make-up, the importance of gesture, the existence in music of musical meaning not related to words, or of associative musical meaning through previous experience with verbal stimuli. Non-verbal expression has been accorded First Amendment protections as a form of speech not confined to the spoken and written word,[84] and yet in a 1973 case, *State v. Cline*, symbolic speech was not afforded the same protection as ideas communicated by pure speech.[85] A 1970 Tennessee decision held that the growing of hair for purely commercial purposes such as performing in a musical group was not protected by the guarantee of freedom of speech.[86] A similar Arkansas decision in the same year required student participants in a school band program to modify the length of their hair to "reasonable" requirements of the band director. Application of this policy to students claiming "social protest" was not deemed to deprive subjects of their federally protected right. It had not been sufficiently demonstrated that the school was attempting to prevent protests or punish students for protesting.[87] A year later, a Utah decision called the wearing of long hair by students as not akin to pure speech but rather symbolic speech, indicative of expressions of individuality rather than contribution to a storehouse of ideas.[88] But the wearing of a beard was termed symbolic conduct entitled to constitutional protection as a variant exercise of free speech.[89]

While the decisions themselves seem at variance, the chronological progress indicates the growth of tolerance toward the symbolism expressed by performance groups as well as by working men and students. The decision in the case of *Jackson v. Dorrier* seems to present an additional question: were First Amendment rights denied on the basis that hair length was only a commercial "gimmick" rather than a symbolic expression? This seems to be the implication of the decision. Regardless of the attitudes of 1969 and 1970, the trend has appeared to move toward greater acceptance of long hair as the question has become virtually a closed issue.

Three facets of the issues of costume in a theatrical performance and the right of an actor to speak out against the nation's and the U.S. Army's role in Vietnam were revealed in another 1970 case, *Schacht v. United States*.[90] The punishment of an actor for speaking against the Army's role was viewed as an unconstitutional abridgment of the freedom of speech. In addition, the actor had not violated U.S.C.A.: 702, which prohibits an unauthorized person from wearing a United States armed forces uniform. Since unauthorized wearing of the uniform is a crime, the court decided that the portion of 10 U.S.C.A.: 772(f) that permits an actor portraying a member of the armed forces in a theatrical production to wear a uniform "if the portrayal does not tend to discredit that armed force" must be stricken to preserve the constitutionality of the remainder of the section. Now, an actor wearing military uniform cannot be denied the constitutional right to verbally or symbolically attack the armed forces.

CONCLUSION

The increasingly liberal views expressed in many of the court decisions relating to performance of music, dance, theatre, and the other live arts give credence to the "right of the body and the instincts not merely to be a begrudged existence but to hold equal honor with its conscious spirit."[91] The questions of nudity, nuisance, religious disapproval, symbolic expression, and the protection of children seem to be accorded just treatment, regardless of repeated onslaughts throughout the years by individuals or groups who fail to recognize the validity of freedom of expression. Even political freedom of expression within our own country, concerned with our own people, has escaped some of the strictures of Censorship; the decision in the *Schacht* case could easily have been disastrous. The greatest dangers to freedom of expression seem to lie with political issues that involve restraints on performing artists or performing groups as they try to bring greater comprehension of their own civilizations to people of vastly different ideologies. Governmental restraints—regardless of the country imposing them—continually prevent the development of understandings larger than the immediate rapport created between audiences and performers— folk-singers, operatic prima donnas, dancers, rock groups, or school bands. Performing artists are truly free people of unique quality because performance is itself a way of life.

Their faith in freedom is their faith in themselves . . . aggression is not against the man, but against the faith that is in him and against the way of life built upon that faith . . . creative artists in so many ways the avatars of freedom, have in this perennial battle never yielded. Thus . . .

liberty and *liberty of art* express a distinction that makes no important difference.[92]

The Rostropovichs and Dylans of the world have achieved the distinction of making a significant difference; they have lifted thousands of lives from begrudged existence to conscious spirit through the unrestrained live moment of performance.

FOOTNOTES

[1] Edward L. Kamarck, ed., "Censorship and the Arts," *Arts and Society* 4 (Summer, 1967): 2.

[2] Herbert T. Silverberg, "Authors' and Performers' Rights; Radio and Television—A Symposium," *Law and Contemporary Problems* 23 (Winter, 1958): 1.

[3] Plato, *The Republic*.

[4] George Santayana, *The Sense of Beauty* (New York: Dover Books, 1955), pp. 129-30.

[5] Horace M. Kallen, *Art and Freedom* (New York: Greenwood Press, 1942), p. 31.

[6] E.g., *People v. Heller*, 1973, 307 N.E. 2d 805, 33 N.Y. 2d 314, 352 N.Y.S.

[7] *People v. Adler*, 101 Cal. Reptr. 726, 25 C.A. 3d Supp. 24. United States Code Annotated Const. Amend. 1, Note 359, p. 138 (1973-1974).

[8] D. C. Tenn. 1972, 341 F. Supp. 465 affirmed 486 F. 2d 894, certiorari granted 94 S. Ct., 1406, 415 U.S. 912, 39 L. Ed. 2d 466.

[9] Robert Paul Wolff, *Philosophy: A Modern Encounter* (Englewood Cliffs, N.J.: Prentice-Hall, 1971), p. 546:

[10] Walter Kerr, "The Importance of Being Insecure," the *New York Times* (September 7, 1975).

[11] Silverberg, p. 126.

[12] *Republic Pictures Corp. v. Rogers*, 213 F. 2d 662 (9th Cir. 1954); *Republic Productions v. Rogers*, 213 F. 2d 667 (9th Cir. 1954); and *Autrey v. Republic Productions*, 213 F. 2d 667 (9th Cir. 1954).

[13] Silverberg, pp. 163-64.

[14] *CBS v. Democratic National Committee*, U.S. Dist. Col. 1973, S. Ct. 2080, 412 U.S. 94 36 L. Ed. 2d 772. United States Code Annotated Const. Amend. 1, Note 67, p. 46 (1973-1974).

[15] *National Lampoon Inc. v. American Broadcasting Companies,Inc.*, D.C.N.Y. 1974, 376 F. Supp. 733. United States Code Annotated Const. Amend. 1, Note 67, p. 46 (1973-1974).

[16] *State v. Vollmar*, Mo. 1965, 389 S.W. 2d 20. United States Code Annotated Amend. 1, Note 331, p. 256 (1972).

[17] *Figari v. New York Tel. Co.*, 1969, 303 N.Y.S. 2d 245, 32 A.D. 2d 434; and *People v. Stabile*, 1969, 296 N.Y.S. 2d 815, 58 Misc. 2d 905.

[18] Joseph Bensman and Robert Lilienfeld, *Craft and Consciousness; Occupational Technique and the Development of World Images* (New York: John Wiley and Sons, 1973), p. 267.

[19] Galina Vishnevskaya, Rostropovich's wife and a leading soprano at the Bolshoi Opera, was also requested for a role in *Boris Godunow* by the director, Herbert

von Karajan. The request was denied by the USSR Ministry of Culture on the basis that she was a soprano and could not sing the role.

[20] In January 1974, a telegram was sent on the occasion of the UNESCO jubilee in Paris saying that Rostropovich was sick, but he was actually in excellent health.

[21] Mstislav Rostropovich, "It Must Be Possible for One's Hope and Belief to Come True," *Washington Post* (March 9, 1975), E-01-4.

[22] Irving Kolodin, "An American Debut: The Big Bolshoi Brand of Grand Opera," *Saturday Review of Literature* (June 28, 1975), pp. 31-32.

[23] Boris Schwarz, *Music and Musical Life in Russia, 1917-1970* (New York: W. W. Norton, 1972), p. 219.

[24] *Ibid.*, p. 220.

[25] "Russian Composer Shostakovich Dies," *Tampa Tribune* (August 10, 1975).

[26] Anna Kisselgoff, "The Split in Soviet Ballet," *The New York Times*, Arts and Leisure (September 7, 1975), p. 10.

[27] *Ibid.*

[28] Derrill S. Copp, "How Censorship Works in the Soviet Union," *Human Events* (March 10, 1973), p. 20.

[29] Anna Kisselgoff, "Tour by Chinese Troupe Ended on Taiwan Issue," *The New York Times* (March 28, 1975), 16:1.

[30] "Chinese Assert U.S. Violated Agreement by Barring a Song," *The New York Times* (April 4, 1975), 3:6.

[31] John D. Mitchell, Donald Chang, and Roger Yen, "Two Faces of China," *Opera News* (April 20-17, 1974): 27.

[32] Frank Ching, "China Denounces Literary Classic," *The New York Times* (September 7, 1975).

[33] Kathleen Teltsch, "Cantata Lacking a Psalm Verse Causes a Cacophony at the U.N.," *The New York Times* (October 19, 1975).

[34] The exhibition included 30 paintings by Western masters and 13 works by Russian painters of the Pre-Revolutionary era, but no contemporary artists were represented.

[35] Hilton Kramer, "The Dark Side of Cultural Détente," *The New York Times*, Arts and Leisure, April 18, 1975, 18:1.

[36] Eric Larrabee, "The Cultural Context of Sex Censorship," *Law and Contemporary Problems* 20 (Autumn, 1955): 672.

[37] Terrence J. Murphy, *Censorship: Government and Obscenity* (Baltimore: Helicon Press, 1963), pp. 30-31.

[38] Albert Goldman, *Ladies and Gentlemen, Lenny Bruce* (New York: Ballantine Books, 1974), pp. 510-36.

[39] Richard Kuh, *Foolish Fig Leaves? Pornography in and out of Court* (New York: Macmillan, 1967).

[40] Goldman, p. 646.

[41] *Ibid.*, p. 669.

[42] *Jacobellis, Tropic of Cancer*, and *Fanny Hill.*

[43] Larrabee, p. 675.

[44] *Ibid.*, p. 679.

[45] William E. Ringel, *Obscenity Law Today* (Jamaica, N.Y.: Gould Publications, 1970), pp. 39-52.

[46] *Southeastern Promotions,Limited v. City of Mobile, Ala.*, C.A. 1972. 457 F. 2d 340 United States Code Annotated Const. Amend. 1, Note 152a, P. 67 (1973-1974).

[47] *Southeastern Promotions, Limited v. Conrad*, C.A. Tenn., 1973, 486 F. 2d 894 certiorari granted 94.5 S. Ct. 1406, 415 U.S. 912. 39 L. Ed. 2d 466.

[48] *Southeastern Promotions, Inc. v. Conrad*, D.C. Tenn., 1972, 341 F. Supp. 465, affirmed 486 F. 2d 894, certiorari granted 94 S. Ct. 1406, 415 U.S. 912, 39 L. Ed. 2d 466.

[49] *Robinson v. State of Arkansas*, 1973, 489 S.W. 2d 503.

[50] John MacKenzie, "Courts Curb Censoring of Live Theatre," *Washington Post* (March 19, 1975), p. 1.

[51] A. Owen Aldridge, "American Burlesque at Home and Abroad: Together with the Etymology of Go-Go Girls," *Journal of Popular Culture* 5 (Winter, 1971): 565-75.

[52] Serena and Alan Wilson, *The Serena Technique of Belly Dancing* (New York: Cornerstone Library, 1974), pp. 9-10.

[53] *Reichenberger v. Conrad*, D. C. Wis. 1970, 319 F. Supp. 1240 United States Code Annotated Const. Amend. 1, Note 368, p. 280 (1972).

[54] *Wood v. Moore*, D.C.N.C. 1972, 350 F. Supp. 29 United States Code Annotated Const. Amend. 1, Note 152b, p. 67 (1973-1974).

[55] *Salem Inn v. Frank*, D.C.N.Y. 1973, 364 F. Supp. 478, affirmed 501 F. 2d 18. United States Code Annotated Const. Amend. 1, Note 152b, p. 67 (1973-1974).

[56] *Yauch v. State*, Ariz., App. 1973, 505 P. 2d 1066. United States Code Annotated Const. Amend. 1, Note 152, p. 67 (1973-1974).

[57] *Paladino v. City of Omaha*, D.C. Neb. 1972, 335 F. Supp. 897, affirmed 471 F 2d 812. 409 U.S. 109 (1972).

[58] 409 U.S. 109 (1972).

[59] Diane S. Siel and Robert M. Salinger, "Demon Rum and the Dirty Dance: Reconsidering Government Regulation of Live Sex Entertainment after California v. LaRue," *Wisconsin Law Review* (1975): 191.

[60] Anthony Scaduto, *Bob Dylan* (New York: Grosset and Dunlap, 1971), pp. 139-42.

[61] Mike Jahn, *Rock; from Elvis Presley to the Rolling Stones* (New York: Quadrangle/New York Times Book Co., 1973), p. 36.

[62] *Ibid.*, p. 231.

[63] "Rights and Remedies in Rock Festival Litigation and Legislation," *Columbia Journal of Law and Social Problems* 7 (Winter, 1971): 141-46.

[64] *Contemporary Music Group, Inc. v. Chicago Park Dist.*, D.C. Ill. 1972, 343 F. Supp. 505. United States Code Annotated Const. Amend. 1, Note 293, p. 123 (1973-1974).

[65] *Grayned v. City of Rockford, Ill.*, 1972. 92 S. Ct. 2294, 408 U.S. 104 33 L. Ed. 2d 222. United States Code Annotated Const. Amend. 1, Note 172, p. 74 (1973-1974).

[66] *Red Lion Broadcasting Co. v. F. C. A.*, Dist. Col. 1969, 89 S. Ct. 1794, 395 U.S. 367 23, L. Ed. 2d 371, United States Code Annotated Const. Amend. 1, Note 287, p. 243 (1972).

[67] *Columbia Journal of Law and Social Problems*, pp. 148-51.

[68] *Township of Walpack v. Ratcliffe*, No. C-317-69 Super. Ct., Sullivan County, N.J., July 20, 1970 (oral opinion) at 34.

[69] *Planning and Zoning Commission v. Zernel Bros., Inc.*, No. 20242 Conn. Super. Ct., July 27, 1970.

[70] *Town of Preble v. Song Mountain, Inc.*, 62 Misc. 2d 353, 308 N.Y.S. 2d 1001 Sup. Ct. 1970.

[71] *Barker v. Hardway*, D.C.W. Va. 1968, 283 F. Supp. 228, affirmed 399 F. 2d 638, certiorari denied 89 S. Ct. 1009, 394 U.S. 905, 22 L. Ed. 2d 217, United States Code Annotated Const. Amend. 1, Note 174 (1972).

[72] *East Meadow Community Concerts Association v. Board of Education of Union Free School District No. 3, Nassau County*, 1966, 219 N.E. 2d 172, 18 N.Y. 2d 129, 272 N.Y.S. 2d 341, on remand 273 N.Y.S. 2d 736 26 A.D. 2d 819.

[73] "Darn the Law! They'll Dance," *Washington Post* (January 28, 1975), C, p. 5.

[74] "South Korea Banning Decadent Foreign Music, Including Many Protest Songs," *The New York Times* (December 28, 1975), p. 10.

[75] Eric Werner, *The Sacred Bridge* (London: Dennis Dobson, 1963), p. 332.

[76] Gilbert Chase, *American Music* (New York: McGraw-Hill Book Co., 1955), p. 10.

[77] "A Bicentennial Musical Splits Connecticut Town," *The New York Times* (August 24, 1975), p. 44.

[78] "D. C. Presbyterian Church Slates 'Religion in Opera' Program," *Washington Post* (March 7, 1975), B-14-1.

[79] Kamarck, p. 302.

[80] Stuart Nixon, Letter to the editor on TV censorship, *Washington Post* (March 6, 1975), A, p. 15.

[81] See note 53; United States Code Annotated Const. Amend. 1, Note 345, p. 131 (1973-1974); United States Code Annotated Const. Amend. 1, Note 359 (1973-1974), p. 138.

[82] *Cinecom Theaters Midwest States, Inc. v. City of Fort Wayne*, C.A. Ind. 1973, 473 F. 2d 1297. United States Code Annotated Const. Amend. 1, Note 293, p. 123 (1973-1974).

[83] *Southeastern Promotions, Limited v. City of Atlanta, Ga.*, D.C. Ga. 1971, 334 F. Supp. 634. United States Code Annotated Const. Amend. 1, Note 102, p. 135 (1972).

[84] *Sutherland v. DeWulf*, D.C. Ill. 1971, 323 F. Supp. 740. Also, *U.S. v. Cooper*, D.C. Colo., 1968, 279 F. Supp. 253. United States Code Annotated Const. Amend. 1, Note 104, p. 51 (1973-1974).

[85] *State v. Cline*, N.H. 1973, 305 A. 2d 673. United States Code Annotated Const. Amend. 1, Note 157, p. 168 (1972).

[86] *Jackson v. Dorrier*, C.A. Tenn., 1970, 424 F. 2d 213, certiorari denied 91 S. Ct. 55, 400 U.S. 850, 27 L. Ed. 2d 88. United States Code Annotated Const. Amend. 1, Note 178, p. 178 (1972).

[87] *Corley v. Daunhauer*, D.C. Ark., 1970, 312 F. Supp. 811. United States Code Annotated Const. Amend. 1, Note 104, p. 136 (1972).

[88] *Freeman v. Flake*, C.A. Utah, 1971, 448 F. 2d 258. United States Code Annotated Const. Amend. 1, Note 104, p. 51 (1973-1974).

[89] *King v. California Unemployment Ins. Appeals Board*, 1972, 101 Cal. Rptr. 660, 25 C.A. 3d 199. United States Code Annotated Const. Amend. 1, Note 293, p. 247 (1972).

[90] *Schacht v. United States*, Tex. 1970, 90 S. Ct. 1555, 398 U.S. 58, 26 L. Ed. 2d 44.

[91] Aldous Huxley, *On Art and Artists* (New York: Meridian Books, 1960), p. 72.

[92] Kallen, p. 15.

CENSORSHIP AND THE CONTEMPORARY CINEMA
Gail Linda Robinson

In 1922, Havelock Ellis wrote *Little Essays of Love and Virtue*, frankly treating the pleasures of sexuality in an unusual and unprecedented manner. Three years later, another somewhat shocking work appeared—Sigmund Freud's *On Creativity and the Unconscious*, comprised of papers on the psychology of art, literature, love, and religion. Gradually, almost imperceptibly, the lace-edged magenta curtains of Victorianism were drawn apart; man was permitted to view himself in a new physical and psychological light. Much was gleaned from what was revealed, and today we have knowledge about all facets of our beings. We can look upon the human body and mind in a beautifully honest manner, such as Adam and Eve are said to have enjoyed before they succumbed to temptation. Persons who have felt this revelation now seriously doubt that the curtains can ever again be closed. Many of our young people—accustomed to liberal attitudes far removed from those of the Victorian household—refuse to entertain the idea that increasing freedoms in the arts and literature could be reversed.

However, as this chapter will illustrate, the Victorian mind still persists. While the lessening of restrictions on sexual expression has made some individuals freer, other persons remain both untouched and unconvinced that freedom of sexual expression in the arts and in literature is a goal worth attaining and preserving. In relation to the contemporary censorship of motion pictures, Murray Shumack has stated:

> The movie industry has been adjudged an art, entitled to the freedom enjoyed by books, newspapers and magazines. But draped in old and tattered statutes, the censors hand down edicts that have made them the elite among nincompoops.[1]

One film that created an unusual amount of controversy in the 1940s was *The Outlaw*, starring Jane Russell. After a six-year ban on the picture, a Baltimore judge who supported a continuation of the restriction stated that Jane Russell's breasts "hung over the picture like a thunderstorm spread out over a landscape."[2] (Meanwhile, Howard Hughes, the producer, was showing the motion picture without a seal of approval in all theaters that would feature it.) But freedom in the arts increased substantially between the 1940s and the 1960s. For example, a seal of approval was denied the film *Bicycle Thief* in 1949 because one scene showed a man strolling into a house of prostitution, but *Walk on the Wild Side* earned the seal in 1964, even though it dealt with a whorehouse operated by a lesbian madam.

However, before the discussion of contemporary film censorship, a word about the organization of this chapter is in order. Contemporary incidents of film censorship in the United States will be treated first. Such incidents are numerous and will demonstrate the unavoidable verity that human vessels of Victorian prudishness are still harbored in America. Also, contemporary controversial films, particularly those produced since 1970, will be analyzed in terms of content, characters, and reviews. Arguments for film censorship will be presented with existing supporting evidence, and corresponding anti-censorship positions will also be analyzed, along with any substantiating evidence. Then, tentative conclusions will be drawn from these discussions of film censorship.

SEX IN MOTION PICTURES

Although controversial books are often the targets of censors, they are not as vulnerable to censorship as are films, since books do not always depict sex pictorially. For example, most would-be censors appear to be less appalled by printed descriptions of sexual activity than they are about seeing it enacted on motion picture screens. In *The Face on the Cutting Room Floor*, Murray Shumack wrote:

> The first law of censorship—and probably the only important one not inscribed on the statute books—is this: in a democracy, the more popular the art form, the greater the demands for censorship of it.[3]

The ALA *Newsletter on Intellectual Freedom* contains numerous reports of legal actions against motion pictures. Most of the examples of film censorship reported in the following section of this chapter are cited in the *Newsletter*, which is available for consultation in most libraries.

One film that was a prime target for censors in the early 1970s was *The Devil in Miss Jones.* Massachusetts Superior Court Judge James C. Roy sentenced a Boston theater operator to a two-year prison term and a $5,000 fine for showing the film. The judge stated that community standards (the opinion of the average person) should determine which films are protected by the First Amendment.[4] Thus, *The Devil in Miss Jones* was deemed "common trash" and was banned in Memphis. In Manhattan, the film was not viewed as offensive, but on the other hand, Bronx Criminal Court Judge Joseph Mazur declared that *The Devil in Miss Jones* was obscene.

Even more than *The Devil in Miss Jones*, another film, *Last Tango in Paris*, was assaulted with the most caustic criticism, and the film was prohibited in a number of geographic areas of the country. In Idaho, Prosecutor Robert J. Fanning ordered a Booneville theater operator to cease showing *Last Tango*, which was labeled "a slender thread to hang a gross obscenity" by Attorney John A. Richardson. In Jamestown, New York, the city council ruled, in apparent reaction to community criticism of *Last Tango*, that X-rated movies could not be shown. In November, 1973, *Tango* fared somewhat better in Mineola, New York, where a motion by residents of the village of Lynbrook to ban the film was denied.

One of the most controversial films of the 1970s has been *Deep Throat*. Labeled by a Cincinnati court as a film created only for profit, it was banned in January 1974 by Judge Robert L. Black, Jr., of Hamilton County's Common Pleas Court. In San Jose, California, the showing of *Deep Throat* was ended under California's Red Light Abatement Act. Superior Court Judge O. Vincent Bruno called it "a moral epic with sick offerings." Elsewhere, five persons each received five-year prison sentences and $5,000 fines for "conspiring" to show *Deep Throat* in Dallas, but attempts to have the film declared obscene in Jacksonville, Florida, were unsuccessful. Social psychologists would probably be amused to learn that while *Deep Throat* was being fought in Jacksonville courts, 12,000 residents of the city each paid five dollars to view the film.

In 1972, the Arizona Supreme Court declared that the film *I Am Curious (Yellow)* was obscene. A portion of that Court's definition of obscenity stated:

> Obscenity . . . focuses predominantly upon what is sexually morbid, grossly perverse and bizarre, without any artistic or scientific purpose or justification. It is to be differentiated from the bawdy and the ribald . . . depicting dirt for dirt's sake; the obscene is the vile, rather than the coarse, the blow to sense, not merely to sensibility. . . . It smacks at times of fantasy and unreality, of sexual perversion and fitness and represents . . . a debauchery of the sexual faculties.[5]

In *I Am Curious (Yellow)*, the primary character, Lena, is concerned with influencing society to become less violent. The film certainly has redeeming features; it deals with a socially significant contemporary issue: the questioning of the establishment by the young. Sexual encounters depicted in the film occur between Lena and her lover. *I Am Curious (Yellow)* is a film with many levels; nevertheless, it is a rather restrained, non-threatening film, as its treatment is largely satirical. The viewer is allowed to maintain a kind of protective social detachment. The acting in the film is quite good, and actress Lena Neyman possesses considerable charisma. Of the explicit sex scenes in the film, Clyde B. Smith has stated:

> I think it is possible to argue that the sex itself is important in the general scheme of things, and thus a legitimate subject for an artist. . . . Why don't we just do away with censorship and stop having to justify, on the wrong grounds, such obviously worthy films as *I Am Curious*?[6]

Various legal actions were also taken against another motion picture, *Distortions of Sexuality*, which featured sexual activities among members of an encounter group led by a quack psychiatrist. In Washington, D.C., two films, *Hot Circuit* and *Distortions of Sexuality*, were declared to be obscene by Federal Magistrate Arthur L. Burnett. The same fate befell *Distortions of Sexuality* in Norfolk, Virginia, where it was declared obscene by General District Court Judge Llewellyn S. Richardson. The judge stated that the film was so repulsive that it would cause retching among Supreme Court justices.

In Minneapolis, the conviction of Mel Lekowitz for showing *The Art of Marriage* was upheld, and a new local decision relating to sexually oriented films was made: films were no longer to be considered "obscene" or "not obscene" but as "hardcore" or "softcore." Hardcore material was defined as that which has "no pretense of artistic value," and thus is not protected by the U.S. Constitution. Softcore material was defined as "less offensive than hardcore and protected by the Constitution as long as it is not sold to minors, pandered, or shown to unwilling viewers." Considerable confusion among Minnesota state supreme court judges was apparent as the seven legal experts attempted to interpret obscenity laws. Indeed, Chief Judge Oscar Knudson stated: "No one seems to know what the guidelines are. Until there is some clarification, I prefer to uphold the trial court."

Several other films have also recently been the object of official censure, *Vixen* among them. As late as January, 1974, the Ohio Supreme Court upheld a 1971 decision by the Hamilton County Common Pleas Court to ban *Vixen* on the basis of what was interpreted as an exploitation of sexual intercourse for purpose of monetary gain. Melvin Van Peeble's motion picture, *Sweet Sweetback's Baadasssss Song*, was also denounced by Florida's special assistant state attorney Leonard Rivkind (of the Task Force on Obscenity) as obscene, and was therefore prohibited from being shown in south Florida theaters. In Kentucky, protests from local citizens caused the cancellation of Russ Meyer's *Beyond the Valley of the Dolls* at the West Liberty Drive-In Theater. In another case which involved the films *Oh, Doctor!* and *Electrosex 1975*, Franklin County (Kentucky) Court of Appeals Judge Alba Whiteside stated that theater owners who planned to show the films could be arrested before the pictures were actually declared to be obscene. In Baltimore, Maryland, Circuit Court Judge Meyer M. Gardin stated that the language of one scene in *Doctors from Copenhagen* was "by far the worst this court has ever heard in a movie," and he upheld a ban on the film. A complaint was filed by Mrs. Billie Lasher and two hundred other citizens in St. Louis, Missouri, concerning the Woody Allen movie *Everything You Always Wanted to Know About Sex But Were Afraid to Ask*. Although some citizens insisted that prohibitions be placed on the film, no official decision was reached.

A case surfaced in Kentucky where Western Kentucky University students filed suit in the U.S. Circuit Court of Appeals charging that their right to freedom of expression had been denied when university officials declined to allow *The Fly*, by John Lennon and Yoko Ono, to be shown on campus. Although the offensiveness of the film consisted only in the fact that a fly was crawling over a nude woman's body, the students lost their case. In another incident, the Reverend Cecil W. Howard of St. Louis wanted to suppress the film *Super Fly*; he claimed that it could have adverse effects on young blacks. The motion picture depicts young blacks in ostentatious clothes and fancy automobiles who commit crimes in order to maintain their lifestyle. Another film, *Pink Flamingos*, has also encountered difficulties with censors; it was cancelled by the University of Maryland for fear that the film might be illegal.

Even *The Graduate*, a presumably innocuous film, was disliked by censors in Hoboken, New Jersey, where the board of education refused use of a high school auditorium for the film's showing, despite plans to restrict attendance to persons eighteen years of age or older. Education Board President Otto Hottendorf softened the verdict on *The Graduate* by conceding that a showing of the film might be allowed if letters of approval were secured from local clergymen. The familiar case of the banning of *Carnal Knowledge* in Georgia can also be added to this list of recent film repressions and prohibitions in the United States.

While specific feature-length, general motion pictures are the obvious targets of a large percentage of film censorship attempts, so-called "porno" films have also been involved in a substantial number of controversies. In 1974, obscenity convictions of three film exhibitors were overturned by the Ohio Supreme Court, because search warrants had not been obtained to seize the objectionable films. In New York, Manhattan Judge Harold Rothwax ruled that the seizure of thousands of magazines and films by police in raids on 135 book stores and peep shows in the Times Square area was a violation of rights of shop owners under the First and

Fourteenth Amendments. The police had not obtained judicial approval for their actions.

In El Paso, Texas, felony charges were pressed for the first time against eight "adult" movie operators, and bond was set at between $10,000 and $15,000 for each operator. Prior to that case, obscenity offenses in El Paso had been classed as misdemeanors. Another step toward repression was taken in Trenton, New Jersey, where the State Assembly voted 53-3 to allow municipalities the option to ban from drive-in theaters films featuring explicit sex scenes. In a similar vein, an ordinance banning the showing of "obscene" films and the selling of pornographic literature in unincorporated Dade County, Florida, was accepted by Metro commissioners in a five-to-three vote. Leonard Rivkind, special assistant state attorney of Florida remarked:

> We need a strong ordinance. Sex should not be a spectator sport. The law
> is not an infringement of First Amendment rights. The First Amendment
> is intended as a highway, not a sewer.[7]

In a North Carolina case cited in the *Newsletter on Intellectual Freedom* (July 1973), a number of citizens appeared before a state senate judiciary committee to express support of a bill to ban the showing of films transported "in and into the state" which portray nudity, sexual conduct, sado-masochistic abuse, and which appeal to prurient interests. During the hearings in Raleigh, Mrs. Danny Lotz, daughter of Evangelist Billy Graham, remarked that the showing of X and R-rated films is part of a satanic onslaught and moral decadence. The evangelist's daughter also claimed that warning labels are placed on poisons and that television stations should likewise warn viewers before objectionable movies are broadcast. One weeping, Bible-clutching woman appeared at the Raleigh hearing and told the state committee that she would not be what she was then if X-rated movies had been shown on TV when she was a youngster.

The equation of sexual expression in literature and in movies with the concept of sin has also been noted. For example, while a raid was in progress in 1972 on a New York City adult book shop, one man who was actually a bookstore customer pretended merely to be a passing observer of the scene. Rather than putting up a defense of the shop, the man criticized it self-righteously and claimed that it contained filth. When ultimately confronted with the fact that he had been observed leaving the store, the customer stated: "The devil made me do it."

Les Brown, a reporter for *The New York Times*, has observed that increasing pressures by certain groups on TV stations to halt the showing of some films is prevalent in Southern California—especially among Mexican-American, Japanese-America, and black activist groups. The Japanese-American Citizens League has placed some films about the Japanese in World War II on an "off limits" list, including *Across the Pacific*, *Purple Heart*, and *Behind the Rising Sun*. Justicia, an organization of Mexican-Americans, would also like to ban motion pictures which show Mexicans in an unfavorable light, including *The Return of the Magnificent Seven*, *Butch Cassidy and the Sundance Kid*, and *Rio Lobo*. While Jews are generally recognized as opposed to censorship, they have objected to the portrayal of Jewish people in an unfavorable light, such as the case of Fagin in Dickens' *Oliver Twist*.

Although black ethnic pictures such as *Super Fly* and *Shaft's Big Score* were protested by CORE, NAACP, and The Coalition Against Black Exploitation because the films depict sordid aspects of the black experience such as dope pushers, prostitutes, and gangsters, these movies were attended by more blacks than was *Sounder*, which portrays a more dignified black image. *Super Fly* and *Shaft's Big Score* were directed by blacks, while *Sounder* was directed by whites, but *Super Fly* is probably more representative or "true to life" than *Sounder* for blacks who live in a ghetto.

In September, 1973, the U.S. Supreme Court conducted a question-and-answer session to help clarify its new guidelines for recognizing obscenity, limits that were decided the previous June in *Miller v. California*. These guidelines for determining what is obscene are as follows: 1) whether the "average person, applying contemporary community standards" would find that a work in general appeals to the prurient interest; 2) whether a work depicts or describes, in a patently offensive manner, sexual behavior specifically defined by the applicable state law; and 3) whether the work, as a whole, lacks serious literary, political, or scientific value. Under the new obscenity ruling, lay jurors are entrusted with the responsibility of making these decisions; they need to consult only the allegedly obscene work for their evidence. The findings of the lay jurors generally cannot be appealed.

Based upon the realization that the United States is a large and diverse country, the Supreme Court asserted the difficulty of expressing criteria for the identification of obscenity in one formula for all fifty states. The June 21, 1973, Court decision did not elaborate on the "local community" concept, but "sexual misconduct" was defined as the "lewd exhibition of genitals." The Supreme Court rejected the "consenting adult theory" in order to protect the uninformed, the gullible, and the unsuspecting. While a person is permitted, according to the new obscenity standards, to house obscene materials in his domicile, the purchase or transportation of those same obscene items is illegal.

SELF-CENSORSHIP IN THE FILM INDUSTRY

The Motion Picture Production Code was adopted by the film industry on March 31, 1930, and the practice of self-censorship of motion pictures began. Between 1930 and 1961, only one important change was made in the code—drug addiction was finally allowed to be depicted in films. In 1961, homosexuality was also permitted frank treatment on the screen. Joseph I. Breen, who was responsible for enforcing the Code, was given the authority to withhold the seal of approval from any film that flouted the rules. Also, outside of the film industry itself, the Legion of Decency was formed in 1934 to warn Catholics of films that were viewed by the group as threats to their faith and morals.

Hollywood tried in the late 1960s to resist opposition to objectionable films by developing the Code of Self-Regulation of the Motion Picture Association of America (M.P.A.A.). However, the rather tolerant new Code has received considerable criticism from various quarters. William Fadiman has written:

> Criticism of the censorship code stems from die-hard Puritans who would prefer inflexible moral restrictions and from civil libertarians who want no censorship at all. Hollywood is caught in the middle. . . . [8]

Under the M.P.A.A. system, films are rated as follows: *X* (under 17 not allowed), *R* (under 17 admitted, but only with parents or guardians), *GP* (under 17 admitted, parental guidance suggested), and *G* (all ages admitted). Dr. Aaron Stern, head of the rating board, commented about film ratings during an interview:

> What you've got to explain to a producer is that he's got a PG script except for—pardon the language—the word "fuck" three times. The word's not important to the story. So he takes it out and gets his PG.[9]

Many foreign motion picture producers do not stifle enthusiasm by giving such labels to films. Perhaps this factor has contributed to the appearance of more daring, imaginative, and exciting films from foreign countries than from American producers.

In *The Fifty-Year Decline and Fall of Hollywood*, Ezra Goodman has stated:

> Hollywood likes to sound off in high-flown phrases . . . about the evil of censorship and other restrictive controls. But Hollywood never had the character and conviction to fight for freedom of the screen.[10]

If Hollywood has indeed succumbed for years to various pressure groups, an immediate turnabout at the present time does not appear likely. Many of the movie censorship battles have been won by individuals—not by the motion picture industry itself. Joseph Burstyn, a foreign film importer and distributor, carried his cause to the Supreme Court and overturned prohibitions against *The Miracle*, *Ways of Love*, *Open City*, *Poison*, and *Bicycle Thief.* Burstyn has stated:

> I had to fight for each of these pictures. I insist on presenting films as freely as a writer writes a book or a painter paints a picture.[11]

Ephraim London, a noted censorship attorney, also managed in 1959 to lift the ban on *Lady Chatterly's Lover.*

During the old Hays Code period (William Hays was Breen's predecessor as the industry's chief resident censor), which began in 1922, little sex or violence was depicted in movies. With the advent of commercial television in the late 1940s and early 1950s, movie attendance dropped drastically in the United States. To attract people back to movie houses, filmmaking then became more adventurous. The Valenti Code, adopted in 1968, was an attempt to balance the right of the film-maker's creativity against the audience's right to view appropriate subject matter. Charles Champlin, a motion picture critic, has written:

> It is one of the great ironies of present filmmaking that economic distress has resulted in a genuine coming of age of the movie medium. In terms of ability to deal with any theme and to handle it with candor in image and language, the movies now have parity with the novel and the drama.[12]

Champlin has also commented optimistically about filmmakers in the 1970s: "They want to use the screen to discover the possibilities of hope and the existence of idealism—not just the grim realities and the private despairs."[13]

Before further discussion of various controversial films and a review of pro- and anti-censorship arguments, a slight digression will be taken in order to examine England's film rating system. First, the British have an organization which was established for the purpose of censoring films: the British Board of Film Censors (BBFC). When a novelist's work or a script is submitted to the BBFC for a decision as to whether it can be made into a motion picture, the decision will largely depend upon how sexual content is to be presented on the screen. If sex and violence are intertwined, the BBFC will confer with psychiatrists to assure that corruptive influences will not be depicted. The BBFC is especially adamant about presentations in films which depict terrorizations of adults by teenagers (i.e., *Lady in a Cage* and *The Wild Angels*).

Film ratings in England are as follows: *X* (over 18 years only), *AA* (over 14 years, whether accompanied by adults), *A* (warning to parents that the film contains material that they might not prefer their children to see), and *U* (everybody over 5, except in Greater London Council territory, where children can't attend without without an adult until age 7). England's *X* rating appears to be comparable to our *X* rating. The British *A* rating is comparable to the American *GP* rating, and the *U* rating is similar to our *G* rating. The *AA* rating differs somewhat from the American *R* category in the United States because young persons do not have to be accompanied by adults, and only those over 14 are admitted to certain films.

One film which has caused controversy in Great Britain is *Zabriskie Point.* The scene which has elicited the controversy is one in which two men and a girl are shown engaging in sex. The film was passed in Berkshire, Hertfordshire, and Buckinghamshire Counties. However, it was cut before it could be passed in Surrey and was not at all acceptable in Essex. Another film, *Blow-Up*, which featured a sexual romp between two females and a male, did not receive such criticism. Evidently, it is more palatable for British censors to contemplate two females and a male in the sex act than it is to view two men and a woman engaging in similar activity.

SOFTCORE AND HARDCORE FILMS

If ever an award is presented for a "soft porno classic," *Last Tango in Paris* would undoubtedly receive that honor. The film is about a fifty-year-old loser (Paul) who meets a twenty-year-old girl (Jean) of quite amoral character. In *Last Tango*, Paul and Jean engage in various simulated sexual encounters, including sodomy; however, in most scenes both actors are fully clothed. With the exception of a scene in which Paul bathes Jean, there is a conspicuous absence of tenderness in the film; despite this lack of sensitivity, Paul falls in love with Jean who wishes to dissolve the friendship. Paul has served his immediate purpose in her life—sex—and Jean has concealed another lover in whom she is more sincerely interested. The film culminates in Paul's murder by Jean. In reference to the motion picture, Director Bertolucci stated:

I'm not sure what my film says. One never knows what his film is about until much later, but I think one of the things *Tango* is saying is that relationships no longer exist, that people in our society can no longer communicate with each other.[14]

Russ Meyer, producer of *Beyond the Valley of the Dolls*, feels that partial rather than full nudity is more erotic in motion pictures. Putting his theory into practice, Meyer includes only sex scenes which arouse him in his films, and he makes ample use of large breasts and characters with insatiable sexual appetites. Unlike most producers, he casts females in dominant roles. Meyer's *Beyond the Valley of the Dolls* was originally intended to be a sequel to *Valley of the Dolls*, a film based on Jacqueline Susann's novel by the same title. As a result of a lawsuit instigated by author Susann, the character's names had to be altered, and the film was no longer a sequel. The result was a movie with three primary female characters, but it was an exaggeration and a parody, dealing with homosexuality, crippling diseases, and drugs. *Beyond the Valley of the Dolls* ended with four murders and a triple wedding, but it was a high-grossing film.

The film *Carnal Knowledge*, which could be classed as innocent in comparison to truly pornographic or "hardcore" motion pictures, is about the sexual development of four rather superficial college students during the 1950s. Produced and directed by Mike Nichols, the film satirized certain accepted stereotypes: Susan, a good, but frigid coed; Bobbi, who was strictly for sex with her large mammary glands; Jonathan, a suave, polished and experienced fraternity type; and Sandy, a more sensitive and inexperienced young man. All four characters meet, friendships develop, and difficulties ensue. Jonathan finds the achievement of sexual excitement more and more difficult and eventually pays a woman (played by Rita Moreno) to extol his powers of masculinity. At the end of the film, Sandy is shown with a messy, dishevelled village girl.

Although Nichols' *Carnal Knowledge* condemned attitudes of the 1950s, it did not offer more suitable options for the present or the future. Nichols makes the "new women" of the 1960s and 1970s look as bad as the old "good girl" and "bad girl" stereotypes of the 1950s. For instance, he gives us Cindy, the castrative female, and the mute village girl who looks as bad as anyone could on the screen. The two young men are obviously maladjusted and unhappy. In *Carnal Knowledge*, four-letter words are uttered, coitus is shown rather unobtrusively, male buttocks are displayed, and the audience is given a three-minute photographic survey of Ann-Margaret's body above the nipples.

In a *Film Comment* article, Richard Corliss has analyzed the differences between hard and softcore pornography and concludes that *Deep Throat* belongs to the former category. Corliss claims that in viewing hardcore pornography, one knows that what is happening is real. He explained, "The heroine of *Deep Throat* possesses an oral cavity so extraordinary that she makes advances in root canal work beyond the American Dental Association's wildest dreams."[15] Bogdanovich feels that *Deep Throat* lacks a display of talent, is not sexy, and has no humor. Furthermore, he claims that the film's leading actress, Linda Lovelace, is not attractive. He contrasts *Deep Throat* with Altman's *The Long Goodby*, in which creativity abounds and excellent technique is used. In describing *Deep Throat*, Bogdanovich states:

There is some deep self-revulsion at work that no amount of legislation is going to stop. Mr. Altman has given us a vivid glimpse of this in
his new film, and a good work of art is a better cure for what ails
us than any court decision.[16]

Film critic Corliss states that the typical hardcore pornographic film lasts
approximately an hour and is similar to stag films in style and representation of
sexual activity. He also notes that in hardcore films there is neither foreplay nor
a build-up of erotic tension as is characteristic of softcore films. Action in hardcore
films begins in the middle of a sex act, and scenes proceed from there. On the other
hand, emphasis is on the female breast, not on the pubic area, in softcore films.
Hardly any kissing is practiced in hardcore films, and fellatio is performed much
more frequently than cunnilingus. The more popular hardcore films (such as
Mona, *School Girl*, and *Deep Throat*) are about one adventurous woman, rather
than several. Also, in these films, the actors are generally more attractive than the
actresses. In *Deep Throat* numerous attempts at humor are made. For example, the
heroine's first orgasm from her new-found pleasure of oral sex is accompanied by
sound effects consisting of chiming bells and fireworks, and the man's exhausted
organ is then bow-tied with a band-aid. Corliss believes that there is a trend away
from hardcore films and that fewer sexually oriented films will be produced, but of
a higher quality. These pictures will be erotic, affectionate—not mechanical—and
they will be "sexy" as opposed to "dirty," according to Corliss.
    Another film, *Straw Dogs*, based on Gordon M. Williams' novel *The Siege
of Treacher's Farm*, deals with a mild scholar, David, who is forced to protect
his property, and Amy, his sensual but insipid wife. The producer, Sam Peckinpah,
increased the amount of violence in transposing the novel to film. For instance, a
description of a dead cat lying in the snow is provided in the novel, but in the
motion picture Amy discovers the cat hanging by its neck in her husband's closet.
In the novel, an animal trap is merely set in anticipation of a snare, but in the movie
the trap's effectiveness is depicted. Pekinpah's conception of violence appears to
be one in which bullets splatter portions of victims' bodies over walls. Too, there
is a rape scene in *Straw Dogs* in which coitus and sodomy both are performed by
rough townsmen on Amy.
    The merit of films which contain considerable violence is often difficult to
judge. Despite its violence, *Straw Dogs* has a message: man is empowered to make
decisions, to conquer evil, and to protect the weak. However, in *The Cowboys*, in
which a group of boys supposedly learn self-reliance from actor John Wayne's
character, the ultimate message delivered is more negative. After the boys achieve
manhood by engaging in a mass killing to avenge John Wayne's death, their cold,
unemotional faces are shown. Likewise, Kubrick tells us in *A Clockwork Orange* that
man must revel in his capacity for evil if he is to be truly human, but:

Alex is a horrifying metonym for humankind, for he is one-dimensional.
He is incapable of receiving or giving love and is completely dedicated
to his own interests. His freedom consists solely in a capacity for evil
(with Beethoven as his one redemptive trait).[17]

Commenting on violence in *Straw Dogs*, Pauline Kael stated: "I think
Peckinpah is a considerable artist, but what comes out in his movies is a confusion

of mind, and a justification for machismo."[18] Kael would like to see truly erotic sex on film, but she feels that most movie sex falls short in this respect. She considers *The Conformist* to be erotic, unlike *The Last Picture Show*, where she notes that most of the women shown are mindless. Although the film *Carnal Knowledge* treats sex as men like to view the topic in locker-room conversations, Kael feels that this approach is not a true reflection of the behavior of men in respect to women. She claims:

> What upsets a lot of people in these new movies, and bores them finally, is that sex is dehumanized and made impersonal and mechanical, and it's no fun that way. . . . But I think the large audience wants sensuality and eroticism, not just hardcore, mechanized pornography.[19]

Movie viewers' levels of emotion must be considered in any discussion of films. Through emotional detachment, a person experiences a certain distance from the action taking place in a film, and some moviegoers achieve this detachment by viewing vicariously what is merely a representation of reality. Some disenchantment results from a realization that the techniques of production rely on artificialities such as false scenery. Of course, some of these seeming sophistications are merely affectations, and the question of controlling emotional reactions to films remains. Herbert Blumer has stated that censorship as presently used is a negative kind of control but that a better kind of control is exercised when attitudes of emotional detachment are developed. According to Blumer:

> A greater willingness on the part of parent and teacher to talk about pictures with children and adolescents, to interpret them in broad ways and so, to build up attitudes toward them, holds promise of better results.[20]

In *The Exorcist*, a twelve-year-old girl, Regan (played by Linda Blair) is possessed by devils. Two priests, Father Karras and Father Merrin, attempt to exorcise the demon, but they die in the process. The first of these "would-be heroes" is also a guilt-ridden psychiatrist who is upset about having neglected his dying mother. The Catholic Conference's Division of Film and Broadcasting has given *The Exorcist* an *A-4* rating, which indicates that the film is not morally objectionable but may "confuse or offend" some people. Colin L. Westerbeck commented as follows on the Catholic rating for *The Exorcist:*

> This surprises me somewhat because Karras' final succumbing to the demons seems to be a gesture that affirms the power of evil in the total absence of good. . . . If he (the psychiatrist) couldn't bring himself to some human response when his mother was dying, we can't believe he does so now out of compassion for virtual strangers.[21]

Perhaps one of the most brilliantly conceived controversial motion pictures is *A Clockwork Orange*, in which the action, at some future time, depicts a hoodlum being conditioned to perceive violence and rape as repugnant acts. Alex, the protagonist, is cured of his lust for violence by a highly unusual kind of treatment whereby he is forced to view violent acts on a motion picture screen, while his eyelids are forced apart and his eyes are artificially moistened. Only one positive character is portrayed in the film—the churchman who believes in free will. The term "clockwork orange" refers to the fact that Alex, though reformed, is without choice, and functions only as a part of an institution. He becomes a mechanical organism—a clockwork orange. The allegedly pornographic aspects of this film consist of rear views of nude males, a rape scene, several scenes depicting assaults on victims by Alex, and gang scenes of brutal kicking and punching. Anthony Burgess, author of the novel upon which the Stanley Kubrick picture is based, made the following comments about the film:

> We're all inclined to love the pornography of violence, but for me that work was a kind of personal testament made out of love and sorrow, as well as of ideas and theology.[22]

The Godfather, an extremely popular movie during the early 1970s, contained much violence. The film's plot concerns a Mafia family, and it includes shootings, garrotings, and beatings. An apparent attempt to mitigate the violence is made by depicting the victims as loathsome characters. In one scene, an uncooperative Hollywood producer finds the head of his slaughtered prize racehorse in his bed.

Another controversial film, less popular among moviegoers, was *The Decameron*, based on Boccaccio's fourteenth-century tales and directed by Pasolini. In the film, a young gardener is shown in a convent servicing one nun after another as they wait in line outside their cells. Many genital shots are included. One scene shows a husband scraping dirt from a jar while his wife engages in sex with the man from whom the jar was purchased.

THE CRITICS SPEAK UP

Maslow has stated that the prime consumers of pornography are immature individuals who have not achieved a state of self-actualization.[23] I. R. Stuart has described an experiment with pornography conducted among subjects at weekly intervals. Movies shown to subjects displayed either nude or partly nude figures painted by art masters. Subjects were asked to evaluate each movie as to its pornographic content. Although a research assistant kept extolling the artistic and economic worth of the paintings of nudes, some subjects consistently rejected the films after three separate viewings spaced several weeks apart. Those who systematically rejected the films were found to have rigid or authoritarian personalities. Stuart asserted that for a work to be considered as an object of art, the artist's intentions should be known; the artist should desire to treat the complexity of relationships between people and not merely the sexual aspects.[24]

Pornography reduces everything to sexual organs, according to Mark Taylor. Taylor also maintains that the criterion which should be used in determining whether a film is pornographic is the ability of the viewer to recall the face of the female protagonist long after seeing the film. According to Taylor, if the female's face can be recalled, the film probably could be classed as not obscene. Taylor cites a comparison that Steiner and Holbrook have made: unlimited sexual expression in films is similar to a totalitarian environment such as a concentration camp. In both cases, people are dehumanized; fantasies of torture or mutilation are merely depicted in obscene films, but they are likely to be performed in concentration camps. Taylor further maintains that pornography—not censorship—is the enemy of freedom, that pornography reduces people to the level of machines, indistinguishable from one another, and that it causes people to be less concerned about their fellow humans.[25]

Over the clamor of the sparse, yet persistent, conglomerate of film censorship advocates can be heard the quieter, less overt pleas of the proponents of freedom of the arts. Fortunately, these supporters of freedom constitute a majority. Just as Americans have generally cherished freedom, these individuals feel strongly about freedom for the film art.

In the case *United States v. A Motion Picture Titled "I Am Curious (Yellow),"* the court declared that the film was not obscene. (The film contains scenes of simulated sexual intercourse and oral-genital activity.) Although the courts have been more lenient with printed discussions of nudity and sexual activity in books, depictions of these actions in films have been examined more critically. But the court has maintained that while books are read in private and movies are seen publicly, one cannot compare nudity and sex acts in a public place with nudity in movies. In movies, sex acts are part of a complete work of art and based upon plots and characters. Such expression is not at all comparable to a spontaneous sexual act that might take place in a public area. The dominant theme of *I Am Curious (Yellow)* is that of a young girl's search for identity and her attempts to cope with a classless and non-violent society; emphasis is not placed on sex in the film. Furthermore, the court ruled that the film's sexual scenes probably do not arouse prurient interest. Indeed, the film has considerable social value and it presents its ideas in an artistic fashion.

Stephen Farber, another opponent of film censorship, noted in 1973 that if the anti-smut California Proposition 18 were adopted, allowing each community to set its own standards, films such as *Cabaret, Godfather,* and *M*A*S*H* would be forbidden.[26] Most contemporary popular movies are *X* and *R* pictures, such as *Clockwork Orange, The Godfather, Superfly, Deliverance, The New Centurions,* and *Everything You Always Wanted to Know About Sex.* Although many theater operators would like to book more *G* and *GP* motion pictures, they are faced with the economic dilemma that the most successful films in terms of box-office receipts are the *X* and *R* rated pictures.

The *Newsletter on Intellectual Freedom* pointed out that at the same time the Senate Watergate Hearings were being held, the Nixon appointees on the Supreme Court affirmed the authority of the states to maintain a "decent society free of pornography." According to the *Newsletter*: "Too few people can appreciate that the real pornography of our century is not to be found in books and movies." Only works having serious literary and artistic value are now protected from legal repressions. The supposed purpose of the censorship of communication media is to protect the weak, the uninformed, the unsuspecting, and the gullible from their own volition. Determining who the weak, gullible, and unsuspecting are is another matter. Chief Justice Burger, Justice White, Justice Blackmun, *et al.,* removed guarantees of First Amendment protections from "patently offensive" works which appeal to "prurient interest." The Georgia Supreme Court subsequently decided by a 4 to 3 vote in 1973 that the film *Carnal Knowledge* was an obscene work, thus unprotected by the First Amendment, a decision overturned by the U.S. Supreme Court in 1974. Under the new obscenity guidelines, jurors are given the task of applying their standards to determine the artistic merits of works. Although the arts may still be able to prosper in a milieu of censorship, in a free society it is intolerable to tell artists and writers what they can produce or to dictate to citizens what they are not permitted to see or to hear.

Sexuality is a powerful motive in creative enterprises, insists John Adkins Richardson; sexual expression, nudity, and what some persons deem to be "pornography" have been represented in the works of Rembrandt, Goya, Picasso, and other famous painters. Richardson also contends that officials who decide on the appropriateness of films should be guided by what is suitable for adult viewing, not only what can be viewed by children.[27]

In another article, D. W. Gotshalk has expressed the idea that artists should portray a subject according to its proper value stature and that artists alone assume the responsibility for what is shown. In other words, Gotshalk's idea is that artists know what they are doing and that external censorship is useless because reality cannot be disguised. Gotshalk further believes that by viewing forbidden material, young people receive an illicit pleasure which they would not experience if the same materials were freely available so that persons could rely on their personal and cultural values. In a freer atmosphere, Gotshalk thinks that persons would absorb appropriate values, recognize pornography for what it is, and would be repelled by truly obscene works.[28] Catherine Hughes has asserted that 1) artists should use their new freedoms in a responsible manner, 2) they should acknowledge their responsibilities, and 3) they should practice self-restraint. She also pointed out that disreputable filmmakers often use sex for sex's sake, their main concern being box-office receipts, but that sex and nudity should be an integral part of the content of the artist's work.[29]

One surprisingly valid anti-censorship argument was propounded in *Film Quarterly* by Frederick M. Wirt, who commented that repressive activity illustrates Santayana's notion that persons who do not remember the past are condemned to repeat it. Thus, in Wirt's opinion, censorship is futile; its advocates cannot suppress change because change will eventually occur. Wirt believes that censorship is an enemy of democracy because: 1) its standards are vague, giving rise to irresponsible use of power, 2) the state becomes involved in what should be personal matters, and 3) the free expression of ideas is thwarted.[30]

Since legal censorship statutes are rooted in cultural attitudes and values, laws are often written rather subjectively. Thus, various censors or would-be censors interpret films in vastly different ways, and those who attempt to practice suppression are often more emotional than logical. For example, one Ohio censor banned the films of Charles Chaplin merely because of his personal dislike for the actor. Also, as the censor becomes an authority through his own rhetoric, the limits of his power are impossible to discern; therefore, the decision as to whether censors have overridden those limits is difficult to make. Censors tend to assume that parents are inadequate to the task of deciding what their own children can and cannot read and see. Likewise, the censor's position implies that the church and school are also inadequate in this respect.

Fear of censorship causes considerable deceit in film making. Sometimes, an entire film will be concerned primarily with criminal acts, but near the end the plot suddenly departs from its former emphasis and terminates with a lesson in morality (i.e., crime doesn't pay). The disadvantages of ill-advised, external film censorship far outweigh the advantages of internal restraint within the film industry, because producers, frightened about the possibility of censorship, might not be willing to take chances. As a result of these influences, some promising films may very well become mediocrities. A democratic society must produce free art; society would fare better to risk the production of an occasional lewd film than to lose a meaningful motion picture.

Paul Goodman claims that censorship might give rise to a need for sadistic literature and that if the stimulation of sexual desire is considered pornographic, we must concede that any interest in sex is shameful. According to Goodman, while we frequently insist that artists move us emotionally with laughter, compassion, and sadness, we do not always allow them to move us sexually; thus, a dull and passionless community is created. Goodman has also distinguished between "bad" and "good" pornography; "bad pornography" is mere sexuality, lust, and sadomasochism, but "good pornography" contains affection, which increases our pleasure.[31]

In court decisions, sexual facts should be treated as an ordinary facet of human life. If there were no censorship, the criminal market would lose out. Prices of pornography would most probably be lowered, and sexually explicit materials would eventually become dull. As a result, sexuality might become more humanized.

Eli M. Oboler has noted a vast difference between theory and practice insofar as sexual matters are concerned. As an example, he pointed out that, in 1973, the possession of information on birth control was still illegal in Idaho, a state which also had one of the highest percentages of unwed mothers in the nation.[32] Oboler feels that the provision of whatever is good for the individual is more crucial than the consideration of the good of society and that citizens must have the freedom to make even morally wrong choices. Just as people of the opposite sex are generally trusted to be with each other, touch each other, etc., without commiting sexual offense, Oboler feels that they can be trusted to read and inform themselves about sexual behavior in books and films without any attending misbehavior. Danish psychologist Svend Renulf has stated that moral indignation exists primarily in the lower middle class. Renulf has pointed out that the Puritans believed that God causes people to suffer for not being censorious enough with one another, for being too happy, for being self-confident, and for sinning under temptation. According to Renulf, these religious fundamentalists seemed to accept every occasion for the dispensing of retribution and probably experienced a sado-masochistic joy in human suffering.[33]

EXAMINING THE EVIDENCE

As should be evident, most intellectuals oppose censorship in films; many have defended their points of view with varying degrees of success. In addition to the plethora of literature written by those who specifically oppose censorship, there is a significant quantity of evidence to support freedom of expression. Alex P. Allain has echoed an often-rejected truism: "In the case of pornography, no study to date has proved that exposure to pornography has caused antisocial behavior."[34]

In 1969, a study was conducted by psychiatrists at the University of Chicago's Pritzker School of Medicine to determine psychiatrists' opinions about pornography and its effects on viewers. Questionnaires were distributed to 7,500 psychiatrists and psychoanalysts and to over 3,000 psychologists. Over 3,400 other professionals in the mental health field were also surveyed. Pornography was defined in the study as both still and motion picture photography which depicted sexual activity without artistic value. Anti-social behavior was defined for purposes of the study as rape and any sexual assault. The results of the research were as follows: 80 percent of the psychologists and psychiatrists *could not recall a case in which pornography was the cause of anti-social sexual behavior.* Only 7.4 percent of the respondents were convinced that there was a positive relationship between pornography and anti-social behavior in *some* of they cases they had observed; and 9.4 percent encountered instances where they hypothesized, but were not positive, that a link existed. Of the respondents, 62 percent did not feel that pornography depicting violence is more likely to lead to anti-social sexual behavior than non-violent pornographic materials. More than three-fourths of the psychiatrists and psychologists did not believe that the viewing of filmed violence agitates or leads to violent behavior. Of the respondents, 86.1 percent felt that persons who vigorously try to censor pornography possess unresolved sexual problems; 64.9 percent felt that censorship contributes to an atmosphere of oppression and inhibition which stifles creativity; 55.7 percent were of the opinion that true pornography should be censored; and 53.2 percent believed that depictions of violence should be censored. Most of the respondents (90.4 percent) felt that non-pornographic, sexually stimulating materials should not be censored, and 70.6 percent felt that if censorship were systematically practiced, a tremendous problem would be the identification of those individuals who are qualified to judge which books and films should be made available.[35]

Another related study was conducted with 365 male subjects (including 109 prisoners) at Boulder, Colorado. Six films from the Institute of Sex Research at Hamburg University were shown to these men, and their reactions and activities after viewing these films were studied. Those subjects who desired to have heterosexual relationships after the film showings were persons who had already established heterosexual relationships as well as histories of intercourse and petting. The subjects who did not have similar backgrounds were more likely to become very aroused and to masturbate.[36]

In another experiment at the University of Connecticut, a selected sample of 194 single male and 183 single female undergraduates were shown two pornographic movies from the Institute of Sex Research in Hamburg. The first film depicted face-to-face coitus; the second showed oral-genital sex. Results of the study indicated that both men and women experienced some sexual arousal upon viewing the films. Men were more excited by the film depicting oral-genital sex, and the women were more excited by the film showing face-to-face coitus. During the two-day period subsequent to viewing the films, more sex fantasies were experienced by subjects, but other sexual activities such as coitus, masturbation, and petting did not increase. Those individuals who had guilt feelings about sex or who were sexually inexperienced felt more negative toward sex after having viewed the films.[37]

CONCLUSIONS

Now that both pro- and anti-censorship arguments have been considered, some conclusions based upon these arguments and their accompanying evidence can be drawn.

First are the pro-censorship arguments. In his decision to censor *I Am Curious (Yellow)*, Judge Lombard claimed that despite the fact that sex scenes in the film occupy only ten minutes, the viewing of pornography in a dark room will have an adverse impact on viewers. But results of the Boulder experiment, where 365 men watched six sex films, seem to refute this fear. While subjects were sexually aroused during the pornographic films, those who had experienced heterosexual relationships expressed an interest in continuing that pattern, while those who were autoerotically oriented continued to masturbate. Also, in the pornography film experiment conducted with undergraduate students, both male and female subjects were aroused as they viewed pornographic films. After a 24-hour period, however, the subjects' sexual activity did not increase.

Critics of films containing sexual expression have often claimed that a public display of sexuality is obscene because the emotions of actors or performers are not visible, and the viewer is only aware of the animal coupling. But these critics assume a lack of imagination on the part of the audience. If film viewers are sexually mature, they are apt to assume from their own experiences and desires that emotion probably would have accompanied the sexual acts. For example, when a person reads a book, neither the pictorial aspect nor the emotions of the protagonists are "seen." But no one criticizes books because readers experience only that which is printed in black and white—only the written word—not the picture or the emotion. Neither literature nor films are monodimensional media.

While some critics of sexual films have maintained that sex must be both a physical and an emotional experience, the question remains as to whether the censor approves at all of the physical aspect of sex. And persons who assert that many consumers of pornography are immature persons might be correct; however, whether that is a sufficient reason to censor sexually oriented films is another question. In the experiment conducted with nudes painted by the old masters, subjects who consistently rejected the paintings were later discovered to be rigid, authoritarian types. In consideration of this finding, perhaps such persons will become our most staunch censors.

In contradiction to Mark Taylor's assertion that the question of whether a film is obscene can be determined by the degree to which the face of the actress can be recalled, some persons generally remember all faces of film heroes or heroines in both pornographic and non-pornographic films. Perhaps Taylor's "dehumanization" theory has little basis; it appears as though this concept exists more in the minds of certain viewers than in the films themselves. Taylor's comparison of pornographic films with concentration camps is, of course, a grotesque exaggeration. If we can compare fantasy with gross reality, we might as well compare an occasional hostile feeling of a normal person with the overt atrocities of murderers.

Pro-censorship arguments contain many flaws, but let us now consider some anti-censorship viewpoints and discover how well they can stand on their own merits. Judge Hays rather accurately contradicted Lombard's comparison of public sex with that shown in movies by noting that sex is only a facet of a complete work of film art, whereas public sex is an event in and of itself, unrelated to anything else and quite unlikely even to occur.

Many censors point out that censorship protects weak, uninformed, and unsuspecting persons from the exercise of their own volition, but the problem remains of how to single out these individuals from the more sophisticated audience. In addition, we have noted that by declaring that so-called "patently offensive" motion pictures which "appeal to the prurient interest" are obscene, such films as *Carnal Knowledge* can be banned by unsophisticated and uninformed jurors. As free citizens, as well as filmgoers, Americans should be seriously concerned about such decisions, which represent extreme restriction of freedom of the arts.

Richardson made an accurate observation when he noted that despite Victorian prudishness, the nineteenth century was notorious for prostitution. If we project his observation a little further, we can conclude that if censors are allowed to pervade our century, we may eventually reap a plethora of similar covert sexual activities as a result of repressiveness. Richardson also recognizes that adults should be offered adult films, not just pictures that are also suitable for children.

Both Gotshalk and Hughes have asserted that censorship is not realistic in a democratic society and that artists should use their freedoms responsibly. Hughes also feels that when nude scenes are needed in films they should be integrated into the whole and related to the work's message. Certainly, many readers will agree with this idea.

Censorship is indeed an enemy of democracy, as Frederick Wirt proclaimed. This truism has been very clearly demonstrated in the Georgia decision to ban *Carnal Knowledge* and in the decisions of some college officials to ban such films as *Pink Flamingos* and *The Graduate*. Wirt is perfectly correct in his statement that censorship statutes are stated in subjective terms; hence, they are open to as many interpretations as there are censors. He makes an equally valid assertion in stating that many censors are emotional, rather than logical, and that they are generally not well versed in the arts. In addition, it should be noted that motion picture producers and directors who are fearful of censorship do not tend to put their best into their works and the end product is frequently mediocre. Certainly, artists must be free to create in a free society.

Paul Goodman concludes that if the excitement of sexual desires is pornographic, everybody's normal interest in sex is a kind of pornography. This statement should be kept in mind when considering the entire matter of censorship. It is true, as Goodman has pointed out, that artists are allowed to move us emotionally, but not sexually.

Oboler makes a valid observation which is so logically simple that it is difficult to understand why someone has not thought of it before: young people of the opposite sex see and touch each other every day without any attendant sexual misbehavior; thus they can generally be trusted to read and view sexually related materials without any misconduct.

Attitudes of more and more Americans have changed toward what should and should not be depicted or expressed in films. Sexual expression appears to be more acceptable in the 1970s than in any previous period of the nation's history. Fortunately, fear of sexual expression in films and in literature has subsided among a large segment of the public. The findings of the President's Commission on Obscenity and Pornography have underscored the theory that fear of pornography is related to a confusion and ambivalence about sexuality; preconceived, prejudicial attitudes about sexually explicit materials are a much greater social and cultural ill than the production and distribution of pornography itself. In brief, the Commission's findings indicate that pornography has absolutely no harmful effects on society. On the other hand, evidence was uncovered to support the contention that pure pornography might have a socially redeeming value for some persons. According to the Commission's recommendation, anti-obscenity laws applying to adults should be repealed. Thus, the so-called "problem of pornography" is actually a problem relating to cultural attitudes toward sex. The official report of the Commission on Obscenity and Pornography contained the following statements:

> The Commission believes that much of the "problem" regarding materials which depict explicit sexual activities stems from the inability or reluctance of people in our society to be open and direct in dealing with sexual matters. This most often manifests itself in the inhibition of talking openly and directly about sex.

The Commission's report further stressed the importance of sex education by recommending:

> that a massive sex education effort be launched . . . aimed at achieving an acceptance of sex as a normal and natural part of life and of oneself as a sexual being. It should not aim for orthodoxy; rather, it should be designed to allow for a pluralism of values. It should be based on facts and encompass not only biological and religious information. . . . It should be aimed, as appropriate, to all segments of our society, adults as well as children and adolescents.

Bernardo Bertolucci's *Last Tango in Paris*, produced by a major motion picture studio and starring Marlon Brado, has been classified by some viewers as a pornographic film. But the frank and rather explicit sexual acts simulated in the motion picture are very much a part of a central plot which centers on the idea that sex without love produces loneliness and chilling isolation. The movie contains simulated sex acts; however, the film's erotic explicity is not designed to sexually stimulate viewers but to enhance the harsh reality of the message. The film has artistic and social merits, and it should be seen for these merits, rather than for its "pornographic" aspects. *Last Tango* would not be a box-office success in a seedy "adult" theater because it is not in any sense an erotic film. Rather, its approach to sex is intellectual and sophisticated, and the plot would not appeal to the typical patron of X-rated films.

Deep Throat has been described as "pornographic trash," "a force for evil," "a nadir of decadence," and "a feast of carrion and squalor." But in 1973, thousands of Americans flocked to motion picture houses over the nation to see this low-budget film in which sex is exploited to the ultimate. In New York City alone, the film brought in an estimated one million dollars in 1973. That amount was supplemented by additional millions from theaters in other areas of the nation. Condemnation of the film by city, state, and county government officials, anti-pornography leaders, and courts only seemed to stimulate box office receipts, leading to the conclusion that certain hardcore pornographic films are accepted and enjoyed by a large segment of the nation's population. The enormous market in the 1970s for hardcore pornographic films, such as *Deep Throat*, and softcore films, such as *Last Tango in Paris*, appears to be related to the changing attitudes toward sexual expression among a significant number of persons. The sexual revolution which began in the late 1960s and the proliferation of sexually oriented literature and films in the 1970s appear to be irreversible developments. Despite cries from moralists who view these developments as evidence of social and cultural decadence, a growing number of ordinary people, artists, psychiatrists, social scientists, and scholars are becoming more open and receptive to sexual expression.

In view of the evidence presented, it seems quite logical to draw the conclusion that censorship is useless, ineffective, and is indeed a foe of our democratic principles. Little evidence has been produced thus far to support many pro-censorship ideas, while much evidence is available to encourage anti-censorship forces to continue their struggle to maintain freedom of expression in all communication media. Unfortunately, too few censorship cases have been solved in a logical, intelligent manner, and much self-righteousness and emotionalism has prevailed when individual films have been condemned. We must staunchly defend the rights of talented filmmakers to produce to their fullest capacity as well as the corresponding liberties of film audiences to select the motion pictures which they wish to see.

FOOTNOTES

[1] Murray Shumack, *The Face on the Cutting Room Floor* (New York: William Morrow and Co., 1964), p. 185.

[2] *Ibid.*, p. 59.

[3] *Ibid.*, p. 3.

[4] "Film Reviews," *Films in Review* 23 (April 1972): 243.

[5] *Phoenix Republic*, October 21, cited by *Newsletter on Intellectual Freedom* 21 (January 1972): 20.

[6] Clyde B. Smith, "I Am Curious (Yellow) and (Blue)," *Film Quarterly* 22 (Summer 1969): 42.

[7] "Is It Legal?," *Newsletter on Intellectual Freedom* 22 (July 1973): 73.

[8] William Fadiman, *Hollywood Now* (New York: Liverright, 1972), p. 19.

[9] Jack Langguth, ed., "Doctor X; Interview," *Saturday Review* 55 (December 2, 1972): 11.

[10] Ezra Goodman, *The Fifty Year Decline and Fall of Hollywood* (New York: Simon and Schuster, 1961), p. 423.

[11] *Ibid.*, p. 423.

[12] Charles Champlin, "A Critic Sounds Off About Film in the Seventies," *The PTA Magazine* (April 1974): 25.

[13] *Ibid.*, p. 25.

[14] "Film Reviews," *Films in Review* 24 (April 1973): 239.

[15] Richard Corliss, "Cinema Sex: From *The Kiss* to *Deep Throat*," *Film Comment* 9 (1973): 4.

[16] Peter Bogdanovich, "Hollywood," *Esquire* 79 (June 1973): 60.

[17] R. A. Blake, "Violence: The Price of Good Box-Office?" *America* 126 (February 12, 1972): 151.

[18] Pauline Kael, "Pauline Kael Talks About Violence, Sex, Eroticism and Women & Men in the Movies," *Mademoiselle* (July 1972): 133.

[19] *Ibid.*, p. 173.

[20] Herbert Blumer, *Movies and Conduct* (New York: Arno Press and The New York Times, 1970), p. 140.

[21] Colin L. Westerbeck, Jr., "The Screen," *Commonweal* 99 (March 1, 1974): 532.

[22] "Playboy Interview: Anthony Burgess," *Playboy* 21 (September 1974): 70.

[23] Abraham H. Maslow, *Toward a Psychology of Being* (Princeton, N.J., 1962), p. 37; quoted in I. R. Stuart, "Personality Dynamics and Objectionable Art: Attitudes, Opinions, and Experimental Evidence," *The Journal of Aesthetic Education* 4 (July 1970): 109.

[24] *Ibid.*, p. 116.

[25] Mark Taylor, "Censorship or Pornography," *Commonweal* 48 (1973): 263.

[26] Stephen Farber, "Censorship in California," *Film Comment* 9 (1973): 33.

[27] John A. Richardson, "Dirty Pictures and Campus Comity," *The Journal of Aesthetic Education* 4 (1970): 95.

[28] D. W. Gotschalk, "A Note on the Future of Censorship," *The Journal of Aesthetic Education* 4 (1970): 100.

[29] Catherine Hughes, "Art and Responsibility," *Catholic World* 209 (1969): 212.

[30] Frederick M. Wirt, "To See or Not to See: The Case Against Censorship," *Film Quarterly* 13 (Fall 1959): 27.

[31] Paul Goodman, "Pornography, Art and Censorship," *Commentary* 31 (March 1961): 209.

[32] Eli M. Oboler, "Paternalistic Morality and Censorship," *Library Journal* (September 1, 1973): 2396.

[33] *Ibid.*, p. 2397.

[34] Alex P. Allain, "Public Library Governing Boards and Intellectual Freedom," *Library Trends* 19 (July 1970): 52.

[35] *Ibid.*, p. 53.

[36] R. Kathleen Molz, "Report on the Report," *Newsletter on Intellectual Freedom* 22 (May 1973): 51.

[37] *Ibid.*, p. 59.

CENSORSHIP RESEARCH:
Its Strengths, Weaknesses, Uses, and Misuses

Richard E. McKee

Censorship is an issue which evokes emotional responses. People who defend the suppression of communications—as well as those who oppose censorship—often attempt to support their actions by marshalling "evidence." Needless to say, the evidence that has been gathered has often been conflicting. Those who seek facts have encountered published reports of studies which contain contradictory information about restricting freedom of expression. Many "research" reports relating to censorship actually contain oversimplifications based upon untested assumptions that in turn color treatment of the topic. Obviously, a great deal has been written about censorship. Robert B. Downs has noted that over one thousand periodical articles and books on the subject had been published by 1960.[1] Between 1960 and 1972, the *Library Literature* index listed over 1,300 entries under the heading "censorship." Yet, despite an abundance of published articles, only a small percentage of this literature is based upon empirical investigations.

This chapter is not an attempt to review all published research relating to freedom of expression and censorship. Rather, significant contributions based wholly or partly on research in the area of censorship will be examined for the purpose of clarifying conflicting evidence. All studies examined for preparation of this essay had one common quality: each supposedly contained a logical rationale—derived from research—for or against censorship. These studies attempted to explain the procedures used and evidence gathered in support of conclusions. Polemical works and articles which merely reported censorship incidents or statistics were avoided. By concentrating on works based upon systematic or rigorous inquiries, the writer hopes to clarify aspects of censorship so that the issue can be viewed in a less emotional and more objective manner.

At times, governments have played a major role in limiting what the populace reads; at other times, religious groups have taken the initiative in restricting materials. Social organizations have also advocated restrictions on materials deemed to be pornographic, immoral, or unpatriotic, whether in books, films, plays, songs, radio, or television broadcasts. Thus, an awareness of the many types of restrictions is necessary if the confusion relating to control of information is to be eliminated. Knowledge about various kinds of censorship can also be of use in understanding a type of suppression that becomes prevalent after having played a minor role for a number of years. Anyone interested in understanding the complex issue of censorship should rely only upon facts derived from careful studies. While reliance upon personal convictions or opinions may be more self-satisfying, in the long run the only person deceived will be the one who has not closely examined the conclusions of carefully conducted studies.

CONCEPTS OF CENSORSHIP

Unfortunately, few scientifically conducted studies related to the problems
of censorship have been undertaken. Thus, the existing body of theory and
knowledge about this phenomenon is weak. Adequate generalizations cannot be
made, because, as Paul Boyer has noted, most censorship studies lack depth, entertain the reader rather than allowing a comprehensive understanding of issues, possess
a polemical character, and concentrate on ridiculing censors.[2] Indeed, a report
about the suppression of a book, motion picture, or some other medium of communication is not the same as an investigation of *causes* of a repressive act. Such
reports call attention only to the act, but they do not provide readers with an
understanding of the central problem in proper perspective.

In addition to the difficulties one can encounter in attempting to obtain
objective and reliable information about censorship, semantic and philosophical
problems are also common in this area. For example, meanings of words do exist
in the abstract, but they are subject as well to different personal interpretations in
different contexts. Thus, a person opposed to restrictions on speech can view a
repressive act as a denial of freedom of expression, while those who support such
activities often approve of censorship as a protection or preservation of values and
as a means of eliminating unpleasant and radical ideas.

Philosophically, people who favor censorship usually believe that controls are
necessary to prevent the dissemination of objectionable and unpleasant ideas or
images in all media of communication. In other words, censors assume that the
discussion or exposure of "objectionable" ideas or images might be too embarrassing, shocking, harmful, or distasteful for certain segments of the population. Some
people view the presentation of an uncommonly encountered part of reality as
harmful. These censors want to protect "innocents" whose value systems, personal
experiences, and previous training are perceived as too weak to withstand confrontations with whatever appears to be radically different from expected norms.
For example, censors often contend that children are not always capable of deciding
the best course of action; consequently, endorsements are given to the suppression of
media which are seen as capable of distorting, perverting, or destroying their conception of a young person's normal orientation.

However, most anti-censorship forces in the United States look upon restraints
on expression as serious violations of basic human rights. Libertarians view openness as a necessary condition for a full and productive life. By suppressing viewpoints
or images that are perceived as threats to an accepted way of life, a person runs the
risk of subjecting others to fears that could be based upon a lack of knowledge.
Opponents of censorship usually view knowledge as the best deterrent to misinfor-
mation, misrepresentation, and the acceptance of false values. It seems logical to
assume, therefore, that this openness can be fostered only in an environment which
permits and encourages freedom of inquiry. Libertarians look upon censorship as an
activity which prevents individuals from analyzing and judging for themselves the
merits and values of ideas.

OBSCENITY AND CENSORSHIP

The basic argument between persons who attempt to place restrictions on expression and those who seek to reduce such controls centers on the issue of whether physical or mental danger may result from exposure to "objectionable" ideas or images. Some people fear the possibility of injury or drastic behavioral changes on the part of persons exposed to "dangerous" ideas or images. The extent of censorship (range or quantity of people affected) and the intensity of censorship (strength of the effect on an individual or group) must therefore be considered. Thomas Hardy observed that even well-accepted literature might pose a threat, because there is always a chance that a work might adversely change a young person's behavior. However, the change may not always be detrimental, as some people assert. Thus, an unanswered question remains: what constitutes a justification for censorship—the range of persons unaffected by objectionable materials, or intesnity of the reaction of a few?[3] In other words, should works be suppressed because they *might* adversely affect a few persons or should these materials be allowed to circulate without restrictions because the majority will not be affected?

Despite limitations, some progress has been made in the identification of principles, trends, and concepts that allow a realistic appraisal of the relationship between "pernicious" literature and censorship. As a framework for this discussion, obscene publications or materials may be defined as those which offend the senses, stand in opposition to conventional morality, and arouse sexual interests. Although this definition is much too broad, it can serve as a framework for an examination of the often-repeated contention that a causal relationship exists between obscene materials and anti-social behavior.

Paul and Schwartz have outlined seven reasons for the suppression of obscene literature which are paraphrased here: 1) to restrain people from accepting corruptive ideas, 2) to subdue sexual misconduct among adults, 3) to curtail sexual activities among youth and the maladjusted, 4) to protect parental interests, 5) to prevent emotional disorders, 6) to prevent commercial exploitation of psycho-social tensions, and 7) to curb communications that do not convey knowledge or promote the arts.[4] Despite these reasons—most of which are based upon assumptions—the actual *causal* relationship which many assume to exist between the reading or viewing of obscene materials and anti-social behavior has not been authenticated. In any event, both pro- and anti-censorship groups have produced studies that "support" their positions. However, numerous disparities can be identified between what is often reported as the "truth" and the validity of studies which produced so-called "facts."

One rather weak and unreliable research project in this area is the study conducted by the New Jersey Council of the Right to Read.[5] Response rate to the study's distributed questionnaire was very poor; only 17.6 percent of the psychiatrists and 27.2 percent of the psychologists selected as respondents actually replied to an opinion survey which sought to determine attitudes of experts about the relationship between obscenity and crime. The small response rate casts doubts on the credibility of the study, the conclusions of which support the contention that there is no causal link between obscenity and anti-social behavior. Too, this type of research raises more questions than it answers, and it provides ammunition for persons who are eager to convince others of the "truth" about the problem of obscenity. The problem is further compounded by additional non-rigorous studies which utilize weak data collection methods and produce unreliable and invalid results.

In 1933, Blumer and Hauser reported that 12 percent of the 110 male prison inmates they studied were stimulated by erotic movies; yet no effort was made in their study to determine if these findings also pertain to non-incarcerated males or whether a relationship exists between a person's predisposition to crime and his preference for sexually stimulating materials.[6] Another research project, the Haines study of 1955, was undertaken to examine the relationship between the reading or viewing of pornography by juvenile delinquents and their crimes. The investigators first explained to their sex-offender subjects that "Senator Kefauver was interested in the effects of television, movies, and radio on teenagers." Although none of the sex offenders claimed that he was influenced to commit crimes because of any communication medium (and only 14 percent related that a medium stimulated their sexual desires), Haines reported that "television, pornography, and movies play a distinct role in the creation of anti-social behavior in susceptible teenagers."[7] The obvious lack of experimental controls, the lack of a comparison between the subjects and non-criminals, and the poor analysis of statistical data did not enhance the study's credibility.

In another study, Von Bracken and Schafers, European researchers, examined reading preferences of convicted criminals. The investigators concluded that: 1) convicted murders choose books containing quality information and adventure stories, 2) persons convicted of fraud selected novels of little importance, 3) robbers wanted books about practical topics, and 4) sex offenders preferred erotic materials.[8] Findings from a number of other studies by Kinsey, Buchwald, Conger, Clark and Triecher, Musseh and Scodel, Lieman and Epstein, and Pysinger and Ruckmuch can be summarized together: 1) certain stimuli will arouse sexual interests among a large segment of society, 2) both adult and adolescent males are stimulated by female nudity and other direct sexual clues, 3) females are excited by less direct, but more complex, stimuli not usually associated with obscene materials, 4) physical development, intellectual aptitude, and degree of masculine identity play a part in the male's reaction to stimuli, 5) settings used to determine sexual stimulation may affect subjects' conduct because investigators were uncertain whether erotic materials were not stimulating to subjects or whether the laboratory-type atmosphere discouraged subjects' expression, and 6) guilt feelings within subjects may cause unpleasant reactions when subjects are exposed to sex stimuli.[9] These conclusions are by no means definitive; yet, their consistency should be noted.

Long-term effects of sexual stimuli on the values, attitudes, and behavior of viewers have not been adequately explored. Little evidence has been produced to allow either rejection or acceptance of the contention that obscenity leads to sexual misconduct and criminal behavior.[10] In general, completed research has tended to reveal that males are more stimulated by pornography than females. All in all, censorship research has tended to be descriptive, and much of it does not provide definitive answers to significant questions. Also, problems associated with research in this area are enormous, but all the completed studies cannot be ignored. Despite weaknesses, these studies provide some insights into general concepts and theories relating to freedom of expression.

RELIGIOUS CENSORSHIP

Studies of religious censorship which have proved to be useful are primarily historical investigations. Several apparent reasons might be postulated for this, the most likely being that many major controversies were either settled or died down in the past. For example, the Reformation was a period of tension between civil and church authorities for political control; however, its controversies, as well as other significant religious debates, have substantially subsided. For the time being, there appears to be a greater spirit of understanding among most religious authorities, and this tolerance of a diversity of religious beliefs has reduced the need for heated confrontations as well as attempts to suppress dissident ideas. Moreover, religious censorship designed to protect orthodox beliefs has become less prevalent.

In an effort to safeguard morals, religious authorities have justified controls on expression as a preventative measure, especially with respect to the protection of young people from exposure to materials believed to be capable of upsetting the secular order or of creating psychological or sociological problems. On the other hand, the protection of the faiths, morals, and doctrines of various religious bodies is a rather broad and almost impossible undertaking. In addition, religious codes of human behavior are usually stricter than those of secular law. For instance, some religious leaders frown upon the consumption of alcohol, but most state governments permit its sale and use. On the other hand, religious authorities may be more permissive in other areas of behavior, as when a few denominations are opposed to war and support members who refuse induction into the armed forces as conscientious objectors.

Religious bodies are usually replete with codes for moral and doctrinal values. Fundamental beliefs are more often than not rigidly outlined in official church statements, and religious leaders have also fought bitterly to preserve their principles. If a religious body perceives the contents of a medium of communication as a threat to its doctrines or to believers' morals, then censorship may be attempted. In order to remove perceived threats, church authorities might practice censorship to squelch the propagation of undesirable teachings although religious censorship limits one's ability to arrive at independent convictions.

While religious censorship may be directed toward practices and beliefs of an external group, another type of religious suppression is often directed toward internal dissidents. Controversies often develop within a religious organization about interpretations of specific teachings or religious texts. In their concern about orthodoxy, ecclesiastics have often sought to limit the communication of ideas that are perceived as subversive of established creeds. In early Christendom, heresies such as Arianism or Manichaeism caused dissension, and established church leaders sought to suppress undesirable ideas from these groups. Before the invention of the printing press, copying religious manuscripts was a tedious job involving numerous people, and scribes often made errors. Such errors have created difficulties within some groups because fine doctrinal points have often been compromised or incorrectly conveyed. Therefore, corrupt religious texts have been targets of suppression.

It is apparent that most religions have practiced either external, internal, or a combination of both types of censorship. But the effects of internal religious censorship are not always detrimental to individual rights because persons who disagree with ecclesiastical authorities can usually voluntarily withdraw from further active participation in a repressive religious body. However, when restrictions are imposed by one religious group on another, the matter becomes more serious. Both covert and overt acts of censorship have been practiced by church authorities. John Calvin and his followers exercised direct repression in Geneva, witness the execution of Michael Servetus, who was opposed to Calvinistic doctrines about infant baptism and the Holy Trinity. In Scandinavian countries, Catholic Jesuits were banned, and only in recent years have they been permitted to work in these countries.

According to the *Encyclopedia Judaica*, censorship has been practiced by Jews to a lesser degree than it has been exercised by Christians. Nevertheless, Jews have banned the following objectionable materials: salacious or trivial works, incorrect explanations or *halakhic* conclusions, works by apostates, materials produced on the Sabbath, and prayer books with unauthorized editorial changes. Book banning has also been used by Jews as a tool to resist movements such as Hasidism, the Reform movement, and even Zionism.[11] Another example of Jewish censorship was the condemnation of Spinoza's philosophic works in 1656 by Jewish authorities in Amsterdam.[12]

The *Index of Forbidden Books*, published by the Roman Catholic Church, was used prior to 1966 to control the reading of Catholics. The catalog listed books considered by the church to be dangerous to faith and morals, and Catholics were forbidden under penalty of excommunication to possess, read, sell, or transmit any banned books without first obtaining ecclesiastical dispensation.[13] The list of banned publications contained works about a variety of subjects including literature, philosophy, theology, history, law, and political science. Catholics who published works by heretics, schismatics, or apostates, or who defended, retained, or examined books included in the *Index of Forbidden Books* without permission could ultimately be denied sacraments and burial in church cemeteries.

After the Protestant Reformation, the Catholic Church sought to protect its doctrines and practices. Thus, to restore a semblance of order, the Council of Trent (1545-1563) attempted to reverse the drift of Catholics to Protestantism by shielding believers from subversive influences that could raise doubts about established doctrine. Klausler has expressed the idea that persons or groups in positions of insecurity may seek to censor what is perceived as detrimental to old values, and the Roman Catholic Church was certainly in that position during the Reformation.[14] Many more examples of church censorship could be discussed. Without a doubt, controls are being exercised by a number of religious groups at the present time; however, a diachronic or synchronic study of religious censorship is actually beyond the scope of this chapter.

One thorough study of religious censorship was the research completed by Redmond Burke for his doctoral dissertation, *The Control of Reading by the Catholic Church* (1948). Burke's investigation touched upon major issues and theories of Catholic censorship; however, the study was conducted before Vatican II. Nevertheless, the research provides significant historical insights into the Catholic rationale for censorship. Burke points out that the primary purpose of the *Index of Forbidden Books* was to suppress incorrect and unsound theological viewpoints and that the majority of the works included on the list dealt with theological questions. A second purpose of the *Index* was to protect the faith and morals of Catholics by delineating condemned publications. Finally, the *Index* served as a means of enforcing uniformity and common beliefs by controlling personal or arbitrary theological positions.[15] Although these purposes were thought to be lofty, a double standard in the utilization of the *Index* soon became apparent. Scholars could obtain permission to study the condemned works, but the typical layman could not. Librarians and instructors of literature also had implied permission to use materials included in the *Index*.[16] This double standard in reference to the use of banned books can be traced to the Council of Trent in the sixteenth century, which ushered in an era of strict church control. As Protestants gained strength during the Reformation, Rome's political and social power declined, so to prevent additional defections, the Catholic Church placed greater restrictions upon members. For example, in 170 A.D. and again in 405 A.D., the use of spurious or apocryphal books of the Bible was forbidden, but not until 1564 was the term "index" established by Pope Pius IV. Under restrictions of canon law, the following kinds of publications were prohibited: 1) unauthorized editions of the Bible or Biblical commentaries, 2) books or pamphlets concerned with visions, prophecies, miracles, or devotional practices that did not adhere to accepted doctrine, 3) liturgical works that had been changed, 4) books that discussed unauthorized indulgences, 5) devotional pictures of the saints, God, or the Virgin Mary, which were not in accord with Vatican decrees, 6) books that attempted to discredit religion and good morals, 7) books that attacked Catholic dogma or ecclesiastical discipline, 8) religious books that contained concepts contrary to church teachings, 9) books that encouraged superstitions such as fortune telling, 10) works that depicted Masons and other similar organizations in a favorable light, and 11) publications that advocated or supported practices such as dueling and suicide, or which described obscenities.[17]

Burke supported the authority of the church to ban books that could endanger the reader's faith. He maintained that ecclesiastical authorities are more knowledgeable about religious matters, but this rationale was similar to many claims of censors who professed to be able to recognize pernicious ideas or information that could pose threats. Burke set the total number of books condemned by the church at 4,134; yet, one must realize that the *Index* did not contain all works found to be objectionable by the Catholic Church. Restrictions on the reading of other books were allowed according to canon law 1399. Burke drew an analogy between the U.S. Supreme Court and the compilation of the *Index* by indicating that laws are constantly being refined and interpreted by the Court, and the Catholic Church's decisions to place controls on books represented official decisions regarding works brought to the attention of the Vatican. The church also made use of the *Nihil obstat* (there is nothing objectionable) and *Imprimatur* (approval to publish) designations to insure that correct doctrine would be transmitted. However, the *Nihil obstat* and *Imprimatur* labels did not prevent a work from appearing in the *Index of Forbidden Books.* In one instance, Monsignor Louis Duchesne received both designations for *Early History of the Christian Church* (1906); however, the book was included in the *Index* in 1912. Apparently, oversights were made by a diocesan censor who claimed that the work was free of error and permitted its publication.

Church law directs bishops to scrutinize books which are sold or distributed in their geographic areas. In 1907, Pope Pius X urged bishops to form diocesan vigilance committees to scrutinize harmful books and to prevent their circulation. Even books with the *Imprimatur* designation were to be examined. As a part of the church's program for the control of reading materials, Catholics who were involved in the book trade were also provided with official guidelines about forbidden books. Book dealers were instructed not to sell, retain, or allow the use of books containing obscenities unless special permission was received from the Vatican. Moreover, a dealer was required to make judgments about the advisability of allowing a customer to purchase any forbidden book.

Although many of the *Index* titles represented works of little interest to the typical layman, a number of significant fiction and non-fiction books were listed, such as works by Descartes, Voltaire, Croce, Hobbes, Hume, Zola, and Maeterlink. The term *opera omnia* was at times placed after writers' names as an indication that all their works were prohibited. Because the *Index of Forbidden Books* was periodically revised, some books on earlier lists were not included in revised editions. For example, certain works condemned before 1600 did not appear in the 1900 *Index*. Nonetheless, works such as the *Dacameron* and *The Prince* were still under a church ban according to canon law 1399. The last edition of the *Index* was published in 1948. Eighteen years later, in 1966, the Catholic Church announced that it would not publish a new edition of the list of prohibited works, and restrictions were also lifted on books included in all editions of the *Index*. However, the Catholic Church still regards certain works as sinful if readers believe that these publications are indeed harmful to their faith and morals. Rather than publishing a list of forbidden books, the Roman Catholic Church now intends to periodically publish lists of books that are not recommended for Catholics.

Burke also pointed out that the Catholic Church has preserved texts, developed and protected libraries, copied old manuscripts, and encouraged the development of printing. In short, he claimed that these measures by the church have demonstrated that Catholic officials have understood the need for the preservation of knowledge. To accurately evaluate Burke's entire study, however, one should take into consideration that the investigator attempted to explain and to defend to a large extent a theological position on censorship. One needs to be aware, however, that an attempt by a religious group to maintain textual integrity and doctrinal conformity is quite different from efforts to ban the sale, study, or printing of non-religious materials.

Theological censorship is a grave threat when it intrudes on civil liberties. Ecclesiastical authorities may feel that they have an obligation to pass judgments upon literary and social works in an attempt to protect faith and morals; yet, the crucial question is: Where does theology end and secular matters begin? For example, a book might be of excellent literary quality, but its central message could be offensive and unacceptable to a church. Difficulties arise when one attempts to compartmentalize these two areas. The value of Burke's research becomes apparent when one realizes that the *Index* served as an instrument to control what Catholics could read for hundreds of years, but that that control was by no means absolute. No mechanism existed for checking how closely a person observed the church's decrees about what could or could not be read; control was more internal than external. A close examination of the *Index* reveals further that a number of works listed there dealt with controversies and rivalries within the church between Franciscans, Dominicans, Augustinians, Benedictines, Carmelites, and Jesuits. Often exaggerated claims were made for the merits or shortcomings of one or another of these orders; hence, petty published arguments (i.e., controversy over what kind of hood was worn by St. Francis) were often forbidden. Many publications of the Jesuits appeared in the *Index*, and a few Protestant writings which attacked the Jesuit order were included.[18]

Closely related to Catholic doctrine is the practice of indulgences for the remission of punishment for sin. From time to time, however, fraudulent indulgence books were published, listing distorted indulgences that made outlandish claims. In one case, the believer was promised that fifteen people would be saved from hell or converted if a recommended prayer were spoken and the fifteen people were specified. Many of these unauthorized indulgence books were included in the *Index*. Oddly, a curious stance toward Protestant reformers is evident if *Index* listings are carefully examined. One finds works by Luther, Calvin, Zwingli, and Oecolampadius; however, all the works of leading reformers were not suppressed. Controversial books by some authors were ignored, yet insignificant tracts were often listed. It seems somewhat paradoxical that non-controversial works were often banned but that some books that could have been potentially damaging to the stability of the Catholic Church were not mentioned.

In his 1906 study of church censorship, George Putnam pointed out that early editions of the *Index* were carelessly compiled. Bibliographical accuracy of the listings left much to be desired. Authors' names were sometimes misspelled, appeared only under a surname or local name, or were listed in Latin or in the vernacular. In an attempt to end duplication in the *Index*, some heretical books were inadvertently omitted by copyists. Undoubtedly, the limited amount of bibliographical information available about certain condemned works also contributed to inaccurate listings.

Universal acceptance of the concept and purpose of the *Index* was never achieved by the church even within its own ranks. The Jesuit Lainez felt that the list of banned books was more harmful than beneficial. A German theologian was even more adamant: St. Peter Canisius characterized the *Index* as a "stumbling block" and "the ruin of schools."[19]

The present value of Burke's description of a type of religious censorship that no longer exists is that the work provides a historical perspective of the church's control of reading. Contemporary society often finds itself faced with the same protectionist attitudes that Burke carefully details. Indeed, parallels presently exist between the conditions that Burke described and some contemporary censorship activities. Burke explained in detail the mechanisms used by the Vatican to control materials which were considered objectionable, yet, as other sources indicate, both the acceptance and effectiveness of the *Index* were not universal. Scholars interested in certain aspects of church theology could obtain permission to use forbidden works; however, the process of doing so was time consuming and burdensome. Thus, persons who were more predisposed to use the forbidden books were restrained from doing so, and those who were less likely to read them were simply admonished not to do so.

Contemporary repressive conditions exhibit some related incongruities. Although some uneducated persons presently attempt to ban literary works such as *Catcher in the Rye* or *Ulysses* from bookstores and libraries, these groups make it more difficult for intellectually mature persons to obtain books. At the same time, those persons who are interested in sexually oriented materials are more likely to turn to more stimulating, easily available hard-core pornography rather than a more literary work.

Another correlation between Burke's findings and current trends is evident. Burke outlined his rather sympathetic rationale for the Roman Catholic Church's censorship program, and many contemporary censors also devise similar complicated, detailed, and defensive philosophies for their actions. They use sweeping terms such as "pornographic," "potentially harmful," "immoral," and "contrary to American values" to defend their attacks on materials that they find objectionable.

Inappropriate and inaccurate terminology is often substituted for vague or undefinable attitudes, ideals, or concepts.

GOVERNMENT CENSORSHIP

Adequate research has not been conducted related to the suppression of information by governments. Numerous investigators have gathered and tabulated data, but answers to some significant questions about governmental control of ideas and information do not exist. Additional inquiries need to be made in this area because knowledge about governmental suppression is presently derived solely from limited historical and descriptive studies. While church efforts to ban publications may affect only selected groups, governmental censorship is enforceable by law and affects all citizens. A restrictive declaration by a church or other private group is quite different from a statute which legally forbids the production or distribution of certain materials.

Most governments have exercised controls on information at one time or another, and to make an unqualified statement that governmental censorship should not be practiced is a much too simplistic approach to the problem. When government officials determine policy or engage in diplomatic negotiations, the reporting of all details of these activities may not be possible or wise. Yet the systematic withholding of embarrassing information, or the deliberate distortion of facts to achieve a political end, is contrary to the democratic ideal. Unfortunately, all suppressive attempts cannot be categorized so neatly. Nebulous concepts of what is or is not beneficial to the social development of a community can often lead to censorship by the government.

An important aspect of the problem of government censorship involves defining the common good. Governments plan and execute policies which are designed to enable men to live together without strife and disruption, and dangers which political leaders perceive as threats to social and political stability are usually discouraged. Consequently, legislation and judicial steps are often taken to restrict the spread of "harmful" ideas or practices. So that governmental leaders are more aware of dangers to societal order, pressure groups express their concerns to leaders in political power; and as political leaders experience increasing pressures from persons or groups who support or disapprove of certain ideas or practices, these officials will often respond by word or deed in order to maintain good relations. However, the groups which politicians seek to please may be either small or large, and restrictions on communication media have often resulted from pressures exerted on a government by a relatively small but loud group. Thus, Lebanon has banned motion pictures that deal with Zionism, Thailand has restricted films that cast its monarchy in a bad light, and the Union of South Africa has censored movies that advocate equality for blacks. Even the pharaohs of ancient Egypt attempted to limit certain influences on their subjects; inscriptions were chipped off monuments in order to restrict the reading of undesirable information.[29] In all of these examples, pressure groups—the anti-Zionists, the monarchists, the white minority, and the rulers of Egypt—expressed sufficiently strong opposition to certain ideas or images that they were able to shape governmental policy relating to communication.

Although United States citizens generally agree that they enjoy considerable freedoms, various incidents in the nation's past have demonstrated that the government has sometimes limited what the citizen could read, publish, or transmit. For instance, a tenuous relationship has been hypothesized between the reading of obscene materials and vice. The Tariff Act of 1842 established a precedent for the suppression of what was thought to be obscene literature. Later, the New York Society for the Suppression of Vice and its leader Anthony Comstock contributed heavily to increased government censorship in the nineteenth century and the early decades of the present century.

A careful examination of the history of nineteenth-century American will reveal a nation beset with some of the difficulties that still face our society. Racial strife, economic problems, crime, war, and population changes were major concerns, and all of these problems inspired men to work for a better and more stable environment. Hence, Anthony Comstock's plans to stop the spread of publications containing objectionable ideas or images were met with little opposition. Although they were simplistic, Comstock's solutions to social ills appealed to persons who were then occupied with more serious problems. His efforts helped to bring about passage of the Comstock Act of 1873, which allowed the U.S. Post Office to refuse delivery of materials deemed to be obscene or crime-inciting. Comstock's cause was that of eliminating vice in the society, so few people vigorously opposed that "noble" objective. However, Comstock's overbearing personal tactics eventually irritated the public.

The Tariff Act of 1842 and the Comstock Act were by no means effective in eliminating all objectionable materials, even though authority was also given to customs officials to confiscate pornographic materials before these works entered the United States. The Library of Congress was authorized to receive and to preserve erotic works seized by customs officials, and it in turn added the materials to its collection of erotica, which is available to scholars and researchers.[21] Disputes about the literary merits of James Joyce's *Ulysses* and the legal battle which was lost by the Bureau of Customs in its attempt to suppress the novel did little to strengthen the contention that censorship was practiced in the best interest of citizens and for the common good.

The concept of personal freedom is firmly entrenched in American life, and official attempts to censor seem contradictory to the democratic spirit. While the disparity between values and practices may be difficult to understand, it must be seen that the era that fostered the passage of the Tariff Act of 1842 and the Comstock Act of 1873 was characterized by social change. Prior to the Civil War, abolitionists pursued their cause by distributing anti-slavery publications, especially to Southerners. To stop the flow of these materials to the South, President Andrew Jackson proposed legislation to give postal officials authority to censor anti-slavery materials. However, outcries by congressmen put an end to that plan.[22] On the other hand, the violence and social changes wrought by the Civil War set the stage for repressive measures imposed in the post-war era. Although there was a heavy loss of lives in battles, civilians also experienced a shaky civil order and many hardships. For example, in July, 1863, anti-draft rioters looted stores and homes in New York, and the strife ended only after four hundred demonstrators had been killed.[23] Also, following the Civil War, social change was inevitable. More people migrated to unsettled territories, industrialization progressed rapidly, and urban centers spread across the landscape. These rapid social changes and the resulting upheavals in American society were particularly distressing to some leaders. Persons whose origins were small towns or farms, which tended to be provincial, did not always know how to cope with social transformations that were occurring in the nation. Some persons thus directed their money and influence to the preservation of values and morals which had been inculcated into their lives at an early age and in another place.[24]

Other nations have been influenced by additional factors when strict censorship laws have been passed. In Ireland, for example, nationalistic motives came into play because of the abundance of British publications, which created problems in a republic that was predominantly Roman Catholic and comprised of a population that was relatively uneducated. The Irish did not always agree with the moral values or views expressed in English establishment literature, and with the emergence of the Irish Republic, a general sentiment developed for the control of foreign materials. The Irish wanted to assert their own cultural values without official approval from the English Parliament. Publications, especially those originating in Britain which advocated brith control, anti-religious sentiments, or unorthodox moral viewpoints were banned in Ireland. Thus, attempts to suppress various kinds of information satisfied the nation's need to prove that Ireland was truly independent, as well as to demonstrate that the Irish were masters of their own destiny.[25]

Ireland has not been the only country to attempt to protect its nationalistic and cultural identity from an onslaught of foreign influences. Parallels occurred in ancient Rome, where Cato, the notorious Roman censor, sought to protect Romans from corruptive influences from Greece and North Africa since he thought that the transfer of foreign cultural concepts was intrinsically bad.[26] In more modern times, the constitution of India, as well as the basic laws of several African states, have incorporated censorship provisions designed to control obscene materials.[27]

Despite the fact that motives and degrees of censorship may differ, the thrust of official restraints on freedom of expression must be outlined in legal codes which specify prohibitions if censorship is to be effective. But such policies are then subject to judicial interpretation and refinement. According to Donald B. Sharp, absolute consistency among legal statutes does not exist, and when a legal system is dynamic and flexible enough to cope with new situations, precedents can be negated. As we have seen, conflicts over freedom of expression that arise between persons with opposite values often result in court decisions that are either unclear or conflict with other rulings. To resolve difficult questions, a judge often relies upon legal precedents; thus, decisions tend to be more authoritative since judges do not usually act capriciously. When precedents are overthrown and others are established, judges must attempt to resolve contradictions, or otherwise, a new precedent might be completely ignored after being established.[28]

The United States Supreme Court has heard numerous free speech cases related to the question of obscenity and expression; however, the basic problem of conflicts between First Amendment rights and restrictions on free speech remains unsolved. One of the earliest decisions dealing with the problem of obscenity was the *Hicklin* case, in which the court attempted to provide a standard for determining what was or was not obscene. The major elements of the *Hicklin* decision were the concepts of the "most susceptible person" and "isolated passages." Thus, if a work had short, objectionable passages and if the passages were deemed to possess characteristics that might adversely affect a person who did not understand the true intent of the work, the publication could be considered obscene. Another set of criteria for the identification of obscenity was later outlined in the *Roth v. United States* decision (1957), which stipulated that isolated passages could not be considered as grounds for determining whether a work was obscene. A new criterion, the work's appeal to the "prurient interest," was established. In light of the *Roth* decision, a book such as *The Catcher in the Rye* could not be judged obscene. Another *Roth* guideline was the "average person" concept, under which an objectionable publication had to be of such a nature that the typical, not the maladjusted, citizen of a community would be affected. Following *Roth*, another case, *Manual Enterprises v. Day*, provided further clarification in that "patent offensiveness" was deemed to be that which would affront community standards.[29]

Between the *Roth* decision and the *Ginzburg* decision of 1966, the U.S. Supreme Court consistently strengthened First Amendment interpretations of the Constitution, and writers and producers of artistic works were provided more leeway in discussing sexual topics. However, the assumption that the liberalizing trend of the Court would continue was shattered first by the *Ginzburg* decision and later by *Miller*. Ralph Ginzburg, a publisher and distributor of sexually-oriented materials, mailed advertisements for his publications, but some of the distributed brochures fell into the hands of children. Ginzburg incurred the wrath of parents who did not want their children to examine the graphic advertisements for *Eros*, a periodical about the erotic in art and literature; *Liaison*, which was supposed to deal with salacious news; and a book, *The Housewives' Handbook of Selective Promiscuity*. Although some court-watchers anticipated that Ginzburg would be acquitted, the Supreme Court upheld a lower court's conviction of the defendant for distributing obscene materials. The Court did not declare the publisher's materials obscene but decided that his methods of advertising and distributing his materials were illegal. The element of "pandering" thus entered into the *Ginzburg* case.[30] (The *Roth* decision had not been concerned with the issue of pandering.)

Confusion quickly arose as to the impact that the *Ginzburg* decision might have on the judicial process in respect to subsequent obscenity cases. *Ginzburg* blurred the distinction between the mode of selling sexually oriented materials and the content of what was sold. Legal obscenity problems were further complicated in the late 1960s, when the composition of the Supreme Court underwent a major change. As vacancies occurred on the Court, President Nixon nominated justices who espoused more conservative philosophies of constitutional interpretations of the law. As a consequence, the Court's decisions soon began to exhibit a marked difference from those handed down by the "Warren Court." Tensions had built up as a result of liberal constitutional interpretations, and problems associated with earlier rulings needed to be resolved. Key words which appeared in previous obscenity rulings had never been adequately defined. The terms "obscene," "indecent," "lewd," "prurient," "hard-core pornography," "community standards," and "prevalent attitudes of the community" had been used previously as though an agreement had been reached on the bench as to their exact meanings.[31]

On June 21, 1973, a major development in the legal control of obscene materials unfolded. The Supreme Court decision in *Miller v. California* gave both the states and the federal government more power to restrict the distribution of offensive sexual materials. Several major changes were made in previously established guidelines. First, a sexually oriented work having utterly no redeeming social value and lacking important political, scientific, literary, or artistic value is now subject to being considered as obscene. Second, local rather than national community standards can be used to determine degrees of offensiveness of sexually oriented materials. Third, commercial outlets and theaters which sell or exhibit sexual films are still subject to state regulation. Fourth, the importation or interstate transferral of obscene works intended for private use can be controlled by legislation passed by Congress.[32]

After the Court's 1973 ruling in *Miller*, the question arose as to how new obscenity guidelines are to be interpreted and applied. Libertarians even claim that the potential exists for a return to the restrictive measures against sexually oriented materials in effect before the *Roth* decision. Despite its failures, the "Warren Court" had provided general obscenity guidelines for application at the national level for the control of obscenity in communications. Literary classics, works of social value with sexual themes, writings with an occasional use of four-letter words, and materials which did not adversely affect "the average man" were thus previously protected.[33] Under guidelines for determining obscenity handed down in *Miller*, formerly protected categories of materials may now come under attack. More private vigilante groups have been created over the nation since the decision was handed down, and these groups have pressed for strict controls on the sale of materials with sexual content, including some modern novels of literary merit as well as selected quality films. Local attitudes tend to be more conservative and restrictive than national ones, and they can wipe out the more sensible national standards for obscenity which were used in the past.

Max Lerner noted that the average person's view of what is offensive is an environmental product. Recognition of important literary or scientific values, however, will not vary greatly among the states, according to Lerner.[34] The implications of this concept are very clear. If local community standards are too heavily relied upon, broader considerations of the worth of materials will not be made. Not all persons are experts in scientific or literary matters, and the merits of a publication or a non-print medium of communication are not always widely recognized by laymen.

As the research relating to government censorship in the United States is limited both in quantity and quality, it is difficult to make generalizations relating to the official control of ideas and information. Political considerations of all problems create difficulties for the investigator. In this brief overview of the legal aspects of official censorship, the complexity of the matter should be apparent. The flux of attitudes and philosophies relating to obscenity complicates any attempt to establish general principles. If the position is taken that the law will be interpreted in light of the needs and concerns of society at any given point, one is faced with continuous attempts at probing the changing values of mankind. Certainly the various value judgments which officials employ in their conceptualizations of the common good add to the difficulties of examining censorship of an official nature.

EXTRALEGAL CENSORSHIP

As with other forms of censorship, there is a paucity of research in the area of extralegal suppression, a form of censorship initiated by unofficial agents in the form of social pressures. Tactics such as boycotts, adverse publicity, or harassment can be carried on against book dealers, theaters, supermarkets, drugstores, or other communications outlets. Schools and libraries are both often faced with attacks from unofficial groups that do not approve of certain textbooks or library materials. Unlike direct forms of censorship, however, extralegal suppression is more subtle in nature, but it may be quite effective. Organizations which foster extralegal censorship are not always readily identifiable, since a local group of citizens may unite to attack works sold in a bookstore or materials in public or school library collections.

Pressures to censor books and other materials can be exerted by the far right, by the far left, by religious bodies, or by radical or ethnic leaders.[35] One of the more prominent pro-censorship associations is an organization called Citizens for Decent Literature (CDL), founded by Charles H. Keating, Jr., a Cincinnati lawyer who was appointed by President Nixon to fill a vacancy in the President's Commission on Obscenity and Pornography. While other organizations direct pressures on booksellers or distribution points with a community, the CDL is an organization dedicated to eliminating obscene literature by means of stronger censorship legislation. Working to change the laws by letter-writing campaigns to city, state, and national leaders and other measures, the CDL has attempted to limit the sale of materials found to be objectionable to it. The CDL receives support from a wide variety of religious faiths.

Another organization which sought to control pornography and obscene literature was the National Office for Decent Literature, a Catholic group formed in 1938 by the Catholic bishops of America for the purpose of investigating the "menace" that sex literature posed to youth. Father John Courtney Murry characterized the organization as a service group rather than action-oriented, with emphasis placed upon the evaluation of comic books, magazines, and paperbacks. Writings of questionable character were placed on the NODL list of objectionable books. Although Father Murry maintained that the NODL list was not compiled as a guide for purposes of boycott or coercion, the list was actually used occasionally for those purposes. Msgr. Joseph Howard (executive secretary of the NODL between 1963 and 1969) characterized the stance taken by the group in these words:

> The National Tabloids and the Shadows stand as monuments to the stupidity of a society which is willing to raft its youngsters down the slough of delinquency just to keep the boat of Free Speech in the harbor. The slick, suggestive cover poses and their accompanying Shadowy titles . . . are cruel monuments to the impracticability of the Douglas-Black-ACLU philosophy of everything goes. It is a dirty trick on Thomas Jefferson and James Madison, who never dreamed of any constitutional protection for this kind of stuff.[36]

A Protestant group, the Churchmen's Commission for Decent Literature, has also served as a watchdog over the literary marketplace, but it has been much less successful in its efforts to control the dissemination of certain kinds of materials than either the CDL or the NODL.[37]

Acting as a counterbalance to the so-called "clean" literature movements in the United States are the "right to read" associations, which take a strong anti-censorship stance. Members of these groups believe that the most effective way to avoid warping the personalities of young persons is to expose them to all viewpoints and to discuss problems related to distorted value systems. In this way, it is believed that children can receive proper guidance when they face conflicting opinions. Attempting to prevent children from being exposed to certain social problems, the right-to-read organizations feel, both shields and cheats the young. Proponents of the right to read feel that society cannot protect the young from all adverse influences. Thus, they believe that when children are exposed to a situation in which they must think or act for themselves, they will not have the necessary background to deal with the unexpected situation if they have not been prepared to do so. One typical example of a right-to-read association is the New Jersey Committee for the Right to Read, founded in 1964 by Harold Flanders and other concerned persons.

The New Jersey Committee for the Right to Read and the Citizens for Decent Literature group have both sponsored research related to censorship or freedom of expression. The findings from their research efforts are questionable because the studies were produced from less-than-rigorous investigations; consequently, these projects are best seen as examples of what can occur when investigators are not sufficiently objective. Rather than taking the position that the data must either support or negate an asserted hypothesis, the investigators in question apparently attempted primarily to secure data that would lend weight to pre-conceived pro- or anti-censorship ideas.

In the late 1960s, the CDL distributed questionnaires to collect information about citizens' attitudes toward pornography and its effects on readers or viewers. Results of the survey were as follows: 1) 63.5 percent of the respondents felt that pornographic movies and reading materials were positively related to incidents of venereal disease, 2) 67.5 percent of the respondents were convinced that pornographic films and literature are factors contributing to incidents of illegitimacy, 3) 75 percent were of the opinion that pornographic movies and reading materials play a part in stimulating homosexual tendencies, and 4) 92 percent felt that delinquency is related to the reading of pornographic works and the viewing of sex movies. These findings are questionable because the survey employed to collect the data used weak methodological measures. For example, unbiased responses were not encouraged because the questionnaire did not allow respondents an opportunity to express doubt about the consequences of viewing pornographic materials. Indeed, bias was even evident in the report of the survey. The introduction discussed the difficulty of establishing a relationship between anti-social actions and pornography, but a statement was presented from the New York Academy of Medicine which implied a positive relationship between these two variables.[38]

A similar survey by the New Jersey Committee for the Right to Read also produced questionable results. The NJCRR selected 546 respondent psychologists and psychiatrists from 1963 to 1965 professional directories. According to the NJCRR findings, 1) 60 percent of the respondents who completed the questionnaire felt that sexually oriented publications serve as an outlet to minimize anti-social behavior, and 2) 80 percent believed a person would not have a healthier and more viable outlook on sex if sexually oriented reading materials were not available. On the whole, the psychologists and psychiatrists endorsed sex education, the improved facilities for the treatment of mental illness, and the use of state funds for constructive rather than censorship purposes. Although results of the survey support some of the claims of anti-censorship groups, certain shortcomings of the research cast doubt on the validity of the study. Despite the careful selection of participants for the survey, only 17.6 percent of the surveyed psychiatrists and 27.2 percent of the psychologists responded to the questionnaire. In view of the low response rate, generalizations can hardly be made from the survey's data. Also, the NJCRR used the term "pornography" in the introduction to the report of the survey results; a number of statements that suggested that pornography has no relationship to anti-social behavior were inserted in the report, and statements from Kinsey's research reports in regard to pornography were also included. Whether these statements were used to affect the reader's attitudes does not matter. In reality, they probably did bias some of the opinions against censorship measures on obscene materials. In addition to these weaknesses, some of the questionnaire items were inappropriate. For example, one question requested opinions about the statistical significance of the relationship between pornography and behavior. Obviously, the question of statistical significance is not a matter of opinion; it must be answered by carefully analyzing quantifiable data.[39]

Extralegal censorship has an adverse effect on freedom of inquiry. Persons or organizations may scrutinize and police their own actions in order to avoid offense to anyone or to avoid adverse public relations. By concentrating on the avoidance of all possible controversies, librarians practicing self-censorship can adversely affect the building of library collections. Thus, self-censorship can be almost as restrictive on freedom of expression in libraries as external suppression on an institution. Scholarship will not be supported if educators or librarians voluntarily close off avenues of exploration simply because they do not want to offend someone or some group.

Another danger inherent in the practice of extralegal censorship is its pervasive threat to society as a whole. When a small group can override or subvert the values and goals of a majority, the spirit of democracy is crushed. Likewise, the rights of a minority should not be overlooked, but the use of repressive tactics to achieve a goal may not always be the most satisfactory means of resolving a problem to the best interest of the minority. For example, some groups may view Mark Twain's *Huckleberry Finn* as a demeaning and racist work, but the book actually presents a rather honest view of prevailing attitudes in a period of the nation's past. Under the skillful guidance of a qualified teacher, *Huckleberry Finn* could provide students with insights about hypocrisies and misconceptions associated with racial prejudices in nineteenth-century America. Suppression of the book only contributes to a failure to understand Twain's desire to convey the idea that all men share the same human condition, seek many of the same goals in life, and deserve equal treatment under the law.

CENSORSHIP IN SCHOOLS AND LIBRARIES

Because a great deal of information has been generated about censorship in public schools and in libraries, and because these institutions share some common characteristics and goals, both will be discussed herein. A great deal has been written about the interference of organized groups with formal public education, and censorship problems in schools and libraries that result in bans on books, the firing of teachers, or demonstrations against a school normally receive considerable attention in the news media. However, the real causes of such actions may not be understood because of the lack of thorough investigations. Only by careful observation and analysis of a number of repressive attempts can a substantive understanding of censorship be achieved. The mere reporting of censorship attempts does not add to the general body of knowledge about reasons for repressive acts.

Censorship in
Schools & libraries

	1987	1986	1985	1984	1983
988	2477	2586	2842	3028	3051
203	2582	2898	3540	4098	3998
	3767	4014	4532	4832	4771
	1880	2381	2513	2774	2992
0	2233	2473	2615	2968	2992
0	2597	2917	3349	3652	4079
3	2739	3114	3332	3486	3820
47	18,275	20,383	22,723	24,838	25,703
−9.5%	−10.3%	−10.3%	−8.5%	−3.4%	+0

*SOURCE: SPAS screens, thro
HW, MX, TR; 1/19/88 for DA

Fortunately, more rigorous research has recently been undertaken in the area of library censorship. While not all relevant questions can be answered, a beginning has been made in the long process of identifying variables and their relationships in respect to this form of censorship. Studies by Aherns, Fiske, Busha, Knudson, and others contain basic information which can provide direction for future research.

A significant study was conducted by Nyla H. Aherns in 1965 among public school English teachers. Aherns sought to identify censorship incidents that were experienced between 1962-64 by these teachers in selected secondary schools. Pre-testing of a questionnaire and the elimination of certain questions from the instrument strengthened the study's methodology. Every twenty-fifth person on membership lists of the Secondary Section of the National Council of Teachers of English was asked to serve as a respondent in the survey. The questionnaire return rate was 81.6 percent. Replies only from respondents who were actually employed as English teachers were utilized. In addition to information about censorship incidents which teachers encountered, Aherns sought data about the qualities of the teachers and schools that had experienced book controversies, characteristics of would-be censors, the nature of the books that were the objects of repressive attacks, the process for choosing materials in schools, and the handling of would-be censorship incidents from initial complaints to resolutions of problems. Aherns discovered that 12.6 percent of the teacher-respondents (N=616) had been involved in at least one censorship controversy. Teachers who had experienced censorship attempts had completed more formal education than those who had not experienced complaints or attempts to remove books from reading lists. Those who had experienced censorship attempts had also only recently completed their education, and these teachers were educated at liberal arts colleges rather than at state universities or teacher's colleges. In addition to having less teaching experience, these instructors had taught in the upper rather than the lower grades. Teachers who had experienced censorship were often perceived as "liberal" or as significantly different than most of the citizens in the communities in which their schools were located, and schools in which these teachers taught were fairly large, with several curricular tracks in addition to a college preparatory program. Generally, most complaints about school books, centered on: 1) materials that had been recommended by teachers as supplementary reading, 2) literature chosen by the student, or 3) readings selected by a committee or departmental faculty.[40]

Aherns concluded that of the twenty-nine states that had experienced controversies about books in high schools, the highest number of incidents (56) was recorded in California. In second place was New York, and Wisconsin placed third in number of incidents. Statistics of the various geographical regions of the nation provided a rather good overview of the intensity of book banning activities in high schools. The percentage of censorship incidents in high schools by geographic regions were: New England, 8.2 percent; Middle Atlantic, 16.1 percent; Southeast, 10.6 percent; Midwest, 13.7 percent; Southwest, 4.1 percent; Northwest, 9.5 percent; and Far West, 17.3 percent.[41]

After carefully analyzing reasons for censorship in schools, Aherns concluded that controversies of this nature in educational institutions are cyclic in nature. She indicated that during the late 1950s and early 1960s, high schools experienced an increased number of attempts at censorship. At the time of the study (1965), social studies textbooks were more frequently criticized than books used in English classes and were being attacked for their "liberalism" and "anti-Americanism."[42] Thus, one can speculate on the basis of Aherns' research that certain school-centered censorship patterns exist. As would-be censors turn their attention from one subject area, they appear to place other topics or forms of communication under closer scrutiny. When teachers desire to promote freedom of expression, they usually attempt to formulate a philosophy which will guide them in defending what is presented in the classroom. On the other hand, teachers who tend to be less opposed to censorship will usually support various suppressions and will agree that "objectionable" works should not be read and discussed. However, no matter how concerned or careful a teacher may be about avoiding controversial works, someone can find a way to characterize even the most innocuous work as potentially harmful. For those teachers who are not totally committed to either a strong pro- or anti-censorship position, the methods for avoiding an attack are less clear.

One finding of the Aherns study is that two-thirds of the books which provoked repressions were in paperback form. This finding suggests that paperbacks might be considered as capable of influencing student behavior more so than hardbound books.[43] The exact reasons for this high incidence is in need of investigation, but perhaps the lower prices and mass circulation capabilities of paperbacks contribute to both the utility and popularity of these works for conveying contemporary—thus often more provocative ideas. Obviously, more knowledge in this area would be of use in preparing for the complaints that arise relating to literary materials used in public schools.

In order to compare book controversies in junior and senior high schools and those in institutions of higher education, Rozanne R. Knudson examined English programs in California junior colleges. In many respects, Knudson's research appears to be characterized by objectivity and rigor. The response rate of the survey was relatively high; 98.12 percent of all persons selected as respondents returned their questionnaires.[44] By choosing English teachers listed in the junior college section of the *California School Directory* (and four college catalogs of institutions not listed in the 1965 and 1966 editions of the *Directory*) and by excluding non-English teachers from the sample's population, Knudson was able to identify English teachers in California junior colleges. A sample was then selected with a table of random numbers. Knudson attempted to obtain a 10 percent sample from a population of 1,415 teachers.[45]

Knudson devoted particular attention to self-censorship, anticipatory censorship, and "censorialness." Self-censorship is a personally imposed limitation designed to avoid confrontations with a person or group that might be offended. Booksellers, publishers, educators, and librarians can practice self-censorship by avoiding the purchase or use of controversial materials. Anticipatory censorship, as defined by Knudson, is that which begins with the author. For example, writers could feel that certain ideas or images might handicap the acceptance or sale of their works, so they might deliberately limit their own creative expression. This type of censorship is particularly ominous when the public's interest is sacrificed. Yet, after a writer has anticipated objections and has made deletions from his materials, the publisher in turn may attempt to eliminate what he considers potentially offensive. Likewise, a bookseller can practice anticipatory censorship by stocking only well-accepted and non-offensive books. Teachers can also modify what is presented to a class in order to avoid parental objections. Another special type of self-censorship is "censorialness," which Knudson identifies as the tendency to oversee morals and behavior or to protect the reader's sensitivity.[46] A censorial teacher, according to

Knudson, might eliminate the reading or discussion of fiction and non-fiction books because these works may contain objectionable language, characters, incidents, subjects, or passages which are considered to be obscene, immoral, profane, un-American, or contrary to widely accepted religious doctrine. A censorial teacher who exhibits little confidence in the intelligence and maturity of students and less determination to make the reading of controversial books by students a profitable and meaningful experience acts in an unprofessional manner.[47]

Because a scientific approach was taken in the California study, Knudson was able to test hypotheses. She found a positive relationship between teachers' anticipatory responses and the supervisors' announcements that neither fiction or non-fiction works should be recommended or required reading. A relationship was also found between anticipatory responses and the conviction that certain kinds of fiction or non-fiction should not be permitted, required, or recommended for use in courses. A positive relationship was also found between restrictions placed on book selection for courses and anticipatory responses of teachers. Finally, the investigator rejected the hypothesis that no observable relationship would exist between anticipatory responses and well-known complaints about books used or considered for use in English courses. On the other hand, Knudson did not find a relationship between anticipatory responses and objections that were expressed between 1962 and 1966 to books either used or planned for usage in English courses. Too, no relationship was found between anticipatory responses before 1962 to works used or planned for use in English courses. Anticipatory responses and sex of respondents were not related. In addition, no relationship was found between anticipatory responses and the educational attainments of respondents. Finally, no relationship could be established between anticipatory responses and the tenure status of those professors who were surveyed.[48]

The value of Knudson's research becomes apparent when one realizes that censorship activities arise even in a junior college. While the frequency and vehemence of the objections might not be so great as those brought against elementary, junior high, and senior high schools, the controversies that arose in California junior colleges caused considerable problems for those involved. For example, at the Shasta College Library, students were once not permitted to sit while using *The Dictionary of American Slang.* In another incident, two Christian Scientists pressured the State Board of Education into removing the *Primer of Physiology* from schools, and, for a brief period, two Roman Catholics were also successful in banning the *King James Bible* from Fresno school libraries.[49] It is not surprising that 13.8 percent of the respondent-teachers reported that certain works could not be utilized in junior college English courses, but these teachers represented 17 colleges or 22.4 percent of all the junior colleges in California.[50]

Earlier studies were attempted in order to investigate some of the same problems explained by Knudson; however, they do not appear to be as reliable as the research carried out in California. For example, Burress conducted an investigation (the "Wisconsin Study") of the effects of censorship in junior and senior high schools. A total of 606 questionnaires were returned—a response rate of 36.9 percent. Burress found that about one-fifth of the Wisconsin respondents reported that they had been involved in censorship incidents and that some teachers anticipated potentially troublesome situations and attempted to eliminate possible grounds for objections. Unfortunately, Burress's methods leave much to be desired. Open-ended questions were used, which required respondents to reply with a phrase or short sentences, and as a result, a variety of unstructured and irrelevant replies were received. Burress also based his conclusions only on random responses from the questionnaires of teachers who had experienced censorship problems. A gap between the data and the interpretation of data is evident because Burress had to make some value judgments in order to analyze all the replies. In addition, the intensity of responses was not solicited in regard to the severity of repressive episodes encountered by teachers. Because the questionnaire response rate was low, the results of the survey might also have been biased.

Another study was conducted by the Utah Council of Teachers of English in 1963. English department chairmen in schools were asked to identify the sources of complaints about books (i.e., from parents, school administrators, or other organizations). Of the 160 chairmen surveyed, only 43 percent returned questionnaires. Thus, the significance of the 16 teachers who reported minor problems and the 21 who listed serious problems was not clearly determined.[51]

The scientific approach of the "Fiske Report," a study among librarians in selected California communities, allowed the exposure of some revealing self-censorship practices of school and public librarians. Unlike the methods used by Aherns, Knudson, and Burress, Fiske and her associates employed face-to-face interviews with librarians. To insure that findings would be highly reliable, preliminary interviews were conducted both to train interviewers and to improve the rigor of questions to be asked in the survey. Twenty-six California communities were selected for scrutiny in order to obtain a broad data base. Extensive reports were prepared immediately after each interview had been conducted with school librarians, administrators, and municipal and county librarians.[52]

Fiske conducted her study for the purpose of identifying relationships between factors which discouraged or encouraged the selection and circulation of controversial materials. Her conclusions about school librarians and censorship was rather disheartening. Only eight out of forty-five school librarians felt that they were truly equal partners with teachers in the educational process in schools, and many of the school librarians also believed that their role was not held in high esteem by students. Indeed, a significant number of the school librarians felt that their social status decreased after becoming a librarian. Despite the fact that school librarians were not as old (on the average) as similar subjects employed in public libraries, they tended to be more receptive to the practice of censorship. Fiske speculated that the willingness of school librarians to limit the spread of certain information or materials might be related to their professional isolation.[53]

Two noticeable contrasts between school and public librarians emerged from the Fiske study. First, school librarians were definitely more convinced of the adverse effects of books on students; one-half of them, in contrast to one-fifth of the public librarians, believed that some books can result in harm to readers. Issues such as sex and political propaganda were considered by school librarians as topics which immature young people might not readily understand. The second point of difference appeared in concepts of the scope and types of collections that libraries should maintain. School librarians were very concerned about the quality of books included in their libraries, and they gave considerable attention to the educational objectives of the school and the role that materials in their collections might have in furthering these goals. On the other hand, public librarians were more interested in meeting the demands of the public at large; they attempted to please the public more than to instruct it.[54]

In another study which examined controversies about the book *Catcher in the Rye*, James F. Symula utilized information obtained by John Farley in an earlier investigation. Farley had discovered that only 2 percent of his selected schools had a book selection policy and that 50 percent of the school librarians felt that they would not receive support from school administrators if a dispute arose over books. The prevalence in school libraries of voluntary rather than involuntary censorship was also noted by Farley. In Symula's study, a similar pattern was evident; librarians in 20 out of the 28 schools investigated had voluntarily censored *Catcher in the Rye* or kept it on a closed shelf. Symula strongly condemned the librarians' practice of choosing only what was termed "polite books" or of waiting to handle each book controversy as it occurred. In Symula's opinion, this procedure only created more problems, and he pointed out the importance of the student's right to examine a wide range of information. He also recommended that complaint forms be made available in school libraries so that objections to books could be recorded and processed.[55]

Public school libraries and public libraries have some commonalities; however, they also have a number of differences. The public library has often been regarded as the "people's university," so books on all topics and at all levels of difficulty are usually included in their collections. By making use of special library services such as reader's assistance, library users were theoretically given an opportunity to uplift themselves culturally. However, the present-day public library does not usually perceive its role so restrictively. Rather than concentrating on the "cultural uplift" concept, more recognition is currently being given by public librarians to the library's potential to serve a broad spectrum of publics. The tastes and interests of the public library's clientele are quite varied. Certainly any interjection of librarians' personal tastes into the selection of books could have an adverse effect on intellectual freedom; librarians' personal tastes may not coincide with the interests, reading abilities, and aspirations of library users or potential users. As a consequence, public librarians appear to be turning toward the "demand" theory of book selection, whereby the library collection is developed, to a large extent, with the realization of a need for materials of immediate or potential use. On the other hand, as was previously noted, the school librarian seeks primarily to develop a collection that is orientated to the instructional programs of schools. User demand usually plays a less significant role in the development of the school library collection.

Another difference in relation to materials selection exists between public and school libraries. Because the former serve a broader clientele, they are more subject to pressures from various groups to obtain controversial materials, and, at the same time, they are pressured by other groups to avoid all controversial works. This dynamic tension appears to be rooted in the public library's service to diverse publics. Public librarians are also responsible to boards of trustees. While a school corporation has a school board, this board often has less time to devote to library issues in individual schools. The boards of public libraries, however, do have more time to deal with specific problems that face libraries. As a result, public library trustees have more opportunities to either encourage or to discourage a permissive or restrictive book selection policy.

Censorship can also take the form of a carefully controlled book purchasing policy. An example will perhaps clearly demonstrate this point. *Library Journal* conducted a survey among small, medium, and large public libraries of their holdings of twenty troublesome works of fiction, including *Lady Chatterley's Lover*,

Lolita, Tropic of Cancer, and *Rabbit, Run.* Books chosen in the sample represented a wide spectrum insofar as quality and controversial content were concerned. The editors of *Library Journal* discovered that public libraries in the Northeast owned the highest percentage of the controversial books (10.5 titles). Libraries in the West and in the South both recorded the same number (9.1 percent) of the titles in question. In contrast, Midwestern public libraries reported a much lower percentage (7.5) of the titles per library.[56] The results of this survey appear to give some credence to the Fiske finding that one-fifth of the California public librarians shunned controversial materials. Nevertheless, other factors should be taken into consideration; additional reasons may enter into the rejection of a particular title by a library. Both the *Library Journal* survey and the Fiske study, however, do confirm that censorship in the guise of careful selection is practiced. Fiske found that two-thirds of all the librarians interviewed who were responsible for book selection indicated that, in certain cases, the reputation of an author led to a decision not to purchase a book.[57]

Public librarians are usually concerned about securing materials that will meet the information needs of all the groups that they serve. To a certain extent, they should be able to determine what these publics want, taking into account other relevant factors such as population mobility, changing interests, and level of education. When librarians believe that they are attuned to the patrons and their needs but they actually are not, the potential for voluntary censorship arises. The critical question becomes, then, the real basis for the selection of materials. While a book, film, periodical, or some other medium could be described as "too mature" or "not geared to the reading tastes" of the community, the real reason for rejection of the work may be the avoidance of a controversy. However, fear of a controversy may exist only in the mind of the librarian.

In addition, librarians can also impose their own value systems upon the selection process. Rather than considering the community at large, some librarians seek to determine how a work agrees with their personal views or tolerances. To avoid the possibility of confrontation, the librarian should not be guided by vague fears. If a highly recommended, authoritative, and well-written work about a controversial matter is being considered for purchase, the librarian should prepare a strategy for defending the work. Favorable reviews, a thorough understanding of the work, and a strategy for handling complaints are needed should the librarian decide to include a controversial book in a public library collection. Unless these steps are taken, the librarian can be less than certain about how to control a potential controversy. Indeed, many controversies over library materials have arisen because a simple procedure for dealing with complaints was not formulated and utilized.

Additional insights about public librarians and selection problems have been obtained from other studies. One study that deserves attention is the research undertaken by Charles H. Busha to determine the attitudes of public librarians in the Midwest toward censorship. Busha's investigation provides a reliable profile of what a large group of public librarians feel about intellectual freedom (as expressed in the Library Bill of Rights and the Freedom to Read Statement) and censorship. The study also examined the connection between librarians' censorship ideas, their authoritarian opinions, and the relationship between intellectual freedom and censorship attitudes.

Busha's research represents a scientific approach to the problem of ascertaining what public librarians actually feel about censorship. Every facet of the opinion research was carefully planned and executed to provide a clear picture of librarians' attitudes toward intellectual freedom in the Midwest. Steps were taken to insure that the questionnaire actually measured the desired attitudes and opinions, and the questionnaire was pre-tested four times and was revised after each test. The final pre-test of the instrument was conducted among a group of public librarians in Iowa, Minnesota, and Missouri in order to determine which items differentiated between pro- and anti-censorship attitudes. To obtain a standard by which results of the study could easily be interpreted, Busha incorporated into the questionnaire eighteen items from Adorno's F-scale designed to measure authoritarianism and anti-democratic trends.

Because of the impracticality of questioning all public librarians in the Midwest about their views in regard to intellectual freedom, Busha chose a random sample of respondents in Illinois, Indiana, Michigan, Ohio, and Wisconsin. From a population of 3,253 public librarians in the East North-Central states, a total of 900 respondents were randomly selected. The respondents were chosen by stratification procedures. For example, if 31 percent of the public librarians in a given state held positions in communities with a population of less than 5,000, a corresponding percentage of respondents from that state were selected from this population category. A total of 684 or 76 percent of the respondents returned questionnaires; 624 or 69.3 percent usable survey forms provided the actual data for the study.

The majority of the pro-censorship librarians held positions in communities with populations of less than 35,000 inhabitants. Nearly all (93 percent) of the librarians with high censorship scores were in the 45-years-or-older age bracket. While 62 percent of the pro-censorship librarians served as directors of public libraries, a total of 50 percent of the survey's respondents held that position. More women than men were in the pro-censorship group; women accounted for 92 percent of those who would restrict books or other materials for one reason or another. Even when one considers that the female-to-male ratio of respondents was 4 to 1, the proportion of pro-censorship women to pro-censorship men was 11 to 1. The survey data also revealed that the amount of formal education completed by librarians was related to respondents' attitudes toward censorship. Most librarians (74 percent) who were opposed to restrictions on freedom of expression had obtained a master's degree in library science; a smaller percentage (20 percent) of those with a master's degree or equivalent degree looked favorably toward restrictions. Thus, the most typical librarian who favored the suppression of some library materials was female, 45 years of age or older, and a director of a library serving less than 35,000 inhabitants. In addition, the typical pro-censorship librarian had earned a few college credits, but more often than not she had not earned a college degree.[58]

Furthermore, Busha was able to measure correlations between independent variables and the tendency of certain librarians to approve of censorship. Positive relationships were found between pro-censorship attitudes and state of employment, education, community size, position, sex, and age. Busha also noted that formal education appeared to be related highly and positively to liberal attitudes toward freedom of expression. For example, the more formal education librarians had completed, the less inclined they were to approve of the suppression of materials. A high degree of correspondence was discovered between respondents' authoritarian ideas and their pro-censorship attitudes. Librarians who received high authoritarian scores were also more favorable toward censorship.[59] Although Busha's inquiry did not examine public librarians' attitudes over the nation, his study complements the earlier Fiske study in several ways. First, what Fiske did for the study of librarians in California, Busha has done for public librarians in the Midwest. Second, Busha has provided statistically significant measures of many of the concepts or findings which Fiske only briefly discussed. Finally, Busha's research provides significant information about the characteristics of librarians who are most likely to be censorial.

Although the Fiske and Busha studies reveal how some librarians approve of restrictions on library materials that patrons might use, one should not be surprised by these findings. When the history of librarianship in the United States is examined, a lack of a firm commitment on the part of many librarians to principles of intellectual freedom is evident. For example, in the early 1900s, a symposium was held with the theme, "What Shall the Libraries Do About Bad Books?" Arthur Bostwick, president of the American Library Association, called for the censorship of books which were "immoral," since he perceived the librarian's duty as one of protecting the immigrants, *nouveaux riches*, and others from the harm of objectionable books.[60]

The present concern of librarians for intellectual freedom has grown out of a somewhat belated anti-censorship movement. As the various findings outlined here have indicated, not all librarians are presently committed to resisting censorship. Yet, the occurrence of censorship in American libraries can be understood more clearly if a number of significant factors are considered. First, the social climate of the late 1800s and early 1900s favored—even encouraged—a restrictive attitude toward discussion of controversial matters. Second, various government restrictions, church regulations, and crusades by vice societies encouraged libraries to adopt restrictive selection procedures. Finally, library association leaders were slow to formulate a firm position in regard to intellectual freedom. When the American Library Association's position toward the freedom to read is examined in its historical context, one recognizes that professional librarians did not begin to seriously promote the concept of freedom of access to library materials until 1939.

Although ALA adopted an anti-censorship position, David Berninghausen has pointed out that there was little real activity in this area of concern until 1946. As a matter of fact, a committee established to deal with problems relating to the maintenance of intellectual freedom in libraries (ALA's Committee on Intellectual Freedom to Safeguard the Rights of Library Users to Freedom of Inquiry) announced in its 1944-45 annual report that " . . . the fact remains that the Committee has received very little indication of interference with the freedom to read in libraries."[61] Not until 1949 did the Committee recognize that censorship was indeed causing difficulties in libraries. In previous years, 1946-49, the Committee was still attempting to determine if censorship was actually occurring. A decision to condemn the practice of labeling books was finally recommended by the Intellectual Freedom Committee in 1951.[62] Thus, the intellectual freedom movement has relative recent origins in librarianship, and many members of the library profession may have witnessed these developments in their own lifetimes.

As many recent attempts in schools and in libraries to control access to materials have been related to the sexually oriented content of various media, the *Report of the Commission on Obscenity and Pornography* should be discussed as a significant study. This report, released in 1970, reviewed in considerable detail contemporary studies related to the real or imaginary effects of pornography. The major conclusion of the report was that no relationship exists between exposure to pornography and anti-social sexual conduct. However, a minority of the Commission members did not agree with the views of the majority. Three out of eighteen members concluded that a positive relationship does exist between pornography and sexual crimes, deviance, and promiscuity. As a result of this divergence of opinion, the *Report of the Commission on Obscenity and Pornography* provides a summary of arguments and tenets of both the anti-censorship and the pro-censorship groups.

The Commission's majority position can be briefly summarized as follows: home environment and peer groups are more influential than pornography in affecting deviant sexual conduct; sexual deviates or persons convicted of sexual offenses were exposed to pornography at a much later period in their lives than individuals who are sexually adjusted; and most purchasers of sexually oriented materials are white middle-class males who are married and in their thirties or forties—not adolescents and young adults. The Commission majority noted that sex education must be improved because a number of studies have concluded that many inadequacies exist in sex education programs of schools. The report concluded that exposure to pornography leads to temporary sexual arousal, which often takes the form of increased talk about sex or sexual practices of a previously established rather than a new form.[63]

According to the Commission's three dissenters, a definite relationship existed between exposure to pornography and subsequent sexual misconduct. They pointed to a number of studies which contradicted claims made by the majority. Sex education was criticized as an ineffective means of controlling or preventing sexual problems. Finally, a long list of model laws for the control of obscenity was presented by the minority group.[64] The dissenting report was entitled the *Hill-Link Minority Report of the Presidential Commission on Obscenity and Pornography*, having obtained its name from the Rev. Morton A. Hill, S.J., a Catholic priest, and the Rev. W. C. Link, a Methodist minister, both of whom were members of the Commission. The Rev. Hill is president of Morality in Media, a national interfaith organization working to counter the traffic in pornography "constitutionally and effectively."

A comparison of the two viewpoints within the *Report of the Commission on Obscenity and Pornography* permits the drawing of certain conclusions: 1) the anti-censorship majority appeared to be more objective in their approach to pornography than the dissenters and 2) the majority of the Commission members placed much more reliance upon studies of a scientific nature in arriving at their conclusions. Thus, the majority made a strong case for its stance by utilizing data obtained from a variety of rigorous studies and experiments conducted by qualified investigators and scholars. On the other hand, the minority, which favored strict controls on pornography, presented a much weaker defense. Apparently, the Commission's minority members lacked a scientific understanding of the concept of causality. At the beginning of the minority report the dissenters pointed out their belief that it was not only impossible but unnecessary to attempt to prove or disprove a cause-effect relationship between pornographic materials and criminal behavior. If the minority members of the Commission actually felt that way, they have admitted that no direct link has been established between pornography and any harmful effects of this material. However, it was most curious that the minority continuously referred to the "eroding," "debilitating," and "dangerous" effects that pornography has on individuals. Secondly, lacking an understanding of the concept of cause and effect, the minority took a haphazard and subjective view of the relationship between pornography and social conduct. Incidents of sexual misconduct and deviance were vividly and laboriously described in the Commission's minority report, and the subject of pornography was invariably carefully brought into the sordid descriptions of these activities. The issues of what is symptomatic of a psychological disorder and of what caused the misconduct were confused in these descriptions of incidents. For example, left unanswered was the question of whether the presence of pornography was an indication of a lack of psychological adjustment or the actual cause of the maladjustment. Finally, many of the investigations cited in the minority report as evidence in support of the suppression of pornography were not conducted in a rigorously scientific manner.

SUMMARY

In summarizing this report on research about censorship, several points should probably be reiterated. First, insufficient scientific research in this area has been conducted. Numerous articles and reports have described censorship controversies or incidents which led to censorship controversies; however, studies matching the rigor of those conducted by Fiske, Knudson, Aherns, and Busha are less common. Only as more scientific research about censorship is conducted will definitive answers be obtained. Second, linguistic problems arise when one attempts to discuss censorship in an intelligent manner. Concepts such as "obscenity," "corruption of morals," and the "harmful effect on youth by pornography" are frequently used loosely and vaguely. Third, attempts at censorship are always less effective than their proponents may claim. Numerous inconsistencies are clearly evident in regard to censorship by the Catholic Church, the federal government, and the courts. Fourth, inadequate attention has been given to the problem of self-censorship, especially among librarians who fear controversies over books or other library materials. Practices such as restrictive and negative book selection or self-imposed restraints in regard to library materials are definite examples of self-censorship. Finally, one must realize that as long as men have differences in tastes, habits, or training, and as long as they are intolerant of the rights of others, problems will persist in relation to freedom of communication. Because each person perceives events, materials, or people according to his own experiences, librarians must be prepared to defend their selections of material. Censorship is truly a difficult matter to treat objectively and precisely since the abstractions that are involved sometimes cannot be translated into the reality of our contemporary world. Yet, given the problems summarized above, the attempts at such translation must continue, even at the risk of failure, if the democratic tradition is to be served.

FOOTNOTES

[1] Robert B. Downs, ed., *The First Freedom; Liberty and Justice in the World of Books and Reading* (Chicago: American Library Association, 1961), p. xii.
[2] Paul S. Boyer, *Purity in Print; The Vice-Society Movement and Book Censorship in America* (New York: Scribner's, 1968), p. xix.

[3] Wayne C. Booth, "Censorship and the Values of Fiction," *The English Journal* 53 (March 1964): 156.

[4] James C. N. Paul and Murry L. Schwartz, *Federal Censorship; Obscenity in the Mail* (New York: Free Press of Glencoe, 1961), pp. 191-200.

[5] Max L. Marshall, *The "Right-to-Read" Controversy* (Columbia, Mo.: Freedom of Information Center, 1969), p. 11.

[6] Donald B. Sharp, ed., *Commentaries on Obscenity* (Metuchen, N.J.: Scarecrow Press, Inc., 1970), pp. 160-61.

[7] *Ibid.*, p. 161.

[8] *Ibid.*, p. 167.

[9] *Ibid.*, pp. 174-75.

[10] *Ibid.*, p. 177.

[11] Moshe Carmilly-Weinberger, "Censorship," in *Encyclopedia Judaica* (New York: Macmillan, 1972), 5:276-81.

[12] George H. Putnam, *The Censorship of the Church of Rome and Its Influence Upon the Production and Distribution of Literature* (New York: Putnam, 1906), 2:254.

[13] Redmond A. Burke, "The Control of Reading by the Catholic Church" (unpublished Ph.D. dissertation, University of Chicago, 1948), p. 63.

[14] Alfred P. Klausler, *Censorship, Obscenity, and Sex* (St. Louis: Concordia Publishing House, 1967), p. 11.

[15] Burke, pp. 43-49.

[16] Burke, p. 76.

[17] Redmond A. Burke, *What Is the Index?* (Milwaukee: Bruce Publishing Company, Inc., 1952), pp. 26-27.

[18] Putnam, pp. 35-37.

[19] Klausler, pp. 16-17.

[20] Sharp, p. 11.

[21] Paul and Schwartz, p. 201.

[22] *Ibid.*, pp. 7-8.

[23] Boyer, p. 4.

[24] *Ibid.*, p. 6.

[25] Michael Adams, *Censorship: The Irish Experience* (University, Ala.: University of Alabama Press, 1968), pp. 13-17.

[26] Klausler, p. 14.

[27] Sharp, p. 11.

[28] *Ibid.*, pp. 9-10.

[29] Harry M. Clor, *Obscenity and Public Morality; Censorship in a Liberal Society* (Chicago: University of Chicago Press, 1969), pp. 16-64.

[30] Sharp, pp. 42-48.

[31] Rozanne R. Knudson, "Censorship in English Programs of California Junior Colleges" (unpublished Ph.D. dissertation, Stanford University, 1967), p. 9.

[32] "A Divided Court Rewrites the Definition of Obscenity," *CQ Weekly Report* 31 (June 23, 1973): 1571.

[33] Knudson, p. 8.

[34] Max Lerner, "What Community Standard?" *Current* 154 (September 18-19, 1973): 41.

[35] Marshall, p. 1.

[36] Harold H. Hart, *Censorship For and Against* (New York: Hart Publishing Co., 1971), p. 41.

[37] Marshall, p. 5.

[38] *Ibid.*, pp. 12-13.

[39] *Ibid.*, pp. 11-12.

[40] Nyla H. Aherns, "Censorship and the Teacher of English: A Survey of a Selected Sample of Secondary School Teachers of English" (unpublished Ph.D. dissertation, Columbia University, 1965), pp. 1-56.

[41] *Ibid.*, pp. 65-67.

[42] *Ibid.*, p. 19.

[43] *Ibid.*, pp. 98-99.

[44] Knudson, p. 56.

[45] *Ibid.*, pp. 72-73.

[46] *Ibid.*, pp. 27-31.

[47] *Ibid.*, pp. 198-99.

[48] *Ibid.*, pp. 179-80.

[49] *Ibid.*, pp. 20-23.

[50] *Ibid.*, p. 107.

[51] *Ibid.*, pp. 44-45.

[52] Marjorie Fiske, *Book Selection and Censorship; A Study of Schools and Public Libraries in California* (Berkeley: University of California Press, 1959), pp. 2-4.

[53] *Ibid.*, pp. 86-91.

[54] *Ibid.*, pp. 21-24.

[55] James F. Symula, "Censorship of High School Literature: A Study of the Incidents of Censorship Involving J. D. Salinger's *The Catcher in the Rye*" (unpublished Ed.D. dissertation, State University of New York at Buffalo, 1969), pp. 46-109.

[56] Eric Moon, ed. *Book Selection and Censorship in the Sixties* (New York: Bowker, 1969), p. 45.

[57] Fiske, p. 64.

[58] Charles H. Busha, *Freedom versus Suppression and Censorship* (Littleton, Colo.: Libraries Unlimited, Inc., 1972), pp. 141-42.

[59] *Ibid.*, pp. 145-46.

[60] Boyer, p. 31.

[61] David K. Berninghausen, "The History of the ALA Intellectual Freedom Committee," *Wilson Library Bulletin* 27 (June 1953): 813-14.

[62] *Ibid.*, p. 816.

[63] U.S. President's Commission on Obscenity and Pornography. *The Report of the Commission on Obscenity and Pornography* (Washington, D.C.: Government Printing Office, 1970), pp. 128-290.

[64] *Ibid.*, pp. 386-509.

CONTRIBUTORS

Charles H. Busha is the author of *Freedom versus Suppression and Censorship* (Libraries Unlimited, 1972) and articles about intellectual freedom in a number of professional journals. He was graduated from Furman University, Rutgers University, and Indiana University.

Rebecca Dixon was head librarian at the Institute for Sex Research, Bloomington, Indiana, from 1967 until 1974. She presently directs the Library Services Division of the Center for the Study of Youth Development, Boys Town, Nebraska.

Stephen P. Harter received the Ph.D. degree from the University of Chicago. He is an assistant professor in the Library Science/Audiovisual Department, University of South Florida, Tampa.

Barbara Connally Kaplan formerly taught at the University of Texas in Austin, where she directed the 1966 Institute for Advanced Study in Arts and Humanities. She is now a music professor at Saint Leo College.

Richard E. McKee received the master's degree from the Graduate Library School, Indiana University. Since 1973, he has been a member of the staff of the Concordia Senior College Library, Fort Wayne, Indiana.

Yvonne Linsert Morse was trained as an artist before she began her career as a medical librarian. She is now director of the medical library of the Veterans Administration Hospital in Fayetteville, North Carolina, where she also continues to paint.

Gail Linda Robinson is a graduate of Brooklyn College, the University of Missouri at Kansas City, and the University of South Florida. She has taught high-school biology courses and has also served as a school media specialist.